CULTURES IN CONFLICT

# THE FRENCH REVOLUTION

**Recent Titles in**
**The Greenwood Press Cultures in Conflict Series**

Cultures in Conflict—The American Civil War
*Steven E. Woodworth*

Cultures in Conflict—The Arab-Israeli Conflict
*Calvin Goldscheider*

Cultures in Conflict—The Viet Nam War
*Robert E. Vadas*

# CULTURES IN CONFLICT
# THE FRENCH REVOLUTION

Gregory S. Brown

The Greenwood Press Cultures in Conflict Series

GREENWOOD PRESS
Westport, Connecticut • London

**Library of Congress Cataloging-in-Publication Data**

Brown, Gregory S. (Gregory Stephen)
Cultures in conflict—the French Revolution / Gregory S. Brown.
p. cm.—(The Greenwood Press cultures in conflict series ISSN 1526–0690)
Includes bibliographical references and index.
ISBN 0–313–31789–5 (alk. paper)
1. France—History—Revolution, 1789–1799—Personal narratives.
2. France—History—Revolution, 1789–1799—Sources. 3. France—History—Revolution, 1789–1799—Social aspects. 4. Culture conflict—France—History—Revolution, 1789–1799—Sources. I. Title. II. Series.
DC148.B76 2003
944.04—dc21 2003044072

British Library Cataloguing in Publication Data is available.



Library of Congress Catalog Card Number: 2003044072
ISBN: 0–313–31789–5
ISSN: 1526–0690

First published in 2003

Greenwood Press, 88 Post Road West, Westport, CT 06881
An imprint of Greenwood Publishing Group, Inc.
www.greenwood.com

Printed in the United States of America

The paper used in this book complies with the Permanent Paper Standard issued by the National Information Standards Organization (Z39.48–1984).

10 9 8 7 6 5 4 3 2 1

Though I never studied with him directly, Robert R. Palmer must necessarily be considered an inspiration to every American student of the French Revolution. His passing in the summer of 2002, as I approached completion of this book, reminded all of us who teach and study the Revolution of the tradition progressive, liberal, and emphatically democratic interpretation that Palmer represented among American historians, from Carl Becker to the present. I hope that this book makes some small contribution to that tradition, by passing a piece of Palmer's legacy on to a new generation of American students.

# Contents

# Preface

The French Revolution remains one of the crucial events of modern European and world history. For more than 200 years, it has been celebrated, commemorated, and debated. This book will introduce students to the topic through the documents of everyday experiences of ordinary people who lived through the dramatic cultural conflicts of the years 1789 to 1799.

These conflicts brought many changes, great and small, to French society. By tradition, the social system placed some people above others, and the Revolution replaced this hierarchy with a society of individuals enjoying equality under the law. The Revolution transformed the old political system, which had been an absolutist monarchy, first into a constitutional monarchy and then the first modern republic, based on democratic principles. In religion, the dominant position of the Catholic Church gave way to tolerance, reform of the clergy, separation of church and state, and finally, a civil religion based on reason. Culturally, French men and women came to think of themselves in new ways—as individuals, as citizens, as patriots, and as belonging not to social orders but to social classes. These changes were neither easy nor complete. All involved intense and sometimes bloody struggles to shape a new society, political system, religion, and culture.

These changes affected all levels of French society in cities, towns, and villages across the country. Though the Revolution began with a conflict between nobles and the king, ordinary people waged the most intense conflicts of these years, and the conflicts of the Revolution became part of their everyday lives. This book is intended to help students understand the impact of the Revolution at this level—the everyday lives of ordinary people. In this respect, it is intended as a complement to textbooks or other document readers, which may focus on the political, intellectual, and constitutional issues raised by the Revolution. It is also intended as a complement to those books that emphasize the Revolution's leaders or those that reflect the people's experiences during the Revolution. This book seeks to present the Revolution as ordinary French men and women might have experienced it, by using documents and images from its participants to tell their own story.

The introduction is in two parts. The first chapter provides an overview of the event itself—a narrative framework for what follows. This chapter describes, first and foremost, the political changes of the period. The next chapter describes different ways of life of the French people prior to the Revolution. Eighteenth-century French society was not divided simply into two opposing sides, but into many different groups. Accordingly, Chapter 2 describes multiple ways of life under the Old Regime. Chapters 3 through 7 then explore the Revolution's effect on these different ways. These chapters are thematic; each discusses a different theme central to the Revolution. Each chapter includes a discussion of a theme, based on several dozen original primary documents (edited and translated by the author). The documents chronicle the everyday lives of ordinary people, sometimes in their own words and sometimes, by necessity, in the words of more elite contemporary observers. The final sections include a glossary, a set of study questions, and a guide to further readings, films, and multi-media resources on the Revolution.

# Acknowledgments

I am grateful to many colleagues and students for their ideas and references that have contributed to this book. I would particularly like to express my gratitude to Jack Censer, Anthony Crubaugh, Nira Kaplan, Laura Mason, Jeremy Popkin, Stéphane Van Damme, and especially Isser Woloch who has done so much to inspire my own interest in teaching and studying the Revolution. I am indebted to the Department of History and the University Faculty Travel Committee of the University of Nevada, Las Vegas, for research and technical support that enabled me to collect the documents and images included in this book. Special thanks to John Mess of UNLV Lied Library for his help in preparing the maps included here and to Melise Leech for her highly professional and intelligent editorial and research assistance in preparing the manuscript. Finally, I am grateful for the patient guidance, attentive readings, and creative suggestions of my editor Wendi Schnaufer at every stage in the preparation of this book.

# Timeline of the French Revolution

On October 5, 1793, a republican calendar devoid of all Catholic religious associations was adopted. It was officially used until January 1, 1806. The following chronology is based on the Gregorian calendar with occasional references to those dates in the republican calendar associated with certain famous events.

The republican calendar year begins on September 22, 1792 (the first day of Year I of the Republic); it provides for months of equal lengths, three weeks of 10 days (called decades) in each month, and five extra solar days grouped at the end of the year (known as the *sans-culottides*, or days of the sansculottes), and a leap year day every four years.

The months were *vendemiaire* (September–October), *brumaire* (October–November), *frimaire* (November–December), *nivose* (December–January), *pluviose* (January–February), *ventose* (February–March), *germinal* (March–April), *floreal* (April–May), *prairial* (May–June), *messidor* (June–July), *thermidor* (July–August), and *fructidor* (August–September).

**1787**

| | |
|---|---|
| February 22: | The First Assembly of Notables discusses new taxes, but rejects them as a solution to the bankruptcy of the royal treasury. On May 25, this Assembly is dissolved. |

| | |
|---|---|
| April: | Etienne Charles de Lomenie de Brienne replaces Calonne as Controller General of Finances. |

## 1788

| | |
|---|---|
| August 8: | King Louis XVI announces he will call the Estates General (the three orders of nobles, clergy, and commoners), which had not been assembled since 1614. |
| August 24: | Jacques Necker, a Swiss citizen and Calvinist, replaces Lomenie de Brienne as Director-General of Royal Finances. |
| July–September: | Throughout France, a poor harvest results in grain shortages, high prices, hunger, and financial difficulties. |
| November–December: | Debate over the procedure that the deputies to the Estates General should follow. |
| December 27: | *Parlement* of Paris rules that the Third Estate will have twice the number of representatives as the Orders of the Nobles and the Clergy, but each order will meet and deliberate separately, thus giving the assemblies of nobles and clergy a combined majority vote. |

## 1789

| | |
|---|---|
| January: | Publication of Abbot Sièyes's, *What is the Third Estate?* This patriotic pamphlet argues that the Third Estate essentially is the nation. |
| February: | Selection of representatives to the Estates General and drafting of petitions of grievance *(cahiers de doléances).* |
| April 27–28: | Riots in Paris directed against two owners of factories, Reveillon and Henriot, who are charged with underpaying their workers. |
| May 5: | The Estates General meets in Versailles. |
| June 17: | The Third Estate proclaims itself the National Assembly and invites the other two orders to join. |
| June 20: | The Tennis-Court Oath. The king orders the meeting hall of the Third Estate closed. The Third Estate, still calling itself the National Assembly, removes to the Royal Tennis Court of Versailles |

| | |
|---|---|
| | (Salle du Jeu de Paume). The deputies swear an oath not to disband until a constitution is approved. |
| June 27: | The king concedes and orders the nobles and clergy to join the National Assembly. |
| July 2: | Demonstrations and speeches in the gardens of the Palais-Royal (a fashionable public gathering place) against the menacing increase of government soldiers in Paris. Protests against high price of bread in public marketplaces. |
| July 7: | The National Assembly proclaims itself the Constituent National Assembly, with full authority to decree law, subject to royal approval; the deputies set as their primary task is to draw up and adopt a constitution. |
| July 11: | Jacques Necker, a popular finance minister, is dismissed by Louis XVI. |
| July 14: | The taking of the Bastille (royal fortress and prison) and revolt against Parisian municipal government. |
| July 16–17: | At the insistence of the Constituent National Assembly, Necker is recalled to his post. The next day, the king travels to Paris and appears before the Assembly. The work of designing the new constitution begins. |
| July–August: | The so-called Great Fear, in which peasants rioted in many regions of France. |
| August 4: | The National Assembly abolishes all privileges. |
| August 26: | The National Assembly adopts the Declaration of the Rights of Man and of the Citizen. |
| September 12: | First appearance of Jean-Paul Marat's radical newspaper *L'Ami du peuple (The Friend of the People)*. It is at first sympathetic to a constitutional monarchy, but becomes increasingly in favor of a republic and for more egalitarian economic policies. |
| October 5–6: | Parisian market women, accompanied by soldiers of the Parisian National Guard, march to Versailles and force the royal family back to Paris. The National Assembly also moves to Paris. |
| November 2: | All church property becomes national goods. |
| December 9: | The administrative reorganization of France into 85 administrative departments. |

December 19: The Assembly issues assignats backed by the nationalized church lands as a paper money.

## 1790

February 13: Most religious orders are abolished.

June 19: All hereditary titles are abolished.

July 12: The Civil Constitution of the Clergy is adopted.

July 14: The first anniversary of the taking of the Bastille (symbolizing the beginning of the Revolution) is celebrated on the Marching Fields (Champ-de-Mars) with a Festival of Unity (Fête de la Fédération).

November 27: All public officials and priests are required to pledge an oath of loyalty to the French nation.

## 1791

March 2: All guilds, which regulated artisanal crafts, are abolished.

June 14: Workers' unions and strikes are prohibited by the Le Chapelier law.

June 20–25: The royal family, Louis XVI, Marie Antoinette, and their children, is arrested at Varennes while attempting to flee the country. They are returned to Paris, and the Constituent National Assembly suspends the king's authority. The Parisian press begins, citing the king's flight, reports on possible secret conspiracies and foreign invasions.

July 6: Emperor Leopold II of Hapsburg demands the release of Louis XVI.

July 17: The Marching-Fields massacre. In response, the Parisian Cordeliers Club demands the overthrow of the king and the founding of a republic. The Jacobin Club is divided on the question; those against a republic quit the Jacobins to form a new faction, known as the Feuillants. Fear of internal and foreign conspiracies against the Revolution spreads widely in the press.

August 27: The Declaration of Pillnitz. The monarchs of Austria and Prussia declare their intention to invade France and end the Revolution.

September 3: The Constitution of 1791 is proclaimed.

September 18: Louis XVI swears to uphold the new constitution and is restored to power over the objections of many patriots, who favor a republic.

September 27: Jews in all regions of France are granted full citizenship.

September 30: Last session of the Constituent National Assembly.

October 1: First session of the new Legislative Assembly under the Constitution of 1791. It will quickly fall into divisive debate whether to declare war against Austria and Prussia. Jacques Pierre Brissot, a Parisian deputy, urges war. Maximilien Robespierre (a radical deputy from Arras) argues against war, fearing defeat would mean the end of the Revolution.

## 1792

January–March: Sharp increase in food prices, followed by food riots, in Paris.

March 9–10: King's ministers resign, and Louis XVI replaces them with Jacobins.

April 20: France declares war on Austria and Prussia.

April 25: Rouget de Lisle composes his war hymn, which will become known as "La Marseillaise."

June 20: A large crowd of Parisian sansculottes ("without britches") invades the Tuileries palace and force the king to don a liberty cap.

July 28: The *Brunswick Manifesto* is distributed throughout Paris. The Duke of Brunswick, commanding general of the Austrian and Prussian combined army, warns Parisians to obey Louis XVI and threatens violent punishment if they do not. The manifesto creates both fear and anger in Paris, and preparations for war intensify.

July 29: At a meeting of the Jacobin Club, Robespierre calls for the removal of the king and establishment of a republic, arguing his weak leadership is a threat to the country in a time of war.

Week of August 3: Forty-seven of the forty-eight sections of Paris petition the Legislative Assembly to abrogate the king's powers by August 10.

August 10: Massive demonstration when sansculottes march on the royal palace of the Tuileries, and fight with a

| | |
|---|---|
| | contingent of French soldiers. The crowd takes the Tuileries, and the king and royal family are forced to seek refuge in the Legislative Assembly. In the afternoon, the Assembly strips the king of his powers and declares him a prisoner of the nation. It then calls for a constitutional convention. |
| August 11: | The now lame-duck Legislative Assembly authorizes the arrest throughout France of suspected enemies of the Revolution and the suppression of royalist newspapers. |
| August 15: | In the west of France, Jean Cottereau, known as Jean Chouan, refuses to be inducted into the national army in protest of the king's arrest. This begins the guerilla revolt against the national government, known as the Chouannerie. |
| August 19: | The Marquis de Lafayette, commander of the Paris National Guard, abandons his post and flees to Austria. Prussian armies, including French emigrant nobles, invade France. |
| September 2–7: | The September massacres in Paris. |
| September 20: | The French army defeats the Prussians at Valmy. |
| September 21: | The new assembly, known as the Convention, is seated. The Convention intends to draft a republican constitution, serve as a provisional revolutionary government, and decide what to do with the deposed king. The followers of Jacques-Pierre Brissot, known as the Girondins, are the majority. |
| September 22: | The Convention abolishes the monarchy and decrees the establishment of a republic. |
| October: | The French army pushes the Prussians back and takes possession of Frankfort. The army under General Dumouriez enters Belgium and defeats the Austrians. |
| November 19: | The Convention declares its willingness to help all subjected peoples to achieve their liberty by overthrowing their kings and nobles. |
| December: | Jacques Roux, a former priest turned radical leader, demands that the aristocracy of the rich be stripped of its privileges, as had been the nobility in 1789. His followers, the Mad Dogs (Enragés), are influential among the sansculottes in the sections. They |

give speeches against the Girondins, and to a lesser degree, the Jacobins, who defended the sacred and inviolable right of private property.

## 1793

January 21: After a trial by the Convention, Louis XVI is found guilty of treason and guillotined.

February–March: Severe food shortage in Paris leads to high prices, riots, and attacks on shops.

February 24: With France now at war with Britain and Holland as well as Prussia and Austria, the Convention calls up 300,000 citizen soldiers. This conscription is unwelcome in some regions, especially in the western region of the Vendée, where draft resistance leads to open revolt against the Republic.

In response, the Engragés revolt in Paris, charging that the Convention is not doing enough to defend the Republic or to redistribute wealth among its citizens.

March 10: Facing open revolt, the Convention establishes an extraordinary criminal tribunal, later to be called the Revolutionary Tribunal. In these courts, juries will try those suspected of being enemies of the Republic. The goal of the tribunals is to restore order and rule of law where civil war has already broken out.

March 18: The Convention, seeking to suppress the Enragés, decrees capital punishment for anyone who attacks the principle of private property.

March 21: Revolutionary committees are created in each town to draw up a list of those suspected of being enemies or traitors to be tried by a jury.

April 5: General Dumouriez, after suffering a significant defeat in Belgium, deserts to the Austrians. Like Lafayette before him, Dumouriez urges his army to abandon the Republic and march with him in Paris to dissolve the Convention. His treason spread rampant fears that Prussia and Austria, now backed by Britain, the Netherlands, and Spain, will again invade France. A panicked population in Paris holds the Girondins, the dominant party in the Convention, responsible.

| | |
|---|---|
| April 6: | The Convention forms an executive committee, the Committee of Public Safety, to supervise the war effort for both the civil war in the Vendée and the foreign wars. |
| April 21: | Robespierre, at the Jacobin Club, proposes a new version of the Declaration of the Rights of Man and of the Citizen, in which the right of private property can be restricted, if necessary, to improve the well-being of the nation as a whole. |
| April 23–24: | Marat, denounced by Girondins, is arrested and tried by the Revolutionary Tribunal. He is set free, but this event intensifies the frustration of the sansculottes with the Girondins. |
| May 4: | The Convention decrees price controls on grain, known as the Maximum. |
| May 18–24: | The Girondins, using their majority in the Convention, establish a commission to arrest extremist elements in the Commune of Paris, specifically the Enragés, and another radical faction, which is led by Jacques-René Hébert. This announcement further angers the sansculottes and the Jacobins, much of whose support is in the Commune of Paris (Paris city government). |
| May 25–June 1: | A contingent of deputies from the Commune enters the Convention to demand the liberation of their arrested colleagues. The Girondins resist, leading to a full-scale attack by sansculottes from the sections on the Convention; with the tacit support of the Jacobins, the deputies of the Girondin majority are arrested. |
| June 24: | The remaining deputies of the Convention, now dominated by Jacobins, approve the Constitution of 1793, also known as the Constitution of the Year I. It assured every citizen not only political liberties, including universal manhood suffrage, but also the right to work, the right to education, and it recognized the "sacred right and duty of a people to revolt" against a government that does not serve the people. It would be adopted by a national referendum on August 4, but was never actually applied. |
| July 13: | Charlotte Corday assassinates Marat. |

| | |
|---|---|
| July 23: | The French surrender at Mainz. Combined with the assassination of the popular Marat, Parisian sansculottes fear another plot by royalists. |
| July 26: | The Convention votes hoarding of grain a capital offense. |
| August 1: | The metric system is decreed the new national standard. |
| August 23: | To prepare for upcoming battles on France's own frontiers, the Convention decrees a mass levy, calling upon the entire population of able-bodied males between 18 and 25 who are unmarried or widowers without children. |
| August 27: | Toulon, a crucial French naval port, is taken by the British, ensuring that Britain will soon invade French soil. |
| September 5: | A large demonstration by sansculottes at the Convention demands the immediate arrest of suspected traitors, the establishment of a revolutionary army, to put down internal revolts. In a state of urgency and fear, the Convention agrees to these demands and makes terror the order of the day. |
| September 21: | The Convention declares that all women must wear a tricolored ribbon to show their support for the Republic. |
| October 5: | The republican calendar is adopted as part of the "dechristianization" program. |
| October 9: | Revolt against the republic government is put down in the city of Lyon. |
| October 16: | Marie Antoinette is guillotined. |
| November 10: | The Festival of Reason is celebrated in the Cathedral of Notre Dame in Paris. This event illustrates the replacement of Catholicism with a "civic cult" celebrating human knowledge, reason, and political liberty. Soon thereafter, all Catholic churches are ordered closed. |
| December: | The Vendée revolt is, for the most part, suppressed. |
| December 4: | The Convention decrees the Law of 14 Frimaire, which centralizes administrative power until a new constitution can be put in place. Though designed to bring order to the provinces, it results in near |

| | |
|---|---|
| | dictatorial authority for the Committee of Public Safety. |
| December 5: | Desmoulins publishes the first issue of *Le Vieux Cordelier,* a newspaper supporting the indulgent policies of Danton, who urged peace negotiations with foreign powers and an end to the Terror. |

## 1794

| | |
|---|---|
| February 4: | The Convention abolishes slavery in French colonies. |
| March 3: | New laws, known for the Revolutionary month of Ventose, authorize the seizure and redistribution of property belonging to those suspected of treason against the Republic. |
| March 24: | Robespierre and the Jacobins turn against Hébert and his followers in the Convention, charging them with extremism, conspiracy, and collusion with foreign powers; most are executed. |
| March 29: | Robespierre, in turn, attacks Danton and his followers, who are arrested and executed on April 5. |
| June 4: | Robespierre is elected president of the Convention. |
| June 10: | The Convention passes the law of 22 Prairial, which accelerates judicial procedures against those suspected of treason. |
| June 26: | French military victory at Fleurus over the Austrians. |
| July 27–28: | A contingent of Jacobin deputies in the Convention deputies charge Robespierre with tyranny; when the Convention convicts him, he attempts but fails to commit suicide and then is captured and guillotined. Justice is declared the order of the day. The Girondins are freed; they return to the Convention as a majority; this will be known as the Thermidorian Convention. |
| September 18: | The Convention declares separation of church and state, meaning both Catholicism and the Cult of Reason. |
| November 12: | The Convention, now back in the control of the Girondins, orders the Jacobin Club closed. |
| December 24: | Price Maximum is repealed. |

## 1795

March 21: The Convention appoints a commission to draft a new, more conservative constitution.

April: Food shortages and riots in Paris. Sansculottes demand bread and Constitution of the Year I.

April 5: The Convention declares peace with Prussia, soon to be followed by peace with Austria and Britain.

April 10: The Convention calls for the disarming of all terrorists, meaning the Jacobins. An extra-judicial, White Terror breaks out across the country, and many Jacobins are lynched.

May 20–23: Sansculottes protests against high bread prices are forcibly suppressed by the army.

June 8: The king's son dies in prison. Royalists look to the next in line, the arch-conservative brother of the king the Count d'Artois, who is in exile in Italy.

June 23: A new constitution is proposed, which states that "those most worthy of governing are those who own property." It also includes a Declaration of the Rights and of the Duties of Man and Citizen, which emphasizes respect for the law. It will be approved on August 22.

June 26: The guerilla Chouans join 4,000 emigrant soldiers who land in Brittany, but are defeated by republican forces. Fighting will continue in the west until 1799.

October 5: A royalist revolt in Paris is suppressed by troops led by Napoleon Bonaparte, who is shortly named commander-in-chief of all French armies.

October 27: The new constitution, known as the Directory for the five-man executive branch it creates, is put into effect.

December 5: Gracchus Babeuf is arrested for conspiring against the government; he will be captured and tried the following year.

## 1796

February 19: Paper assignats are suppressed in a move to cut inflation.

## 1797

| | |
|---|---|
| August 22: | Renewed fighting in the colony of Saint-Domingue, where a slave revolt had been suppressed in 1791–92. Now backed by the British, Toussaint L'Ouverture and other former slaves will establish (in 1804) an independent Republic of Haiti. |
| September 2–4: | A right-wing coup against the Directory fails. Conservatives in the Directory are replaced with former Jacobins. |
| September–December: | Public debt is invalidated. |
| December 29: | A second coalition uniting Russia, Great Britain, and eventually Austria against France is formed. Warfare resumes and will continue intermittently for the next 17 years. |

## 1798

| | |
|---|---|
| May 11: | A Jacobin majority wins national elections, but the directors declare the wins invalid. |
| July 1: | Napoleon launches his Egyptian campaign. |

## 1799

| | |
|---|---|
| August 23: | Napoleon returns to France after his expedition failed. |
| November 9–10: | On the 18th of Brumaire, Napoleon—led by his brother Lucien and the prominent revolutionary Sièyes—stages a military coup. |
| December 15: | Napleon proposes a new constitution, the fourth since 1791, which assures no guarantee of individual rights and only a minimally representative government. It is approved by a plebiscite. Napoleon proclaims himself First Consul and announces the French Revolution over. |

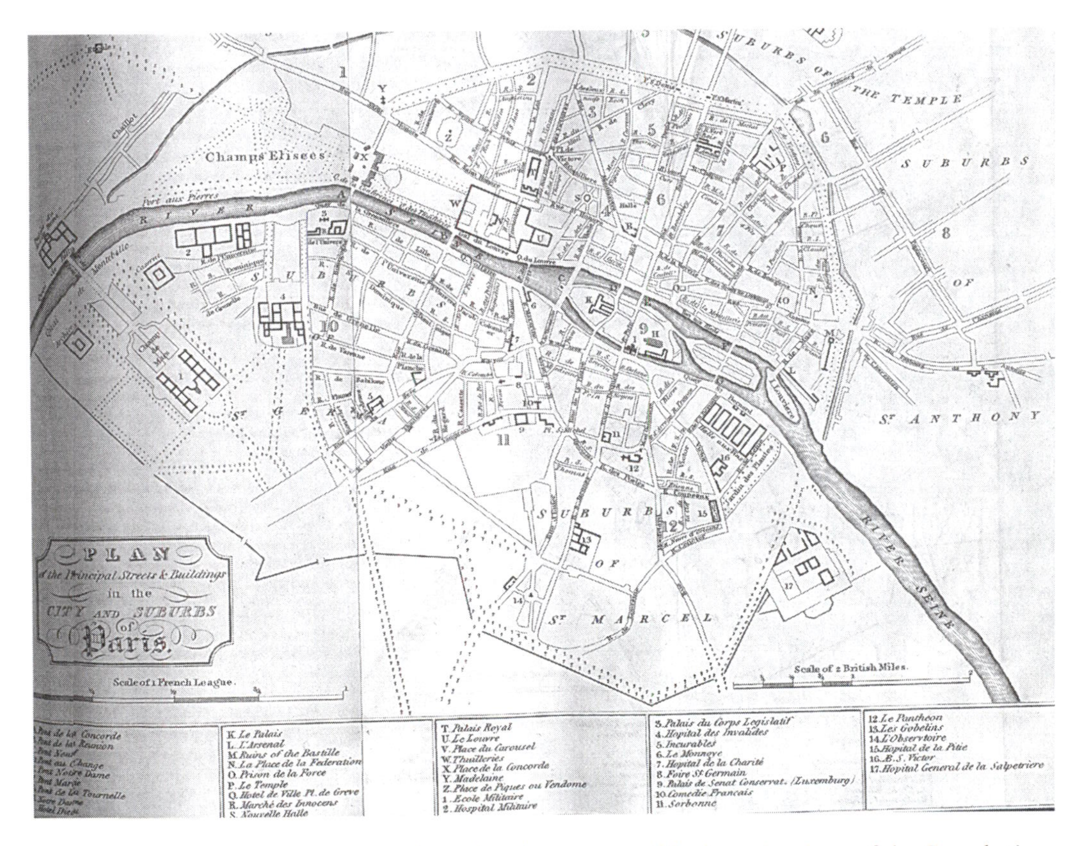


This map shows the neighborhoods and major streets of Paris at the time of the Revolution, with a key (at bottom) identifying the location of many of the major events of the Revolution. *Source:* John James McGregor, *History of the French Revolution*, 10 volumes (Dublin: Christopher Bentham, 1820–1827) vol 2. Reproduction courtesy of University of Nevada, Las Vegas libraries.

This map shows the territory of France, c. 1789. The regional names are those of the 85 Departments of roughly the same surface area created by the Revolutionaries rather than the traditional provinces of the Old Regime. *Source:* John James McGregor, *History of the French Revolution,* 10 volumes (Dublin: Christopher Bentham, 1820–1827) vol 1. Reproduction courtesy of University of Nevada, Las Vegas libraries.

# *Chapter 1*

# Historical Overview

The sudden death of the French king Louis XV due to small pox in 1774 only temporarily resolved the decades-long political and social problems that had divided France. The new king, Louis XVI, sought for a while to reconcile himself with the *parlements* (the 13 regional courts that advised the king on royal decrees and provided the primary check on royal authority). He also published, for the first time, a royal budget hoping to win back investor confidence. He would rule as a patriotic monarch for about 10 years, devoted to his people and respectful of the liberties of the different social groups and regions that made up his kingdom. However, in 1786, faced with imminent bankruptcy, he sought once again to decree tax reforms. Once again, the *parlements* blocked the king. The next year, seeking to build support for fiscal and judicial reforms, the king reluctantly agreed to call an Estates General to Versailles for 1789. The Estates General was the kingdom's traditional assembly of clergy, nobles, and commoners from each region. It had not met since 1614.

## THE OUTBREAK OF THE REVOLUTION (1787–89)

To choose delegates, small assemblies of each order—clergy, nobles, and commoners—gathered in each of six hundred districts. This procedure forced many people, such as financiers and lawyers, who thought of themselves as bourgeois gentlemen (the well-off, well-educated commoners), to assemble with artisanal workers or even peasants, with whom they had very little in common culturally. This election process, therefore, seems to have created, rather than resulted from, anger among these gentlemen.

Each district assembly also prepared *cahiers de doléances* (petitions of grievance) proposing measures for the Estates General to consider. The king also requested the opinions of his people by revoking censorship, generating a flood of pamphlets and newspapers that called for changes far beyond tax policy, such as a representative assembly in the government and the end of many privileges. Many demanded a constitution for France, without necessarily making clear what that meant. Some certainly may have thought of the newly drafted, but as yet, unratified, U.S. Constitution, though the only explicit references were to state constitutions, such as Virginia's that included a bill of rights.

Before the Estates General could meet, an important question had to be addressed: How would the assembly function? The king and the *parlement* of Paris, for once in agreement, called for it to adopt the "forms of 1614," meaning the same procedure that had been used 175 years earlier; each order would deliberate separately. That meant that to pass, any measure would have to win support in two of the three houses. Patriotic pamphleteers charged that this tactic meant the nobility and clergy would block any meaningful reform. They proposed instead that the body vote by head, so that all votes would count. Moreover, to ensure fair representation for the 85 percent of the people in the Third Estate, patriots called for this order to have twice as many deputies, so that the clergy and nobles could not outvote the commoners. Under pressure in the patriotic press, the king did agree to "double the Third," but did not allow voting by head.

Nevertheless, when the Estates General met on May 5, 1789, people all across the kingdom had high hopes that it would address many of France's economic, social, and political problems. This was due in part to an expectation that, in the face of such serious problems, the three orders—indeed, all of French society—would unite behind a king who would rediscover his own patriotic love for the people. Some were skeptical of the king's intentions and worried he would use royal troops to dissolve the gathering before it could enact any meaningful reform.

This suspicion was most prevalent among the delegates of the Third Estate, who declared on June 17 that they represented not merely the commoners but the *entire* nation. One week after making this bold claim, these delegates found themselves locked out of the assembly hall. Suspecting that the king had ordered the building locked, the delegates moved to the only open building in Versailles, the capital, large enough to accommodate them, the indoor tennis court! There, after a short debate, they agreed that their mandate came not from the king but from the people collectively—that is, the nation. On that basis, they resolved to continue their assembly until they had drafted a constitution for France. In the week that followed, liberal-minded delegates from the First and Second Estates decided to join these deputies. Having taken on this new mission, the body gave itself a new name, the National Assembly. Seven tense days later, the king relented and ordered all the deputies to form a single body, which would vote by head rather than order. Moreover, it would no longer represent the traditional society, divided into three parts, but the entire nation, united together!

While there were many pamphlets for people to read in Paris in the summer of 1789, there was not a lot of bread for them to eat. Indeed, there was a dire shortage of food, which led to a sharp rise in prices, accompanied by severe unemployment. This economic recession meant that many people, and not only the poorest, suffered great hardship and hoped that the Estates General, while it debated the government debt, would also address their concerns.

Food shortages, caused by harsh winters in the countryside and resulting in increased prices in the cities, were common in early modern Europe. In eighteenth-century France, improved roadways, as well as government reforms of the grain market, had greatly improved the situation, but this did not make those who could not afford their weekly bread feel any better off. They blamed the increase in prices on immoral behavior by peasants who grew the wheat or commercial wholesalers who brought grain to the cities. They expected the city or the royal government to prevent profiteers and speculators from taking advantage of their hardship; after all, bread—they argued—was a necessity of life, and a basic responsibility of the king and the city government was to protect ordinary people.

Those who felt these concerns most acutely were women, who purchased consumer goods in the marketplace daily. By tradition, when prices for necessary food items, such as bread, rose beyond what ordinary people considered a fair price, the people would hold protests. These protests, known as "popular taxation" or "bread riots," involved crowds attacking a baker's shop and taking bread, paying in return the traditional price (usually one *livre* for a large, two-pound loaf of bread). The people involved in these protests believed they were asserting the traditional, moral order against those who would promote their own interests, or profits, against traditional community values.

Food shortages were always the most acute in the summer, when the spring wheat had been used up, but the fall harvest had not yet begun. In the second week of July 1789, a combination of bad winters and short-time summer shortages pushed the price of bread in Paris to its highest level in the entire century. In response, women in the marketplace began to talk about holding a bread riot.

Joining this protest were self-declared patriots, who met in neighborhood assemblies to discuss current political events. These assemblies were the same groups that had formed earlier in 1789 to elect Parisian delegates to the Estates General and now continued to meet. They worried that royal troops would use any excuse to dissolve the National Assembly; they also worried that the royal troops in Paris would seize the armories to prevent the citizens from defending themselves. On the night of July 12, a rumor spread through the crowds in the gardens of the Royal Palace that such an action was imminent. (The gardens belonged to the Duke of Orléans, who allowed the public to enter freely under his protection and engage in such activity as listening to political speeches.) Camille Desmoulins, a young journalist, gave a speech calling for the Parisian men to form a citizen's militia in order to defend themselves, the women in the marketplaces, and, if necessary, the National Assembly. The next day, this call had spread, and many men joined the women in the marketplace to demand affordable bread and arms for a militia. On July 14, a large crowd gathered at City Hall to make these demands and, upon rejection, marched first to the armory known as the Invalides (a military hospital for wounded veterans, set up by Louis XV) and seized cannons, then marched off to demand powder at the fortress on the eastern edge of Paris known as the Bastille.

This building was a remnant of the wall that formerly had surrounded Paris; in the 1700s, it served as an armory and a prison for those arrested by royal order. By 1789, the neighborhood surrounding the Bastille on the eastern edge of Paris had become valuable real estate, and the Bastille was being phased out as a prison and armory. That day, it held only six prisoners, and only a handful of royal soldiers defended it. Their leader, named De Launay, opened the drawbridge to receive the delegation into the courtyard; however, one of the soldiers panicked and fired. This set off a riot, in which the demonstrators killed or arrested the soldiers defending the prison, then marched back to the city hall and seized it, arresting the city councilors and killing the mayor.

The next morning, the royal troops as well as the royally appointed Lieutenant-General of Police withdrew from the city. The neighborhood assemblies formed militias to keep the peace and delegated representatives to a new municipal assembly. The old city government had been made up of representatives of the six largest guilds; by contrast, this new government was composed of three hundred representatives. Though the event, at the outset, had nothing to do with the National Assembly, it led in a few short days to the formation of a new city government formed by the people rather than the king. As news spread, people across France interpreted the taking of the Bastille as a sign that ordinary people, motivated by their patriotic conviction, had become involved in the political affairs of the day. In the next two weeks, similar revolts took place by patriotic activists—against city governments made up of corporations that were backed by royal charters.

The uprisings in the city generated a great deal of excitement, but also consternation, among the literate, politically conscious parts of society. Peasants in the countryside were afraid. They worried that urban protests about high food prices would encourage the new city governments to send out armed troops to force them to sell their produce more cheaply. Rumors began to circulate in rural villages of armed brigands who were attacking farms, threatening to burn down fields not yet harvested and then stealing the grain from the peasant farmers. As a result, peasants also organized militias. In certain regions, these small bands of armed peasants went on the offensive, against the landlords—or more precisely, against their seigneurial privileges, about which the peasants had complained in their petitions of grievance to the Estates General. These privileges required the peasants to pay the lords to gain approval for harvesting or any other use of the land. In this peasant mobilization, known as the "Great Fear," thousands of peasants attacked the symbols of seigneurial power: weather vanes and scales, which only nobles could erect; the walls and roads of royal châteaux, which were built by the obligatory labor of peasants; and *lettres de fief*, or feudal land titles, which were the legal documents on which landlords based their claims to seigneurial obligations owed to them by peasants.

By this point, a clear pattern of political activity was emerging. First, noble magistrates in the royal courts, second, middle-class lawyers of the Third Estate, third, artisans of Paris, and last, peasants in the country had become politically active. The National Assembly, now at work on a constitution, would need years to finish the job, but it needed to send a message *now* that would calm the protests. The obvious targets were the various traditions, privileges, hierarchies, and arbitrary authorities discussed above. Moreover, many National Assembly delegates from all three orders had been emboldened by these dramatic events and were ready to propose farther-reaching changes. On August 4, noble and clerical deputies offered to sacrifice their personal privileges, such as exemptions from taxation, for the good of the nation. This virtuous sacrifice in turn inspired representatives of the Third Estate to give up the privileges of their guilds, cities, and regions. Finally, the delegates voted together to abolish the feudal system entirely, meaning all hierarchies and privileges, so that all citizens were equal before the law. This did not mean the end to rents or the redistribution of land—and said nothing about how a new social or political system would be constituted. But it did make inevitable the end of the nobility and clergy as distinct, privileged groups (these changes would be accomplished by votes of the National Assembly in the summer of 1790) and it made France into what Louis XIV had advocated a century earlier: one country with one law.

The Assembly also set to work on a preamble to the constitution that would make clear the direction in which the delegates hoped to take France. This document, issued in September 1789 as the Declaration of the Rights of Man and of the Citizen, called for a society in which free individuals could—and would—choose voluntarily to associate with one another and form a political society for mutual ends. Whatever form the new government took, it would be designed to defend and promote the good of the people. The guiding principle would be the liberty of each individual: liberty from coercion against one's will; liberty of association, liberty of religious conscience, liberty of thought and expression; and, in the final article, the "sacred and inviolable right" of individual property. These liberties were designed to end the society of groups (or corporations) based on tradition, such as the three orders, the guilds, the church, and seigneurial land-tenure arrangements. The only limitations on these liberties would be those mutually agreed upon by the members of that society—that is, the laws passed by the new government. These laws would apply to all individuals equally, and no individual (including, presumably, even the king) would be above or outside the law; private laws or privileges that applied to one group or person, would no longer exist. This preamble, unlike the Bill of Rights to the U.S. Constitution (which was also being written in the fall of 1789), did not seek to set specific limits on the power of a newly formed government, but instead sought to begin the process of creating a new government by empowering individuals at the expense of traditional social groups. The result, declared the National Assembly, would be a new government and an entirely "regenerated" society.

## THE CONSTITUTIONAL MONARCHY (1789–92)

From this point on, the National Assembly now met as a single body and governed France. It passed laws through which it hoped to reform and regenerate France. It would also develop a new constitution, and for this reason, it became known as the Constituent Assembly. The basic framework for the government was set early on when the Assembly voted to give the king a veto, though this veto could be overridden. Some patriots objected to any veto. They believed that the Assembly, as the representative of all the people, should make the law without interference. Others wanted a stronger veto for the king, to prevent the Assembly from passing laws in favor of one group, such as property owners, at the expense of another, such as the poor. Almost everyone in France and across Europe expected that the Assembly, with so clear a mandate, would produce a new constitution and legal system within a year or two, and the French Revolution would be over.

Between September 1789 and June 1791, the Constituent Assembly worked continually on both the constitution and a new legal code. Its primary goal, for both projects, was to break up the corporations, privileges, and hierarchies of the Old Regime and encourage individual liberty of thought, speech, and, above all, property. In early 1791, the Assembly passed the Le Chapelier law, which abolished the guilds. To further enforce individual liberty, this law also outlawed any workers' associations. On the one hand, this law freed individuals from having to obtain an apprenticeship to enter a craft or obtain a mastership to open a workshop; on the other hand, it prevented the formation of friendly societies, as in England, through which workers pooled resources to provide for the families of unemployed, sick, or dead colleagues.

This law was one of a series of laws abolishing the exclusive privilege of royally chartered bodies, including not only the economic sphere but also the cultural sphere, such as the royal literary and scientific academies and the royal theaters. These bodies became open to all, in the service of the public. One result of this change was the creation, for the first time in history, of public museums, open to all and operated by the government to ensure the promotion of general knowledge.

At the same time, the Constituent Assembly sought to create equality under the law, for all citizens—meaning the law would apply equally to everyone—regardless of their region, religion, order, wealth or sex. Most important, this meant that all positions—in the military, the diplomatic corps, government offices, academia, judiciary, and so on—should be open to the person with the best ability and willingness to fulfill it. The Assembly decreed that to select those most able and willing, the people should vote; as a result, the period from the fall of 1789 through the spring of 1791 brought possibly the most elections of any two years in history. Every town and city elected a new government; every region elected new judges; many professional associations and military units elected their own leaders. Since citizens had to travel to cast their ballots, many of these elections took several days of voting to complete. Voter turnout often stood at about 25 percent. To produce the many new officers, diplomats, teachers, and judges the new society would need, the Assembly also proposed (and eventually created) a system of competitive examinations for entrance to special training schools.

Such a society, of free and equal individuals, without natural leaders born into the elite, did not seem obvious. Indeed, many people very much doubted that such a society could exist, because they feared that individuals, freed of obligations to a group, would pursue only their own self-interests (meaning wealth and power). To prevent a society of self-interested individuals, the Assembly also sought to promote a sense of civic self-sacrifice and patriotism, or in the language of the day, "virtue."

In general, the Assembly sought to re-invent completely the bases of French society. Not only did this mean new names and symbols, but also new ways of measuring and experiencing France. New maps featured regions named for natural geographic features rather than, as before, for the noble family that ruled over that region. A new system of weights and measures made it much easier to calculate; this system eventually became the metric system. And a new calendar established a week as 10 days and a month as 3 weeks, so that people could readily calculate the day of the week for a given date. These changes in the way people understood time and space demonstrated what the Assembly meant by regeneration of the French society. Many of these reforms took years to develop and were only partially completed, but they indicate how far the revolutionaries thought they could go in re-inventing the world.

In September 1789, the most pressing issue for the Constituent Assembly was determining who would be eligible to serve in the new government and to vote in the new elections. In effect, the idea of what it meant to be a free citizen in a large country had to be invented, since no one had ever experienced it or even thought it possible. In the republics that had existed in early modern Europe, such as in the Swiss city of Geneva, only one segment of society were full citizens. Other large countries that had developed citizenship rights, such as England or the nascent United States of America, likewise had granted the chance to participate to only a small segment of society. Most people considered democracy dangerous; it had to be limited sharply if the government were not to deteriorate into anarchy. Those able and willing to rule would have to be determined, so they could define and protect the liberty and equality of all.

The first question, then, was to ask who would be eligible to vote for and hold office. Elections had taken place regularly in Old Regime France, in guilds and in city governments. However, these communities considered themselves single bodies, so when they voted, they expected the results to be unanimous. The selection of delegates for the Estates General in January 1789 had taken place through caucuses, rather than by secret ballot, and the Revolution continued this practice.

Indeed, the idea of elections during this period did not presume that each person should cast a vote based on his own preference. There was great concern that since many people might not understand what was in their interest, democratic elections would lead to anarchy or mob rule. To avoid this, the Assembly sought to promote elections that would be based on the public use of reason, or a rational calculation of what would be best for all of society. Those able to make such a calculation would be those with a stake in society (and thus would be affected by the outcome) and those who had shown they could manage their own affairs. This meant that France granted voting rights only to those who held property as in other eighteenth-century electoral systems, such as Britain and the new United States.

Some Enlightenment writers emphasized that citizens should use reason to calculate what would be best for their own, and for society's, material interest, while others insisted participation had to be based on a sense of civic virtue. The Constituent Assembly sought to establish criteria that would do both. On the one hand, it required voting to be restricted to literate adults, who could use reason; on the other hand, it required voters to speak French and to have resided in one place for at least one year. Those accorded the right to vote would be considered active citizens, who would make the laws through their use of reason, motivated by civic virtue. These laws would apply equally to all, so that everyone would have passive citizenship rights to be equal under the law.

The Assembly did not expect that all passive citizens could become active. Most of the delegates, influenced by traditional European medical and theological doctrine, believed that women could not use reason to deliberate. Therefore, after a discussion, the Assembly voted that only men would be eligible for active citizenship. Although this was the first-ever discussion of women's suffrage, it set a double standard that would endure in France until 1944. The Assembly also had petitions from religious and racial minorities, notably Jews and free blacks in the French colonies. The deputies had to decide if these property-owning men could be motivated by civic virtue. In a decision that became the model argument for the citizenship of religious minorities across Europe and the world, the Assembly decided to give everything to Jews as individuals, meaning active citizenship to all who met the property requirement, but nothing as a nation, meaning no recognition of their distinct community traditions or institutions. The new government would be made up of individuals who had reason and were capable of patriotic, civic virtue.

Speaking for the free blacks in the colonies, Vincent Ogé, argued that so-called *gens de couleur* ("people of color," meaning those of mixed-race descent) were property owners and even slave owners—and, accordingly, should be eligible for active citizenship. Ogé explicitly distinguished these men from black slaves, who made up most of the population in the French Caribbean colonies. However, white plantation owners as well as commercial businessmen in the port cities of Nantes and Bordeaux, argued that the Assembly should not take any action that might disrupt France's overseas trade with its colonies. The Assembly agreed, refusing Ogé's petition (and, in fact, having him arrested) and allowing a colonial assembly of white plantation owners to decide the future of all issues pertaining to race and slavery in the colonies. This fateful decision would lead, as Ogé had warned, to slave uprisings, first in the colony of Martinique and then in the larger colony of Saint-Domingue.

Passive citizens still had many opportunities to participate indirectly in revolutionary politics. For instance, the ability to use new names—such as names of streets, cities, regions, and months—and to use more democratic forms of address, such as "citizen" and "citizenness," instead of "sir" and "madam," symbolized the change that was taking place. Moreover, the end of censorship meant that ordinary people could participate in political debates by reading newspapers and pamphlets, and by attending political meetings and cheering or hooting the speakers. The first such meetings were the small electoral assemblies to select delegates to the Estates General. In Paris, these district assemblies continued to meet and to provide ordinary citizens, including passive citizens, a chance to debate the issues of the day. In September 1790, the Parisian city government reorganized these district assemblies into 48 sections. Though the sections had no legislative authority, they functioned as neighborhood councils and drew many ordinary citizens into political life.

Citizens also formed political clubs, based not on geographical proximity (the same neighborhood) but on a similar outlook. These clubs were, in effect, the first political parties. The first club, the Society of Friends of the Constitution, formed by a group of Breton deputies, gathered every day before the Assembly to decide how to vote on key issues that day. The deputies sought to promote the greatest individual liberty and the greatest opportunity for participation. Because they met in a hall that had formerly been a Jacobin monastery, this group became known as the Jacobin Club. They soon opened their meetings to others who were not members of the Assembly but shared their views; they inspired others to organize similar clubs in other cities, which promoted their goals of greater liberty and democracy through speeches and newspapers and to propose candidates for city and national offices.

The Jacobin Club eventually became the largest and most powerful political force in France, enjoying support primarily from liberal-minded, middle-class professionals and skilled artisans. One of its leaders, a lawyer from the small city of Arras named Maximilien-François Robespierre, argued in the Constituent Assembly for active citizenship for all men regardless of wealth, for the abolition of slavery in French colonies, and for a term limit for deputies in the Assembly.

Another political group, known as the Girondins, for the southwestern region where many of its leaders came from, sought to promote commerce, especially exports of goods. It also sought more power for the king. Other political clubs included the Cordeliers Club in Paris that shared many of the views (and members) of the Jacobins, and the Feuillants, a splinter group of the Jacobins. As the Revolution progressed, such clubs became more widespread and popular, providing a venue for passive citizens to take an active role, especially in the larger cities. These clubs not only held debates and printed pamphlets; they also circulated petitions and organized demonstrations to show their support for the Revolution. One of the most active clubs, the

Society of Revolutionary Women, promoted the new government among market women.

Newspapers were another new aspect that had great political influence on the Revolution. Some of the most prominent newspapers, such as the *Revolutions of Paris,* or the *Old Cordelier,* were associated with the clubs (Feuillants and Cordeliers, respectively). Another, the *Friend of the People,* edited by Jean-Paul Marat, took a strongly patriotic position. It called on the Assembly to protect the ordinary, working people of Paris from those who might use the Revolution for their own enrichment, whom Marat called aristocrats, regardless of their social origins. For ordinary people, the ability to attend sections or clubs and to read pamphlets and newspapers provided the most significant opportunity for political participation in the Revolution. Many took part with a great sense of patriotic duty.

In the winter of 1789–90, the Assembly's Constitution Committee worked out a new framework for the government; other committees drafted new laws to reform French society. Many of these reform measures emerged from the decree of August 4, abolishing the feudal regime. In June 1790, the Assembly abolished all titles of nobility; nobles were stripped of their legal privileges, exemptions from taxation, and powers as landowners over peasants. They remained large landowners, and peasants were required to buy out many of their obligations to the lords through cash payments. The Assembly ruled that only those nobles who openly rejected the Revolution by leaving France would lose their lands. In effect, this change transformed lords into large creditors, people who no longer had seigneurial power over their peasants but remained the most wealthy and prominent segment of society.

Similar thinking underlay the Assembly's decision to transform members of the clergy into ordinary citizens, with all the same rights and responsibilities. Parish priests would be encouraged to continue to serve in the same capacity, but would no longer remain outside French society. Instead, the Assembly liberated them from the church by making them employees of the national government. To ensure their loyalty to the nation, they would be required to take a pledge of allegiance, known as the Civil Constitution of the Clergy. Members of the clergy, under this new plan, would be paid a salary well above the stipend that most parish priests received; in return, the church lands became national goods. Since no individual owned these lands, the Assembly did not consider this confiscation to be a violation of anyone's sacred and inviolable rights. Moreover, money raised from the auction of these lands paid off the national debt. Promissory notes backed by the value of these lands, known as *assignats,* began to circulate as paper money. This plan seemed to combine social reform with responsible management of public finances, an ideal combination of reason and patriotism.

In the summer of 1790, these reforms appeared to be going so well that the Assembly organized a large festival to celebrate the success of the Revolution. The Festival of Unity, held in central Paris on February 14, 1790, gathered soldiers from militia units throughout France to view patriotic plays and participate in a grand ceremony that celebrated the unity of all, under their patriotic king.

## DISSATISFACTION WITH THE REVOLUTION

The Festival succeeded beyond everyone's highest hopes, but from that point on, the Revolution did not proceed smoothly. Over the next year, from mid-1790 to mid-1791, many groups became dissatisfied. The most prominent doubts about the Revolution came, as one might expect, from the former nobles, whose privileges, authority, and land had been challenged by the decree of August 4 and the law of June 1790. While some liberal-minded nobles actively supported the Revolution and took leading roles in it, many others used the reforms of August 4 to renegotiate rent terms with their peasants. Some landowning nobles feared that the loss of their seigneurial privileges augured further reforms, and they decided to leave France. Since such an act of treason meant the government would confiscate their land, many left behind a legal heir, or better yet, hired a good lawyer to defend their estates. Many nobles in the military officer corps abandoned their posts rather than serve under the authority of the Assembly, which decreed such reforms as elections within military units for leadership. Emigrant nobles gathered outside of France's border, in the Prussian city of Coblenz (now Koblenz, in Germany) and in northern Italy. They appealed to the Prussian king Frederick William and the Hapsburg emperor Leopold II (and the brother of Marie Antoinette) to intervene and roll back the Revolution by force; by early 1791, an invasion of emigrant nobles and foreign powers seemed likely, causing great worry in Paris.

Within the clergy, displeasure with the Revolution emerged in 1790; and more than half refused to swear allegiance to the nation. Roughly, one half of the parish priests refused to swear the oath, preferring to lose their pulpits rather than participate in what they saw to be an abandonment of their orders. Among those higher in the church administration, at the level of bishop or above, 95 percent did not swear the oath. These "refractory clergy" were concentrated in rural areas, especially the western and central part of the country where support for the church and nobility had been the strongest. In more urban areas, and in those areas where the clergy were relatively isolated, priests were much more likely to swear the oath.

Even some patriots took displeasure at the actions of the Constituent Assembly. Many patriots felt that the Assembly did not go far enough to create true liberty and equality. Men as diverse as the former Marquis de Condorcet, the *abbé* Grégoire, and the lawyer Robespierre all agreed that the Assembly had erred in distinguishing between active and passive citizens. Condorcet argued that since all people, including women, had reason, then every individual should be eligible to participate in government. Moreover, he warned, society would suffer if it did not benefit from the contributions of everyone, since a rational debate required the broadest conversation possible. Grégoire, similarly, argued that free blacks, Jews, and women could become, if they were not already, both rational individuals and patriotic French citizens. Robespierre objected to the property requirement for active citizenship, arguing that if the new regime granted political rights only to those who could afford to pay taxes worth three days of their wages, it was creating only the illusion of liberty and equality.

Other criticisms came from those outside the Assembly, especially from the people in the Parisian sections and at the newspapers. The patriot newspapers *Revolutions of Paris* and *Friend of the People* strongly supported the Revolution but criticized the king and the Assembly. These newspapers feared that patriots, who had shown their virtue by fighting for liberty on July 14, were losing out to wealthy aristocrats, who had lost their noble status but still sought to control political power in order to retain their wealth. Some patriots, such as Marat, argued that anyone who had benefited from the Old Regime in any way—including seigneurial property owners, bishops who had enjoyed benefits of church-owned land, and those who had been employed by the government, including members of royal academies—should bear the burden of the debt the Old Regime had accrued; Marat also argued that those who had benefited from the Old Regime should pay to lessen the misery and shortage now faced by hard-working patriots who had lost their jobs in the recent economic crisis. He and other patriots criticized the wealthy as aristocrats, whether or not they had been nobles before the Revolution. These patriots argued that aristocrats might be motivated by reason, because they could calculate what was in their material interest, but that unlike patriotic artisans, the wealthy were no way virtuous. Patriots such as Marat hoped that the new constitution, with the liberty it provided all citizens to form clubs and print newspapers, would enable all citizens to agitate for a more democratic government and more just economic policies in the future.

## THE CRISIS OF THE CONSTITUTIONAL MONARCHY

From the beginning, most French people believed King Louis XVI would support the Revolution once his despotic ministers, including the queen, Marie Antoinette, were removed. Despite some critics in the press, the king retained broad support throughout 1789 and 1790. Certainly, he faced some indignities, notably the forced return to Paris from Versailles in October 1789 and the Civil Constitution of the Clergy, which he considered an attack on Catholic bishops. Since the new Constitution granted him a significant veto power (though he could be overridden by the Assembly), the king seemed inclined to support, or at the least, tolerate these changes. The king's support for the Revolution increasingly worried some of his closest advisors, who encouraged him to oppose the new constitution.

On June 21, 1791, King Louis heeded their advice; hidden by disguise and the cover of night, the royal family fled Paris to join the emigrant nobles in Coblenz. There, the royal family hoped to co-ordinate with the Prussian king and Hapsburg emperor an invasion of France. Moreover, the king left behind a statement harshly attacking the new constitution. However, their plan failed when a customs officer recognized Louis at the border town of Varennes; the royal family returned, under arms, to Paris. Some patriot newspapers, notably the radical *Friend of the People,* took the news of the king's failed flight as all the evidence that he could not and would not support a constitutional monarchy. These patriot newspapers, including some Jacobins and most of the more radical Cordelier Club, called instead for a republic.

However, a majority of the Assembly delegates, led by the Girondin faction, hoped to preserve the moderate course they had set. They agreed to overlook the king's flight, arguing unconvincingly that the king had been abducted against his will. These monarchists organized another national festival, during the week of July 14 (1791), to celebrate once more the unity of the nation under its king. At this festival, a contingent from the Cordeliers Club held a demonstration calling for the Assembly to suspend the constitutional monarchy and replace it with a republic. Fearing this protest would get out of hand, and worried for the safety of the king, the leader of the Paris National Guard, the former Marquis de Lafayette, ordered his troops to fire on the demonstrators. The troops killed about 50 demonstrators; to patriots, this Massacre of the Marching Fields demonstrated how little had changed and how the property owners who controlled the new regime intended to preserve their power at all costs. To moderates and conservatives, such as the newly formed Monarchist Club, this event demonstrated the threat of the mob and the need for firm restraints that would keep in place the cooler heads of the propertied and of royal authority. Those already against the Revolution—refractory clergy, emigrant nobles, and the kings of Prussia, Austria, and England—resolved to undo the Revolution by force. They issued the Declaration of Pillnitz calling for an end to the Revolution.

King Louis had retaken the throne after his flight, but the massacre diminished his popularity. Furthermore, he now headed a government threatened with war by his own former nobles and royal allies. Under these difficult conditions, the king approved the new constitution for a constitutional monarchy at the end of August, 1791. The Constituent Assembly, its work completed, dissolved itself—and, led by Robespierre, voted that none of its members could stand for election to the next legislature. This democratic, self-denying law ensured that a new crop of representatives would come into office in the next legislature, known as the Legislative Assembly. Elected by the roughly fifty thousand active citizens, the Legislative Assembly took power on October 1, 1791.

The Girondin faction dominated the Legislative Assembly. The Girondin leader, a former writer, philosopher, and spy, named Jacques-Pierre Brissot de Warville, advocated a commercial economy, an aggressive foreign policy, and a strong monarch. He and his followers believed that all of these goals would be promoted if France declared a preemptive war against Austria, Prussia, and Britain. His rivals in the Assembly, the Jacobins, argued against a war, fearing that a war would only worsen shortages and political unrest at home.

In 1789, the National Assembly had attempted to show how this new government would differ from previous regimes by issuing a declaration of peace to all free peoples of the world. However, now the three greatest powers in Europe, joined by many of France's own most experienced officers who had emigrated, threatened an invasion. In April

1792, France declared war on Prussia and called upon patriotic volunteers to join the army. At the same time, ongoing food shortages in Paris led to regular demonstrations and even riots. Rumors sweeping Paris attributed the shortages to hoarders in the countryside and enemies of the Revolution in the city, especially the refractory priests. Patriots such as Marat called for the deportation of refractory clergy and for the Assembly to arrest peasants who were hoarding grain. In the countryside, many peasants became even more suspicious of the Revolution.

Only the king could pull the country together, but no one knew if Louis could be trusted. Many patriots, including a majority of the Jacobins and the Cordeliers, considered him a weak leader who had already betrayed France by attempting to flee and then ordering his troops to fire on citizens during the Festival. For these reasons, they believed that the king would not defend France from an invasion, and they petitioned for his removal and replacement with a republic. The clubs and sections of Paris and other large cities began to demonstrate regularly in support of these petitions. Others petitioned for forceful action against internal enemies, such as refractory priests and aristocrats, meaning land owners and wholesale grain merchants, whom patriots feared would turn against France in a time of war. Those who believed the Revolution had already gone far enough, including many Girondins and the splinter group of moderate Jacobins known as the Feuillants, pleaded with the king to suppress these petitions and demonstrations. His wife, the queen, openly asked her brother, Emperor Leopold II of Hapsburg, to invade. In June, King Luis mobilized 50,000 soldiers to defend the Tuileries Palace in Paris, where he and the royal family were living.

## THE RISE OF THE JACOBIN REPUBLIC (1792–93)

On July 14, 1792, the third anniversary of the taking of the Bastille, there was no national festival. Instead, many patriots in Paris and Marseilles organized petitions and demonstrations accusing the king of being beholden to foreign enemies rather than the French people. In response, the Prussian Duke of Brunswick issued a manifesto threatening to invade France and besiege Paris if any harm came to the king. This news convinced many activists that the country faced a grave and immediate danger. They chose not to focus their energies on the upcoming September elections but to take direct action; on August 3, all but one of the Paris sections approved petitions calling for the removal of the king.

On August 10, a large demonstration organized by the Parisian sections, with the support of the Jacobins in the Assembly, attacked the Tuileries palace and seized the royal family. That afternoon, the Legislative Assembly voted to arrest the king and to hold new elections for a new constitutional convention. Thus began the second, more radical phase of the French Revolution.

Elections of deputies to a new, constitutional convention took six weeks to carry out. During that time, from mid-August to late September, a provisional government tried to wage war while keeping the peace at home. This was no easy task; the arrest of the king sparked not only an invasion of Prussian troops, backed by French emigrant nobles, but also the resignation of many French officers—including Lafayette. It also prompted some ordinary conscripts in the western region to refuse to enlist as soldiers. These resisters, known as Chouans, began a guerilla war against the still-undeclared republic. The Parisian press identified the Chouans as counter-revolutionaries, but they viewed themselves defenders of the king, the clergy, and the autonomy of their region. Parisians were terrified, fearing not only the end of grain shipments from the countryside (at precisely the time of year, late summer, when food stores in the city were lowest) but also a Prussian invasion that would besiege their city. These fears led to calls, in the most radical newspapers, to eliminate the enemies of the Revolution within their midst, who endangered everyone's liberty—namely, the refractory clergy.

The first week of September, several hundred patriots, acting this time without the support of the sections and against the wishes of Jacobin leaders, massacred more than a thousand priests who had refused to swear the oath. This collective violence further divided the city and the country. Radicals celebrated the massacres as courageous acts of brave citizens saving the Revolution by taking matters into their own hands; moderates and conservatives feared that the rule of law was deteriorating into anarchy.

In this desperate situation, Parisians received the news of an unexpected victory of French troops over the invading Prussians at the French town of Valmy as a sign of salvation. In fact, the battle was really a stalemate, but it showed that an army of patriotic volunteers, led by inexperienced officers not of noble birth, could fight and win against the best-trained army in Europe. The German poet Johann Wolfgang von Goëthe had traveled with the army to Valmy; that evening, he consoled the soldiers by telling them, "Here and on this day begins a new era in the history of the world." In Paris, two days later, the newly seated constitutional convention took a similarly optimistic view and voted to declare an end to France's thousand-year-old monarchy and to found instead a republic. To symbolize the importance of this change, the new government put in place a new calendar that calculated all time from September 22, 1792, the founding of the Republic.

A republic, in early modern Europe, meant many things. Politically, it meant a government ruled not by a king but by the citizens. It also meant a greater degree of equality; in a republic, there could be no distinction between active and passive citizenship, at least among men. Culturally, a republic meant that all people had to feel unity, or fraternity. Republican citizens would have to be willing to sacrifice their personal interests for the good of collective liberty and self-defense. This shared commitment to sacrifice, known as *virtue*, would motivate them to make whatever sacrifice—of their time, of their property, and, if necessary, of their lives—was necessary. It also meant they had to be vigilant to ensure that all their fellow citizens kept up this sense of civic virtue, since a republic would always be threatened by those who sought to take away its liberty. Anyone not willing to defend the republic endangered it. Socially, a republic was associated with a small group of artisans or small landowners; no one had ever imagined that a country the size of France, with as diverse a population, could form a republic. This concern to protect the liberty of the republic, and the obligation of every citizen to do so, greatly influenced the leaders of the Jacobin party as well as the patriots.

To put these ideas into a new constitution was the task of the newly elected legislature, known as the Convention. At the same time, it also had to govern France—to address the food shortages, the inflation, and the now open war with Prussia, as well as the civil war breaking out in the west. The Convention also had to decide what to do with the king. The Constitution of 1791 had declared the king inviolable from all prosecution, yet it also declared no individual could be above the law. Therefore, the Convention first had to decide if it could try King Louis at all. Then, it had to decide the crime. The Girondins, who held a majority in the Convention, argued that the king was now a mere citizen, entitled to the same rights as anyone charged with a crime. The Jacobins, led by Robespierre and a little-known provincial lawyer named Antoine Saint-Just, argued that the French people had already found him guilty when they overthrew him on August 10, and that as representatives of the people, the Convention delegates could only punish him.

Moreover, the Jacobins argued that he must not be charged with the crimes of a man or enjoy the protections of a citizen, since as the king, he had never been a part of society. "This man," Saint-Just claimed, "must either reign or die." This argument carried the day. By a wide margin, the deputies voted to convict the king of treason. Then, by a narrow majority, the deputies sentenced him to death. Thus, on January 21, 1793, King Louis XVI was executed by the guillotine. His wife and children were imprisoned; Marie Antoinette would be tried eight months later and also guillotined. His son, the heir to the throne, would die in prison.

This regicide had two important consequences. First, it made all of those in the Convention responsible for an act that could not be undone, for which the foreign monarchs of Prussia and the Hapsburg Empire had sworn to exact vengeance. The deputies of the Convention knew this act had raised the stakes substantially for the Revolution. Second, it divided the deputies between the Jacobins and the Girondins. The Girondins, who had mostly voted against the execution, lost all support in the Paris sections, whose members now considered them unreliable weak links in the defense of France's liberty.

The Jacobins, by contrast, emerged in the eyes of the politically restive Parisian population as patriotic heroes defending the ordinary people. Though the Jacobins hoped for an orderly transition to the Republic, they also encouraged the sections, the patriotic newspapers, and the city government (known as the Commune) to keep up the pressure on the Girondin majority in the Convention. Indeed, the Jacobins encouraged participation of ordinary Parisians in the sections by promoting Marat's newspaper, *Friend of the People*. Marat's attacks were so effective that the Girondins sought to have him removed from the seat in the Convention that he had won in the election and sought to shut down his paper. This effort failed, which only reinforced Marat's popularity among Parisian patriots, especially those in a new political club, the Mad Dogs (Enragés). Led by a former priest named Jacques Roux, the Mad Dogs sought to alleviate the misery of the poor by redistributing property. Another Parisian leader, Jacques-René Hébert, became a prominent voice in the Commune, leading a radical faction known as the *ultras*. At the suggestion of Georges Danton, a leading Jacobin, the Convention passed a law providing a stipend for ordinary artisans to attend section meetings. In this way, the Jacobins developed a base of support among the ordinary citizens, or sansculottes of Paris.

The Jacobins proposed a series of measures that were very popular with the Parisian sansculottes, notably a new constitution that expanded the right to vote to all men (although women would remain passive citizens). They also proposed that the constitution assure a right to subsistence so that indigent patriots, especially the hard-working artisans of Paris, would not starve while others turned a profit. To achieve this goal, the Jacobins proposed a legally mandated maximum price that could be charged for bread and other essential goods to keep them affordable. These proposals, however, only reinforced the apprehension about the Jacobins among merchants in the provincial cities. The merchants were pleased that the Girondins continued to control a majority and could block these measures and defend the right of private property.

Among the peasants, especially in the west, the Revolution had brought little favorable change—that is, no new land. It had also created some undesirable consequences, such as the loss of parish priests and, in March 1793, a new draft. In response, more peasants began to revolt against the Republic; in the spring of 1793, former nobles and clergy organized a peasant army that attacked the regional capital of Nantes and seized republican tax-collectors and draft officers. Nantes, an important port, also provided a natural point for English troops to land and represented a second front in the war. Months later, the English landed in Spain and invaded France from the south, opening a third front.

This multifront war seemed far beyond any preparations the divided Convention could make. The Girondins, whose leaders had called for war a year earlier, now resisted taking the necessary step of centralizing power in the hands of the government so that an army could be drafted and provisioned. Instead, it was the Jacobins, who had opposed the war, who now took on the responsibility for organizing the national defense. For this purpose, the Jacobins proposed suspension of the new constitution; they argued that in this time of crisis, no elections could be held, nor could the individual liberties enshrined in the Declaration of Rights of Man be respected. Instead, the Convention would have to govern without a constitution, until the Revolution and the Republic were safe. This argument won over the Convention, which decreed that the government will be revolutionary until peace. To lead the way, the Convention created a Committee of Public Safety to oversee the war effort at home and abroad. The Committee of Public Safety was charged with overseeing a successful draft; requisitioning the necessary materials to provide the army with guns, uniforms, and horses; putting down the resistance in the west and southwest; and pacifying the Parisian population by providing food and enforcing the price maximum. The sections of Paris and the Jacobin clubs across France called on their representatives in the Convention, led by Robespierre and Danton, to be more forceful in defending the Republic. Danton appealed for "boldness, boldness, and still more boldness, for France to be saved," by which he meant that ordinary citizens should join the army, attend political meetings, sign petitions, and demonstrate on behalf of the republican government. He also meant that good citizens had a patriotic responsibility to denounce those among their neighbors whom they suspected of treason. For this purpose, citizens formed revolutionary societies, which also helped enforce the price maximum, the draft, and other emergency measures designed to save the Revolution. Moreover, these citizens were encouraged to serve on juries, known as revolutionary tribunals, to try those denounced as suspects. The sections also formed irregular militia units, known as revolutionary armies, to head into the countryside and punish hoarders who were thought to be driving up the price of bread by preventing convoys of grain from reaching the city.

The Girondins opposed this use of force and sought to have the sections dissolved; in response, the sansculottes—believing themselves to embody the heart of the Revolution—rebelled, attacking the Convention and arresting all the Girondin deputies. This purge left the Jacobins, more specifically the more radical faction known as "the mountain," in charge of the Convention, the Committee of Public Safety, and thus the Republic.

## THE COUNTRY IN DANGER: VIRTUE, LIBERTY, AND TERROR

This division split the country further during the summer of 1793. Supporters of the arrested Girondins, especially in the commercial cities of Bordeaux, Nantes, and Lyon, organized militias to resist the central government. These movements were known as federalist revolts, because they sought autonomy for regional and city governments from the national government in Paris. To the Jacobins in the Convention, these revolts seemed to prove that merchants in these cities were speculators, concerned only with their property and profit, and not with the security of France. The Convention sent units of the army, led by Convention delegates on mission, to each of these cities to suppress the federalist revolts, arrest and execute their leaders, and liberate the cities.

Such forceful action appealed to the sansculottes who continued to demonstrate and call for the Republic to terrorize its internal enemies.

As the war situation became more desperate, as an open revolt broke out in the French colonies, and as bread shortages and inflation in Paris worsened, the popular radical journalist Marat was assassinated at his home by a young provincial woman, Charlotte Corday. Many patriots suspected Corday was encouraged by royalist plotters seeking to undermine the Revolution. These patriots worried that the Revolution was being lost for a lack of will to fight. In September, they petitioned the Convention to make terror the "order of the day," by establishing revolutionary tribunals to try those suspected of treason all across the country. Thus began the Terror, in which more than one hundred thousand citizens were arrested, some fifty thousand tried, and an estimated twenty thousand executed, mostly by guillotine although some by firing squad or drowning. This bloodshed, though by no means unprecedented in its quantity, represented to many observers the anarchy and chaos that would naturally result in a society without a king, nobles, and clergy.

To the Jacobins, such extreme measures were regrettable and awful, but necessary to overcome the difficulties placed in the way of liberty and the Republic by its enemies. Robespierre defended the Terror, and, indeed, accelerated it, as the republican forces gradually suppressed the internal revolts and pushed back the foreign invaders. In the spring of 1794, the Convention sought to encourage even more virtue, which increasingly meant support for the Committee of Public Safety. It passed a new law that prevented suspects from defending themselves before the Revolutionary Tribunal. This led to the most intense period of trials and executions, many of them involving political opponents of Robespierre, but also involving some of his closest supporters, such as Danton and Hébert. By 9 Thermidor, Year II (late July 1794), so many members of the Convention and the Commune had been arrested and executed and so many sansculottes clubs had been shut down by the orders of the Committee of Public Safety that Robespierre had no support left. Rivals in the Convention staged a coup, killing him and his closest followers. On the next morning, the Convention declared an end to revolutionary government and proclaimed justice the order of the day.

## HOW TO END A REVOLUTION: THERMIDOR TO BRUMAIRE (1794–99)

The overthrow of Robespierre did not make clear, however, what would come next. Many thought that the Revolution had gone off course, but there was disagreement on how to set it right or if that were even possible. Some argued that France should restore the monarchy and the Old Regime, while others hoped that, with Robespierre eliminated, the Republic might continue as before in pursuit of greater fraternity and social equality.

Most wanted to steer France toward the political center and find a way to end the Revolution. This meant avoiding a return to the Old Regime while also ending revolutionary politics, with its constant demonstrations, riots, political meetings, and food shortages. In late summer 1794, the Girondins returned to the Convention, now purged of many of its left-wing Jacobin members. Once again with a more moderate majority, the Convention set aside the constitution that the Jacobins had drawn up in June 1793, which granted universal suffrage and a right to subsistence. Instead, the remaining deputies, known collectively as the Thermidorian Convention, began work on yet another constitution that, its authors hoped, would resolve the problem of creating a republic without the excesses of the Terror.

The Thermidorians sought a republic based on equality under the law, individual liberty, commercial growth, and a strong stable government. To achieve this goal, the new constitution drastically reduced the right to vote to only about thirty thousand of the wealthiest men in the country—out of a population of 27 million! The new constitution also provided for absolute defense of individual private property, at the expense of any right of the poor to subsistence. The Ideologues believed that by improving agriculture using modern methods, more food—rather than a fairer distribution—could solve the problem of urban shortages. The Thermidorians also believed that the Jacobins had been too susceptible to pressure by Parisian sansculottes, so they discouraged popular activism among Parisian artisans. In May 1795, the Thermidorian Convention called in National Guard soldiers to suppress a group of women and men who were protesting the continuing high bread prices and calling for the Jacobin-authored republican Constitution of 1793 (which had never been put into effect). This event proved for many people that the Thermidorian government—and the new constitution it was drafting—would not serve the interests of the ordinary people in Paris who had been the backbone of the Revolution. Moreover, supporters of the Jacobin movement were horrified that the Thermidorian regime tolerated a wave of revenge across provincial France, known as the White Terror. In a series of incidents, supporters of the Girondins verbally and physically attacked those who had supported the Jacobins or had taken part in revolutionary tribunals. Mobs led by royalists lynched an estimated fifteen hundred former Jacobin supporters, without trials. The cycle of attacks and revenge would divide families and leave a rift in French society that would last generations.

The Thermidorian moderates put into place a new constitution in August 1795. This document, known as the Constitution of the Year III, became the first republican constitution adopted in French history. It created a five-man executive council, chosen by the legislative assembly; this executive council, or Directory, had veto power over laws and authority to keep domestic peace and oversee the military. The new constitution divided the legislature into two chambers, the Council of the Five Hundred and the Council of Elders, each to be elected only by owners of substantial property. Furthermore, only citizens 40 years of age or older could sit in the Council of Elders, to ensure it would be more conservative. This division of power represented a sharp departure from the Jacobin conception of the Republic that had governed the country since 1792 in which the sovereignty of the nation, all the people collectively as represented by the Assembly, was indivisible.

The new government, known as the Directory, kept the domestic peace and prevented further political conflict; this became clear in its first months. In October 1795, with the new legislature not yet seated, a small group of Parisians organized a protest against the continuation of some Jacobin delegates in office under the new government. Fearing this protest might lead to a full-scale uprising of royalists seeking to bring back the Old Regime, the government turned to the military to suppress the crowd. The military officer summoned Napoleon Bonaparte, reportedly stated that a “whiff of cannon powder” would keep the peace and establish a more stable republic.

Once in power, the Directory enacted important reforms, notably in the economy. It removed the price maximum, stabilized the currency, encouraged greater industrial and agricultural production, and promoted wholesale trade and exports. It also strictly enforced bankruptcy laws, reversing the Jacobin Republic’s leniency toward debtors; this favored wealthy financiers and larger enterprises over smaller workshops and stores, creating hardships for ordinary people. For this reason, some criticized the Directory as a regime of the rich that made no effort to make society more moral or fair but was only ruled by money.

The directors included *abbé* Sièyes, who had been a leading patriot in 1789, and conservatives, even royalists, such as Lazare Carnot. Working together, the Directory sought a politics of balance, sometimes tilting to the left and sometimes to the right. In 1797, the directors annulled election results favoring the royalists; then a year later, they annulled elections won by neo-Jacobin candidates. In each case, protests were put down by force. The Directors were determined to govern from the center. One of the most spectacular shows of centrist force was the trial of François Gracchus Babeuf and his Conspiracy of Equals, who had plotted to overthrow the Directory and establish a regime that would ensure each citizen the right to land and a job. The government held a public trial and executed Babeuf and his collaborators.

## THE COUP D'ÉTAT OF NAPOLEON BONAPARTE

The Directory lasted from the fall of 1795 to the winter of 1799, longer than either the constitutional monarchy (1789–92) or the Jacobin Republic (1792–95). It restored a modicum of stability to France, preventing a return to civil war, while preserving the revolutionary principles of equality under the law, individual liberty of speech and religious belief, and a constitutional government. It also had success in fending off France's foreign enemies, though it could not control its own generals. These generals led the French army into the Netherlands, Italy, and even, in 1798, across the Mediterranean into Egypt. This aggressive policy meant that the government had to continue to fund and draft soldiers for a costly war, which decreased its popularity. The Directory also had success in stabilizing prices, in part by canceling two-thirds of government debt and in part by intervening directly in wholesale markets. However, many people still suffered shortages, in part due to the Directory's insistence on maintaining the 10-day weeks of the republican calendar, which meant market days, traditionally Sunday, would occur less frequently. This led many people, especially women in provincial cities, to call for a return to the seven-day calendar—and, while they were at it, for the churches to be reopened. These actions, though not challenges to the regime, undermined the credibility of, and support for, the government in the countryside.

Above all, the Directory had success in calming the political atmosphere. Many former Jacobins formed political clubs known as Constitutional Circles to defend individual liberties and the Republic against royalists and to promote economic fairness in taxation. Though these Circles were tolerated, the Directory suppressed other political clubs, limited the number and content of newspapers, and generally discouraged citizens from taking an active role in politics. For this reason, no one came to the defense of the Republic when in November 1799, a group of conservative politicians aided by the popular general Napoleon Bonaparte, seized the legislature and overthrew the Directory on the 18 Brumaire, Year VIII (November 9, 1799). The next morning, Bonaparte declared himself first consul of France and proposed a revised constitution that announced, "Citizens! Based on the principles with which it was begun, the French Revolution is over!"[1]

Thus began another adventure in French history—the rule of Napoleon Bonaparte. This period lasted 15 years, during which time Bonaparte restored the Catholic Church in France and created religious tolerance for Calvinists and Jews under supervision by the government. He did not restore the nobility's privileges nor the church its lands, and he retained the principle of equality under the law. Moreover, he completed one task the Revolution had set for itself in 1789, drafting a legal code to cover most areas of the law: criminal, penal, civil, and commercial. (A rural code, concerning land ownership in the countryside, was never completed.) To enforce these laws, he established a thorough, well-organized, and powerful national bureaucracy. To govern each department, Napoleon appointed a prefect and for each city a subdelegate; these officials, selected on merit and trained by the government, oversaw all aspects of governance. Their most important task was enforcing the law, which they did with great efficiency: collecting taxes, drafting soldiers, and monitoring the population to prevent any opposition to the regime.

For Napoleon, this orderly administration provided the natural endpoint to the Revolution. When it was in place, he formally ended the Republic in 1804 by following the lead of Julius Caesar and crowning himself Emperor. Shortly thereafter, he took a new wife, Josephine, and had her crowned Empress; finally he declared his son would succeed him. Not only did Napoleon end representative government in France, but his rule reversed some of the Revolution's moves toward liberty and democracy: freedom of the press and of theaters was ended; all political associations were suppressed; only the wealthiest 1 percent of the population enjoyed the right to vote; and the legislative body could not pass new laws, only approve decrees.

Napoleon believed that the Republic had failed because it had tried to base its political and social system on an unstable basis: individuals. He wanted instead to base society on "masses of granite," meaning wealthy property owners, and on families, in which husbands and fathers would provide for and rule over women and children. To this end, the Napoleonic Code prevented workers from forming any association and required them to have their employer's written permission to change jobs. Women could not own property in their own names and had to reside where their husbands moved in search of work. In the colonies still under French control, Napoleon reinstated slavery. All of these measures show how Napoleon sought to create a society that was modern in its orientation toward economic growth but was without what he considered the excesses of individual liberty or active citizenry. During his 15 years in power, Napoleon centralized the government in France and used his power to put a final end to the traditions and hierarchies of the Old Regime. Some historians see Napoleon as a logical conclusion to the Revolution, while others consider him a reversal of the Revolution and a sign of its failure. Another interpretation perceives Napoleon's government as a continuum, beginning with the Old Regime monarchy, passing through the liberalizing reforms of the Revolution and the centralizing tendencies of the Republic, before culminating in the modern state. Many of Napoleon's reforms—such as the Napoleonic Code, the prefects, and the ability of the state to coerce individuals (exemplified by his effective systems for conscription, tax collection, and record-keeping)—were among the most enduring changes of this period of cultures in conflict.

## NOTE

1. John Hall Stewart, *A Documentary Survey of the French Revolution* (New York: Macmillan, 1951).

## *Chapter 2*

# Ways of Life in France before 1789: The "Old Regime"

Only in retrospect—that is, after the start of the Revolution—was French society and government in 1789 referred to as the *Ancien Régime*. Though we usually translate that term into "Old Regime," it also meant the "Former Regime," or the way things were before the great changes. Yet those living in France prior to 1789 considered themselves to be living in the most reformed, modern society in the world, which had already undergone great changes in their century of Enlightenment. So to begin, we must understand what eighteenth-century French people considered the traditional way of doing things before the Revolution.

### TRADITIONAL SOCIETY IN THE COUNTRYSIDE: SEIGNEURIALISM

The social order in France prior to 1789 was considered to be "traditional," in that it was based on traditions that stretched back to uncertain origins in the past. Moreover, the most common, and convincing, justification for anything in the traditional society was that it had been done for a long time. So there was no specific plan for a traditional society; it was simply the ways things seemed to most people to have evolved by nature. Although great changes took place in the eighteenth century, many aspects of French society continued, based on long-standing traditions.

Three principles—hierarchy, privilege, and corporatism—governed the lives of ordinary people in France prior to 1789. *Hierarchy* meant that some people were thought of as inherently above others, rather than all people being born equal; this was most evident in the special status accorded clergy and nobles over common people. *Privilege* meant literally "private law"; to have a privilege meant to have a law or power that applied only to a small group, instead of everyone being equal under one set of laws and having the same sets of rights. *Corporatism* meant that all people belonged to one or more groups or "bodies" of people (hence the term *corporation,* from *corps* for body). The corporation to which a person belonged determined how everyone else in society identified and related to that person. Fellow members of a corporation were considered to be like a family; they looked out for one another and shared the same economic interests as well as moral values. The most common examples of corporatism in Old Regime France were trade guilds, but any group (or body) of people constituted a corporation, such as the citizens of a city, the clergy of the Catholic Church, or (in the sense we use the term today) members of a commercial enterprise.

Where one stood in the social hierarchy, the privileges one enjoyed, and the corporation to which one belonged were determined primarily by one's birth. Owning land, possessing a noble title, having the chance to enter the clergy or another "privileged" group were all matters primarily of birth. Moreover, such important personal characteristics as one's legal status, religion, career, and wealth were all based on birth, and so ordinary individuals could not really establish these personal characteristics for themselves.

Authority all across Europe in this period was more social than political—meaning that most people had no direct contact with any government. Instead, they answered to a class of landowners, known as lords, who controlled not only the wealth of their land (known as their fief) but also all the people who lived and worked on it. Those who worked on the land for these lords were known as subjects, or serfs. This system, known as *feudalism,* was a hierarchical social system, based on a principle of obligation and protection: those higher up in society accepted pledges of loyalty and obedience from those below them; in exchange for making such a pledge, known as "swearing homage," those below (*vassals*) were protected and defended by the lords. The ceremonial nature of swearing homage demonstrated the relationship: the vassal would kneel and kiss the hand of his lord, who would declare, "You are mine, to do with as I wish."

As landowners, lords were considered "free," because they could command (and compel, by force, if necessary) their serfs on their lands; they could also choose, from among higher-ranking lords (known as liege lords), to whom they wanted to swear allegiance.

Their homage would be a promise to put all their serfs to work for their liege lord when he demanded it for purposes of mutual self-defense; this is how liege lords (including princes and kings) constituted their armies. Liege lords could not, however, tell lower-ranking landowners what to do on their own lands.

In reality, this system actually ceased to exist in France (and most of western Europe) in the 1300s, due to the growing power of kings, which limited the power of lords over their own land. Yet many of its principles remained in effect, especially the freedom of lords to command those who worked on their lands. For this reason, the system that did exist in eighteenth-century France is often referred to as "lord-ism," or seigneurialism (to use the French word for *lord,* or *seigneur.*) Under the seigneurial system, lords still owned most of the land and retained some aspects of their autonomy, notably an exemption from royal taxes. This exemption of landowning lords from royal taxes was an example of a privilege, or a law that applied only to some people. As we will see, privileges were so common in Old Regime France that few laws applied to all people equally. So, when people in eighteenth-century France still spoke of feudalism, they generally referred to such privileges.

Those who lived and worked on the land, under seigneurial (rather than feudal) lords, were known as peasants (literally, "people of the land"). Peasants, unlike serfs, owned small plots of lands; peasants were not, as were serfs, tied to the land. They could leave the land and move elsewhere, though they rarely did so. Peasants were, legally speaking, tenants (literally, holders) on their lands. They could possess the land, but they did not have the right to *use* it; the power to use the land (or *usufruct*) belonged to the lord. To make any use of the land—such as to plant on it, harvest what was grown, buy or sell it, or even to use machinery (such as scales, ovens, wine or oil presses) on it—peasants needed the lord's permission. To obtain that permission, peasants had to show respect to the lord, in the form of dues. Dues were payments, such as part of what was harvested, cash or labor, from the peasant to the lord. These payments were neither rent nor taxes. They were, legally, signs of obedience and loyalty to the lord and respect for his power as lord over that land. A symbol of the lord's power, in popular belief (though it never actually existed), was the so-called "lord's right" (*droit de seigneur*): When a peasant married, his lord could choose to sleep with the bride on the wedding night.

Legally speaking, the peasant only had tenancy on the land for his or her lifetime, so upon the peasant's death, the land reverted to the lord unless a payment (known as *mortmain*) was made. For the same reason, a peasant could not buy or sell land without the lord's consent; if the lord gave consent, it required a payment known as *lods et ventes.* Other seigneurial dues included *champart,* the due for harvest; and *bans et fours,* the due for use of scales and ovens. The most important seigneurial power, though, was that of justice; as lord of a fief, the owner legally had the right to enforce laws, including settling any disputes over land that arose among the peasants—or between the peasants and the lord over what dues were owed. Most lords hired lawyers to serve as their judges, but clearly, the lord was the law on his own land. Peasants, then, were really sharecroppers.

About 85 percent of the eighteenth-century French population was peasants. Some were reasonably well off and possessed enough land to support their families comfortably. The symbol of their status was that they often owned plows and draft animals to help cultivate their fields and also to lend to others for additional income. Other peasants had little or no land, working as wage laborers for the lord and for other, better-off peasants. Peasant villagers tended to work the land together, pulling a single plow across all their lands.

Nearly all peasants also shared another attribute: debt. Farming is a seasonal occupation and is always dependent on credit. The French peasantry was particularly indebted because of a growing burden of seigneurial dues for many peasants. Lords hired lawyers to rewrite the "letter of fief," the document that established the terms of their peasants' obligations. Peasants also faced rising royal taxes and tithes to the church. In times of hardship, such as in harsh winters that ruined crops or economic depressions in cities that brought down prices, many peasants went bankrupt and had to sell what little land they owned.

Landowners also varied greatly. The wealthiest families, from the higher ranks of the nobility, had huge estates that generated not only great revenues but also brought them great power and prestige. Such families were literally royalty, in that they were related to the king. On their estates—or manors—they built impressive *châteaux* (castles, though they were really large country houses.) These families were also the ones who held prominent positions in the government, the church, the military, and the diplomatic corps. They left their estates in the hands of hired managers, who were specialists in increasing seigneurial dues as much as possible. They tended to be very socially conservative, and for this reason, they tended to oppose the royal government, which sought frequently to make reforms (as we will see soon.) Other wealthy landowners were lords, but not necessarily nobles, because they had recently bought their estates with money they made in other fields or—more frequently—they inherited their estates through a marriage dowry. Some landowning noble families did not enjoy great wealth or influence at all. They sought to maintain their family lineage and privileges; they were known as "old birds" *(hobereaux)*.

## TRADITIONAL SOCIETY IN TOWNS AND CITIES: *CORPORATIONS*

In cities, the saying went, the air was free, because there was no lord. The citizens themselves ruled the cities. This liberty, symbolized by walls and by city militias to defend those walls, could only be preserved by the collective effort of all the citizens, and so people in cities were expected to act always with "virtue," or a regard for the benefit of others in the community. In their economic lives, virtue meant cooperation among craftsmen in any given trade (such as shoemakers, barrel-makers, print-shop workers, among others). Craftsmen worked as a community or *corporation,* a single body, deciding together (through an elected council) how many people could work in a specific trade, how many workshops and retail stores there could be for that trade in town, and how high to set wages, prices, and production levels. These bodies, commonly referred to today as *guilds,* were governed by owners of workshops (known as *masters*) who sat on a council (known as a *jury*). Each master's shop employed several (on average, four to five) trained workers (known as *compagnons,* or companions), and several adolescent apprentices. The corporations also chose representatives to the city council, who in turn chose a mayor; the mayor's primary responsibility was to use the city police—and when necessary, the citizens' militia—to enforce the corporation's decisions about its own trade, to collect the sales taxes and other duties that the town used to support itself, and to make its common payment to the royal tax collector. The town's governmental structure, including its guarantee of liberty from a lord, the city government positions it could create, and its payment to—and privileges from—the royal government were spelled out in a city charter, a document that most towns received directly from the French crown.

The people who lived in towns were not all craftsmen. Those who considered themselves better off and better educated than craft workers, such as wealthy banker-investors, wholesale merchants (who might also own one or several workshops, though they hired others to serve as masters and run the shops), or lawyers considered themselves "gentlemen." They were not noble, but they enjoyed professional privileges and considered themselves closer to the *anoblis* than to the workers. Below the craftsmen were those who had no skills or trade, who often lived on the margins of poverty and unemployment; they were often dependent on small loans from neighbors to get by, or in times of greater hardship, charity from the church. Cities worried about having too many poor people in town, and city governments often sought to expel those who did not belong to a community of craftsmen.

## DYNAMICS FOR CHANGE

The traditional society we have just described, however, was also undergoing great change in the eighteenth century. This change was not fully evident to contemporaries, but it did manifest itself in every aspect of French economy, society, culture, and government.

In early modern Europe, the size of a country's population was considered the best measure of its health, wealth, and power. For this reason, the French government, in the 1600s, had begun a policy to increase the number of children through payments to families that had 10 children or more. The goal of this program was to offset the inclination of families to limit the number of children, so that they would have fewer heirs among which to divide up their property. In fact, this sort of family planning only affected wealthier families; most French families had many children, since there was no widespread birth control. On average, a French woman in this period had a child every eighteen months, which amounted to an average of eight births during her period of fertility (generally from her late teens to her late twenties). Of those eight, only four would survive to adulthood. Still, this meant a rapidly rising population—from twenty million in the late 1600s to twenty-seven million on the eve of the French Revolution. This population was widely scattered across France, four-fifths living in rural hamlets and villages, where they worked small plots of land. The rest of the population was in the towns and villages, where people worked as artisans in handicraft production or as paid laborers. The increase in population in the countryside meant more families working smaller plots of land, and the increase in the cities meant a growth in the available labor pool for new industries, such as textiles.

Most people's households included more people than the immediate family members. Almost anyone of means in the cities had at least one, and usually several, domestic servants who lived in the household as part of the family. Among artisanal workers, the master's workshop also served as his home and often provided lodging for his apprentices and several of his workers, all of whom would take meals together. Peasant households generally included extended families reaching across several generations, so that the children of the head of household would bring their spouses and raise their children under the same roof, at least until they inherited or could afford some land of their own. As a result, people in eighteenth-century France considered their families to be much broader—and almost no one spent much time alone!

The economy of eighteenth-century France was overwhelmingly agrarian, meaning farming was by far the largest industry. Moreover, farming remained very traditional. The cultivation of grains on hand-plowed fields produced a small yield ratio of five units of grain to every one of seed. Yet even this very traditional sector of the economy saw great change, due to the introduction of new crops (such as potatoes and rice), new methods (of irrigation and fertilization), and more effective use of labor (made possible, in part, by the increase in the population). These changes were made mostly on the estates of wealthy nobles who hired professional managers, rather than on the lands of smallholding peasants who continued to use very traditional farming methods. Yet these changes did contribute to a significant increase in agricultural output. Unfortunately, the limited communication and transportation system, and a desire to export higher-priced agricultural goods such as olive oil and wine, meant that the food supply to French cities remained very precarious.

In the cities, most people worked as handicraft workers. An average workshop employed four to five people, who worked separately on their tasks, using their own tools and skills, and buying their materials from the master, who paid them for each piece or good they produced. Such small-scale production was generally limited to the local demand. Yet French industry also saw change, especially in the textile industry where a growing global market (especially for higher-priced textiles, such as silk or woven tapestries), the growing labor pool, and new production technology (such as the water wheel) made possible larger-scale operations, known as "manufacturies." Though most work in manufacturies was still done by hand by skilled workers, many more goods were produced at a much faster rate. Manufacturies were generally built on the outskirts of the larger French cities, where farm workers migrated from towns or villages in search of temporary work. These neighborhoods, such as the Saint-Marcel and Saint-Antoine neighborhoods of Paris, were sources of both great economic activity and great concern to observers, who worried about the shortage of housing, food and churches for the newly arriving workers.

The greatest changes in the French economy came in the service sector, which experienced a tremendous boom in the latter half of the eighteenth century. Growing literacy rates and the spread of more and better secondary and post-secondary schools both resulted from and led to more people entering intellectual trades, such as teaching, accounting, and especially law. The resulting increase made these trades highly competitive. One consequence, for instance, was a drastic increase in the number of lawsuits—an increasingly attractive option for those hoping to advance socially. One area of the service economy that exploded in the 1700s was finance and insurance, though many considered these not to be trades but merely schemes for speculation. Nevertheless, the growth in both public and private credit—or, put differently, the growth in private and public debt—was the single biggest source of economic growth and change in the eighteenth century.

The transformation of culture in eighteenth-century France is undoubtedly the greatest change of the period. Some historians believe that from 1680 onwards, the French people had a collective crisis of conscience in which they gradually doubted their beliefs in traditional religion, politics and society. While this claim is probably overstated, there was undoubtedly a thorough change in thinking at every level of society. Among the best educated, the Enlightenment extended the Scientific Revolution by promoting the idea that human reason could produce knowledge useful in the organization of literature and the arts, the economy (inventing modern economics and agronomy), society (inventing social science), government (political science) and even morality. This desire to break with tradition and reform all things through the use of reason was one of the most important cultural changes that would be felt strongly during the French Revolution.

One reason for this influence was the explosion in the printing, distribution, and reading of newspapers, pamphlets, and books across the century. In the larger cities, about 80 percent of men and 40 percent of women were literate; in the countryside, the percentages were much lower. Though in both cities and villages, there was ample opportunity for those who did not read to hear new ideas read to them in taverns and public libraries from newspapers by their priests, friends, and neighbors. It is estimated that on average, a given copy of a book or newspaper was read or heard by 20 people. Moreover, a printer issued, on average, 500 copies of a new newspaper or book, and several hundred thousand such books and newspapers were printed across the century. Print therefore reached an audience of millions. Most of this literature was anodyne and traditional, such as the lives of the saints or kings, or romantic stories. Though there was a marked increase in the printing of fiction and theater, and even pornography, these genres tended to include new ideas. There was also a great interest in news, especially scandals involving the rich and famous; pamphlets about scandalous trials sometimes reached the tens of thousands.

One way to measure this influence is to look at evidence of what ordinary people believed. Hundreds of thousands of the best educated and most well-to-do commoners, as well as a large number of nobles and clergy, discussed new ideas in Masonic lodges, reading clubs, literary academies, and informal discussion groups in people's homes known as salons. These people came to see themselves as distinct from the rest of society due to their shared literary and intellectual interests. Yet even among those not as well off, who did not join lodges or create salons, we see evidence of change—for instance, in the decrease of money donated to parish churches for masses said and votive candles lit for the dead and an increase in the amount spent on personal prayer books—suggesting not necessarily a decline in religion, but an increase in piety.

## OLD REGIME POLITICS: HOW ABSOLUTIST WAS THE MONARCHY?

The French monarchy had changed over its thousand-year history prior to 1789. It had evolved greatly from the Renaissance to the eighteenth century. Moreover, there was a great deal of politics within the realm beyond the king's authority. From the earliest French kings, in the sixth century, until the Renaissance, France was ruled by what might be considered a judicial monarchy, meaning the king shared power with noble magistrates. These magistrates, or judges, sat on a special court that would discuss (or *parley*) royal edicts, which is why the courts were known as *parlements*. These courts were not parliaments in the sense that they did not propose legislation, but they did have the power to decide if legislation were consistent with the traditional limits on the king's authority (such as the exemption of nobles and of certain regions of France from taxation.) Each of the twelve historically distinct regions of France had one court; in addition, the *Parlement* of Paris had jurisdiction over most of the country. These courts were also courts of appeal and courts where any suit involving a nobleman would be heard. The leading magistrates on each court, known as presidents, considered themselves to be the natural leaders of their region and defenders of their region's historic privileges and traditions, or what they called liberties.

After a long period of dormancy, these courts became active after Louis XV took the throne in 1715. The *parlements*, acting separately, often opposed royal edicts that they considered to be in contradiction to the liberties of their region. They took particular interest in special taxes, known as "the twentieth," assessed on one-twentieth of the wealth of everyone in the kingdom, including nobles. Due to the costs of wars, which France fought frequently in the eighteenth century, the monarchy constantly needed more revenue, and several times (in 1730, 1750, 1771, and 1786), the monarchy proposed a twentieth tax. Each time, one or more of the *parlements* opposed this policy, arguing it encroached on the liberties of the nation. In response, the King and his supporters argued that these nobles were merely defending their own exemptions, or abuses.

Another issue on which the *parlements* opposed the king was control of the Catholic Church. The *parlementary* magistrates sought to defend those Catholics who subscribed to a doctrine known as Jansenism, which emphasized individual piety of the believers over the leadership of the bishops. This put Jansenists at odds with the higher-ranking clergy including those from the Jesuit order, which had the favor of the king. Jansenism generally attracted better-educated believers, particularly lawyers and judges, who had several reasons to oppose what they considered "ministerial despotism," or too much power in the hands of the monarch and his advisors. They considered prominent Jesuit bishops, including those who advised the king on religious matters, to be unconcerned with ordinary people. This "theologico-political" opposition by the *parlementary* courts to royal power,[1] which had been very minimal from 1650 to the end of Louis XIV's reign in 1715, gained new momentum during the reign of Louis XV (1715–74). By 1770, the noble magistrates on the courts, as well as many lawyers, came to view the 13 different *parlements* as a single body, defending the liberties of the nation.

According to doctrine of absolutism, which the Bourbon dynasty developed in the 1600s, the law courts had been created by past kings and therefore served at the pleasure of the crown, meaning that the king need not heed their rulings on matters of government. The king could, and in several instances in the 1760s did, convoke a special session, known as the "Bed of Justice," in which he delivered a verbal tirade to the *parlements,* and overruled their decisions. This ritual symbolized the absolute authority of the king. Although magistrates and other judges, as well as mayors and counselors to the king all owned their offices (which were passed down through inheritance and could be bought or sold), the absolutist doctrine held that kings could revoke these offices from their holders and grant them to someone else.

Royal monarchs did not believe they held absolute authority for their own good. Rather, they believed that they had been granted this power by God to serve the people. Moreover, the royal monarchs considered the unity of the kingdom to be their first responsibility, especially with the memory of the bloody internal Wars of Religion, which had been fought from 1559 to 1590, foremost in their minds. To prevent a return to such chaos and to improve the country's wealth and power, successive Bourbon kings sought to use their power first and foremost to assure the religious unity of the country, revoking in 1685 the Edict of Nantes that had granted toleration to the more than one million Huguenots (French Calvinists). Moreover, they sought to enhance France's industry and commerce and to standardize tax collection across the entire kingdom. To enforce royal decrees and collect royal taxes more equally, the Bourbons appointed several thousand regional officers, known as *intendants.* These officials took on powers that previously had been exercised by nobles in the *parlements* or in regional assemblies, known as Estates. Bourbon kings argued that the nobles who controlled the *parlements* and regional Estates were not defending regional liberties, as they claimed, but were instead defending their own exemptions and legal privileges.

## PATRIOTS VS. ENLIGHTENED REFORMERS

In the 1760s, Louis XV proposed other reforms to promote industry, including abolition of the guilds and reform of city governments. Artisans in cities opposed these reforms on the same grounds that the *parlements* opposed the "twentieth tax" on noble wealth—that they surpassed the authority of the king and encroached on the liberties of the nation. Faced with consistent opposition to his proposed reforms, Louis XV in 1771 invoked his absolute power and exiled all *parlementary* magistrates. He proposed a total reform of the judicial system and municipal governments. He argued that the crown needed to impose the "twentieth" to balance its budget, strained by the expense of nearly a century of warfare, in particular the Seven-Years War of 1756–63 against the British. This conflict, known to the British as the French and Indian War, had left the French crown nearly bankrupt and deprived of its valuable colonies in North America.

Traditional elites opposed this move as a judicial revolution enacted by ministerial despotism. For four years, the *parlementary* magistrates and their supporters in the legal profession opposed these royal reforms through pamphlets and newspapers. The authors of these pamphlets and newspapers, and those who subscribed to their arguments, called themselves *patriots*. This term, derived from the Latin *patrie* for homeland, meant they were on the side of the people and implied the people should be sovereign in their homeland and be represented in their government. The most advanced patriots called on the king not to restore the *parlements* but to call an assembly of representatives of clergy, nobles, and commoners, an Estates General. Such a body had not met since 1610.

Most of the pamphlets attacking the royal government as despotic, however, did not make a political case. Instead, they argued that the king and his entire entourage, especially his wife and advisors, were morally corrupt. In response to these patriot pamphlets, the royal government at first sought to suppress the press. But then it changed course and authorized the printing of pamphlets making its own case for reforms. These pamphlets argued that in this enlightened age, the government had to modernize the country by ending the abuses of regional and noble tax exemptions. In this intense debate to influence the Crown's creditors, both sides appealed to public opinion. Thus, even before the Revolution, the French had entered into a new kind of politics, one in which cultural conflicts were already much more important, and open, than ever before.

## NOTE

1. Dale Van Kley, *The Damiens Affair and the Unraveling of the Old Regime, 1750–1770* (Princeton: Princeton University Press, 1984); Jeffrey Merrick, *The Desacralization of the French Monarchy in the Eighteenth Century* (Baton Rouge: Louisiana State University Press, 1990).

*Chapter 3*

# The People against the Privileged: Social Differences and Personal Identities

The Revolution, from its earliest days to its farthest-reaching legacies, brought an opportunity, even the necessity, to eliminate traditional ideas and strive for new ones. Most important, the Revolution meant an end to a society in which people had little say over their own beliefs, status, or government. Instead there was a society based on the equality of all individuals under the same sets of laws. The Revolution came to mean that ordinary people were able to determine their own religions, professions, and social groups, based on personal preference and talent. Though these goals were widely shared in 1789, there was no clear way to achieve this great change, and no solution ever really did become clear. This confusion led to conflicts. Revolutionaries debated and, in some cases, fought violently over the ideas and realities of the new society. Differences in wealth, religion, profession, and economic opportunity were not eliminated, but what these differences meant for ordinary people changed profoundly. The documents in this chapter give a sense of the drastic and rapid, but often difficult, changes in social relationships and personal identities during the Revolution.

## THE END OF THE THREE ORDERS

The noble order in eighteenth-century France included a wide variety of people. Nobles ranged from high-ranking military officers and wealthy landowners to principled provincial judges and well-educated advisors to the king to the so-called *hobereaux* or "old birds," who generally had little land or wealth and vigorously defended their privileges This diversity, however, was not reflected in contemporary criticisms of the nobles. These criticisms emphasized the nobles' excessive privileges, wealth, and power, often arguing that the nobles did not use these advantages for the good of society. Such accounts graphically described the aristocrats at the royal court as interested only in frivolous pastimes and orgiastic parties.

Likewise, pamphlets unsubtly minimized the diversity of the Third Estate—ranging from unskilled workers in the cities to poor peasant farmers to well-educated lawyers and wealthy bankers. Many pamphlets presented commoners as the opposite of aristocratic nobles—as guileless, salt-of-the-earth folk whose desire to support their families led them to work harder, and for less, than the rest of society. Such accounts were misleading as documentation of the way people actually lived, but they do give us a good sense of how many people perceived society under the Old Regime and how they wanted the Revolution to change it. These people argued that the problems faced by France arose from the frivolous and self-interested behavior of aristocrats, whose influence had to be supplanted by that of virtuous patriots. We see this argument in the excerpts below from an anonymous pamphlet written by an Englishman who lived in France for 30 years before the Revolution.

## DOCUMENT 1: NECESSITY FOR A REVOLUTION

There was certainly a great necessity for a revolution. For many years, the French Government had imagined that it might with impunity multiply the privileges of an order already by far too much privileged; and it was never suspected that the vilified victims on whom it dared to tread would on their side dare to revolt. The Third Estate [had been] contemptuously thrown into an ignominious obscurity. The military [should have been] open to the emulation and hope of the citizen but [in 1780] a new order [the Ségur ordinance] was issued that required a proof of nobility from those persons who . . . aspired to a dignified rank. . . .

Whenever a man of noble descent devoted himself to agricultural pursuits [on] his estates . . . that land became exempted from the taxes which were levied on commoners. . . . [T]he deficiency in the taxes paid to the government arising from this odious privilege was made up by an additional levy on his unfortunate neighbors. . . . It was not therefore sufficient to be insulted by the privilege of this noble, but the people were compelled even to pay for the honor of being insulted.

[Source: *Domestic Anecdotes of the French Nation* (London: Kearsley, 1794) "Preface," (unpaginated).]

## DOCUMENT 2: FRIVOLOUS AND DEBAUCHED ARISTOCRATS

"Such were the timid, vile and servile courtiers. Disgusted and condemned at court, they crawled in all the dirty and corrupt paths of intrigue but haughty, vain and insolent at Paris, they insulted the nation by an ostentatious magnificence and a continued usurpation of the just rights of their fellow citizens.

At the court at this time . . . there was a great passion for horse racing. . . . Great bets were made at every race and the noblemen turned jockeys and rode their own racers. The Nation . . . saw with indignation the behavior of the dukes and counts. . . . These princes not only . . . entered into all those scandalous combinations which this species of gaming offers but treated the [common] people at the courses with the most ineffable contempt and savage ferocity. . . . They used their whips on the spectators as well as on their horses and . . . employed such grossness of speech and offensive oaths that showed [*sic*] these princes were not unskilled in the language of the vilest part of the nation. . . . These frivolous and debauched courtiers [thereby] exposed themselves to the derision of Paris by other kinds of [gambling].

When their poverty [became] greater than their pride, they condescended to intermarry with families who, without having to boast of the honors of nobility, had acquired the immense fortunes of commercial speculation. The nobles wanted the money the financiers had accumulated and the financiers wanted the honors of the nobles.

There appeared [nevertheless] a disposition in the court to discountenance the nobility for marrying into families that could not boast of as rich blood [noble heritage] as themselves, whatever merits they might eminently profess. . . . It was the nobility of the person, and not his virtues or his talents, which rendered him acceptable at court."

[Source: *Domestic Anecdotes of the French Nation*, 129–65.]

***

This view can be described as patriotic, because it emphasized the goodness and sincerity of ordinary people as the only hope against the corruption of powerful aristocrats. This view heavily influenced the National Assembly, which decreed on August 4, 1789, as one of its first and most important acts, the end of all privileges and corporations. In September 1789, the Declaration of the Rights of Man and Citizen made clear that the new society would be based on principles of individual equality under the law rather than upon hierarchy. From there, it was only a matter of time before the National Assembly abolished outright all titles of nobility, which it did in a decree dated June 17, 1790.

## DOCUMENT 3: ABOLITION OF TITLES OF NOBILITY

Article I: Hereditary nobility is hereby abolished forever; as a result, the titles of prince, duke, count, marquis, viscount, baron, cavalier, squire and all others like them will neither be taken nor given to anyone.

Article II: No French citizen will be able to take other than his family name; he will not be able to wear . . . his coat of arms or have it worn by servants in his livery.

Article III: The title of Monseigneur will not be given to any body or any individual, likewise for the title of Excellence, highness, Eminence, etc . . .

[Source: *Moniteur Universel* CCCXXIV (17 June 1790) 25.]

***

This act fundamentally altered the basis of French society, since it ended the special status of both the clergy and the nobility as distinct bodies or corporations; moreover, it ended the privileges of those orders. However, not everyone perceived this change as an immediate improvement in the lives ordinary people.

The response in newspapers was mixed. The official government newspaper, the *Mercure de France,* worried about the economic consequences of such a change, since the sale and verification of titles of nobility had been an active industry. By contrast, the patriotic newspaper, *Friend of the People,* worried that the decree had not gone far enough to address the rampant inequality in French society.

## DOCUMENT 3B: NEWSPAPERS RESPOND TO THE ABOLITION OF NOBILITY

"This decree will diminish even further the chances for work in the capital [and other large cities] by removing from the public revenue seven million *livres* that were produced by payments from those seeking to verify their quality as nobles. So the [National Assembly] will have to replace these revenues with other means."

[Source: *Mercure de France* (3 July 1790) 71.]

"What have we gained by destroying the aristocracy of nobles if it is replaced by the aristocracy of the rich? If we are going to be put under the yoke of those newly wealthy [through commerce], it would have been better to conserve the privileged orders. . . . Leaders of the country . . . we do not demand that you divide up all your possessions, which the heavens have given in common to all men . . . you will nevertheless become our equals, because you are less numerous than we are so how can you be certain to continue to collect the fruits of our work?"

[Source: *L'ami du people* CXLIX (30 June 1790) 6.]

***

Another idea that the French discussed frequently in 1789 was that the people of the Third Estate had struggled to support the privileged orders. This struggle was emphasized in illustrations such as this engraving that shows a commoner physically held down by chains and forced to carry a nobleman, a bishop, and a cardinal; these elites hold bills for the dues, tithes, and taxes owed to the landowner, the church, and the royal government, respectively. Such images contributed to the idea, widely held in 1789 and the years immediately after, that the key conflict of the Revolution was the liberation of the people who did the physical labor, yet had traditionally been at the bottom of the hierarchy, from their bondage to the privileged, who contributed little and lived off the commoners' blood, sweat, and tears.

The abolition of the nobility, then, represented for many ordinary people a chance to be liberated. Yet, clearly, this measure alone could not resolve all the problems of society. Though the National Assembly

This hand-colored engraving from 1789 shows an unclothed, sinewy commoner being ridden by a nobleman, a bishop, and a cardinal. The nobleman, in a coat, is speaking the words, "Feudalism, faith, and homage to the lord." The bishop, wearing a miter, holds papers reading "Inquisition" and "Tithe, property of the clergy." The cardinal, on the right, holds a paper reading "Hereditary privilege of elites." Courtesy of the Library of Congress, Department of Prints and Photographs, PP 1789.37.

clearly intended to put an end to titles and privileges based solely on birth, it also intended to assure each individual the right to his property, so there would be no re-distribution of land and wealth. By the same token, the Le Chapelier law in June 1791 abolished the corporations that bound individuals into trade guilds. However, this law also outlawed all associations of workers.

Influenced by the theory of individual liberty associated with John Locke, the Assembly believed that only private property rights could serve as the basis for the new society, because only property owners had a stake in what would happen to that society. To most people, that meant land ownership. Most of the landowners, however, had been nobles prior to 1789. What about those who did not own land and lived from the pay they received for work they did in workshops on land they rented from others? Would they be considered full-fledged members of the new society? What about those who made profits from commerce? Was their wealth a just reward for contributing to society or an attempt to accrue more than any one else? In this document, a police report filed in 1794, several years after the abolition of nobility, we see how uncertain remained the question of what it meant for individuals to be able to pursue their private property interests.

## DOCUMENT 4: THE REVOLUTION HAS DESTROYED THE OLD WAYS

"The Revolution has not only overthrown the...nobility; it has done more; it has destroyed the old ways of thinking. Before, vanity was what motivated the French. The first goal of [everyone] was rank and title. A merchant worked to gain enough money to buy an [honorific] office as a royal treasurer or a royal secretary. And after he would be ennobled, he would look down on everyone below him who continued in business.

All that has changed. Titles no longer exist. Fortunes have been revolutionized...everyone needs to work. Hard work rises and opposes itself to idleness.... The old disdain [of nobles] for mercantile professions has been replaced by a widespread mania for going into business. Its not only for necessity; [they go into business] also for the love of money.

The current needs of France open a broad field for business, but how curious to see the varied and bizarre directions that this commercial speculation takes....Everyone says that the well-being and prosperity of their country is their only goal to which the Revolution has opened the eyes of each individual.... Every one...insists on the right he has to pursue his goals on his own—and also to be protected by the government from his fellow citizens."

[Source: Charles-Aimé Dauban, *Paris en 1794 et en 1795* (Paris: 1869) 590–91.]

***

## HOSTILITY TO THE CLERGY IN 1789

Like the nobility, the clergy, or First Estate, was a distinct order in society, with its own laws and its own status as a group. Yet within this group, ways of life varied greatly. The clergy ranged from local village priests, who performed many services for their parishioners and lived off a meager monthly stipend, to absentee archbishops, who enjoyed the benefits of large, landed estates that belonged to the church, but who did little pastoral work. During the eighteenth century, the everyday life of ordinary people in France remained very closely tied to the church. Yet writers of the Enlightenment, known as philosophers, criticized the clergy as intolerant, oppressive, and opposed to reforms. As a result of these criticisms, French religious beliefs and worship practices changed greatly in the decades before 1789. Though nearly everyone still believed intensely in God, many people became critical of the clergy as corrupt, parasitic, and immoral.

These criticisms were not made about most of the parish priests, who were seen as performing the useful work of helping ordinary people. Instead, critics charged that within the clergy, monks and bishops made very little contribution to society. Supporters of the Revolution tended to believe strongly that the church—like the rest of French society—had to be reformed so it would become more useful to society. To this end, the National Assembly, in June 1790, decided that church lands, rather than benefiting absentee bishops or supporting monks or nuns who remained isolated from the rest of society, should be sold off to pay off the national debt. Parish priests, by contrast, were assured a higher income from the new government, in exchange for swearing an oath of allegiance to the nation. This law, known as the Civil Constitution of the Clergy, became a controversial topic. Patriots supported the law as a way to root out corruption from the clergy. However, moderate revolutionaries and conservatives feared that if the bishops of the Catholic Church no longer provided moral authority, society would fall apart. (We will return to this debate in Chapter 7.)

In the following documents, several patriots look back from the early years of the Revolution on the clergy of the Old Regime. First, we hear from the writer, Louis-Sébastien Mercier, who would become an active politician during the Revolution. In the 1780s, Mercier published a very popular series of short articles on everyday life in Paris, known as *Overview of Paris (Tableau de Paris)*. In an article, entitled "*Collèges*" (high schools), he mocks the Jesuit teachers as obsessed with teaching useless subjects such as Latin—the official language of the Catholic Church, but almost never used outside of it. He suggests that this method of teaching prevents French students from taking an interest in their contemporary society.

## DOCUMENT 5: LATIN PEDANTS

"The method of study is vicious and the best students take away nothing useful.... Pedants try to teach Latin to children who do not know their own language...In the ten-year program of the *collèges*, seven or eight years are devoted to learning Latin. And still, nine out of ten students never learn it. These teachers...are ridiculous and insufferable....They do not use Latin to encourage a love of ancient Rome or of republics...[Instead,] the youth is always given strange ideas, and they soon lose any interest in their own well-being. Only an absolute monarch would pays teachers to give boring lectures about those in ancient Rome who spoke so eloquently...against the power of kings!"

[Source: Louis-Sébastien Mercier, *Tableau de Paris* (Amsterdam: 1785) III, 85.]

***

In the next document, another patriot writer compares the higher-ranking ecclesiastics to the disliked aristocrats of the nobility. He lists a series of reasons why bishops and cardinals had become unpopular by the 1780s, even among parish priests who felt that their superiors were exploiting power. In the final anecdote, he mocks the chastity of the clergy. Not only does the bishop in the story carry on an affair with a woman, but when he is discovered and injured by her husband, he claims the wound to be a stigmata—the wound received by Jesus Christ on the cross, which Christians considered a sign of holiness!

## DOCUMENT 6: ANTI-CLERICAL JOKES

"The higher class of the French clergy regarded themselves as the first order of the state. Its honors and privileges were gradually usurped.... From the year 1750, the clergy complained of a sect of 'Philosophers,' whom they distinguish by the epithet of modern... The religious orders were indeed so notoriously infamous that almost every [different order] was distinguished by some dishonorable epithet... 'To drink like a Cordelier,' 'as stinking as a Capucin,' 'as gluttonous as a Bernardin,'... were all favorites...."

In 1770... a Nun on the point of making her last vows hanged herself in the presence of her parents, who obstinately persisted in devoting her to this vocation. This circumstance afforded M. de la Harpe a fine subject for a tragedy,... "The Nun," in which he inveighs against these austere institutions. Such a drama could not be performed at Paris, and... the tragedy was never performed. But every where the author was invited to read it aloud, and it served to excite a warm indignation in the public against similar institutions.

In the month of June [1783] a nun escaped and she was soon detected.... The [others] hastened to inform the superior, who cried out to bring back the fugitive. Her whole flock, animated by their zeal... pursue their late companion through the streets. The runaway... reached the barrier of Saint-Antoine. The other nuns called out to the gate-keepers to shut the barrier, for that she was an apostate. The keepers, seeing in this fugitive nothing which concerned them, nothing that was contraband, no bundles to examine,... allowed her to pass, and then touched by her entreaties, closed the barrier against her pursuers.... They were obliged to return to their superior, who reproved them for committing this scandal and for taking the opportunity to wander about the streets.

In 1777, I observed the lower clergy loudly complaining of the heavy assessments under which they bitterly groaned. That the bishops... are unfeeling masters, who grind their inferiors; and deprive by their unmerciful exactions, the curates of even a bare subsistence.... The curates of the province of Dauphiny, finding insufficient their petty allowance, which had been reduced to the miserable pittance of 500 pounds [a year],... thought it very necessary... to show his Majesty their urgent need for an augmentation of income, without which they could not subsist. For this purpose,... they humbly applied to their respective bishops to ask their permission to assemble, and they were refused. They appealed to the law courts, which authorized them.... Upon arrival in Paris, these priests presented their petition to M. Necker [the Finance Minister]...However, before they could present it, the bishops obtained an order from the King ordering the priests to return to their province the next day. They had taken the wise precaution of printing their memorandum...it was soon distributed and seized by the public with avidity; [which learned that] these oppressed men could not obtain a relief from the despotism of their bishops, amply exposing the true character of the [bishops]...

It is very certain that the higher class of the prelates possess immoderate incomes.... Although their debauched manners were well known at Paris, the bishops at least tried to conceal them and to sacrifice anything rather than to be brought forward as actors on the public stage, by exposing themselves in a court of justice....[One] bishop (who is still living...) was supposed to have as great a lubricity as any man. In one of his amorous pursuits...he pressed a fair lady with a vehemence of passion—but had forgot the usual precaution of locking the door. The husband entered at the unhappiest moment possible; the lady did not lose her sagacity and feigned that the bishop was attempting to violate his honor [by raping her]. She seized the sword of her husband and plunged it in the thigh of the ravisher. The bishop, humiliated, confused, and wounded, retired to his chamber. Others at court considered it a miracle that the bishop should be wounded in the thigh without injuring his pant leg."

[Source: *Domestic Anecdotes of the French Nation*, 45–80.]

***

The next document is from a letter written in 1789 by the English Ambassador to Paris, Earl Gower, to a friend in London. Gower supported the Revolution's early goals. But he opposed the more aggressive action of some revolutionaries, such as those who attacked nuns for their opposition to the Civil Constitution of the Clergy.

## DOCUMENT 7: THE FLAGELLATION OF NUNS

"The only remarkable event that has happened here during the course of this week is the flagellation of some hundred of Grey Sisters and other nuns by market women, because the nuns wanted to hear the Mass celebrated by priests who refuse to swear the oath [of alle-

The text reads, “The monks are learning to march.” One of the monks is saying, “With patience, we’ll get it, like everyone else. In time, the Nation will make good citizens of us.” Courtesy of the Library of Congress, Department of Prints and Photographs, PP 1790.20.

giance]. Such is the feeble state of the police and of the government that the offenders have escaped punishment.... It is hoped that [the revolutionary government] will be able to prevent such events in the future and that [freedom of] religion will be tolerated in this country."

[Source: Oscar Browning, ed., *The Despatches of Earl Gower* (Cambridge: 1885).]

***

Another form of mockery directed against the clergy includes this humorous engraving from 1791 showing monks learning to march as soldiers. The image suggests that those who previously remained separate from society could, through encouragement and, if necessary, force, become good, patriotic citizens who were ready, willing, and able to make their contribution through military service.

## TOWNSPEOPLE: FROM ARTISANS TO SANSCULOTTES

Most people who lived in cities and towns in eighteenth-century France worked in a trade or service rather than in agriculture. For food, they depended on markets supplied by farmers from the nearby countryside. When these supplies ran short, due to bad harvests or when silos ran dry in later summer and in winter, cities suffered shortages. Indeed, food shortages in Paris were one principle cause of the unrest of July 1789. Throughout the Revolution, French cities (especially Paris) suffered chronic food shortages, causing high prices. Compounding this problem, townspeople suffered from rising unemployment and a general disorder in the city. This police report gives us a sense of the hard life of Parisian workers during the Revolution, who endured shortages and resorted to extreme measures for money, and whose lives were full of conflict.

---

### DOCUMENT 8: THE HARD LIFE OF PARISIAN WORKERS

---

"The workers complain very much that they cannot get enough meat or soup at the inns. They eat only bread and herring. In all the inns of the city, there is not one ounce of meat, and vegetables are alarmingly rare and very expensive....

Four individuals employed as grave-diggers at a church report that bodies have been stolen from the cemetery...they say that certainly it was for jewels in the tombs of very rich people and for the silver plates on the coffins. . . .

This city has not only thieves but also shameless men who insult all the women they pass in the street; one such man passed a woman to whom he spoke the most dirty words, then lowered his pants towards her and chased after her. That woman ran away as fast as she could . . . Many other villains approach children that they seek to corrupt . . . "

[Source: Dauban, 71.]

***

For many workers in Paris and other cities, however, the Revolution represented more than just hard times and an occasion to behave badly. For many, it represented the chance to contribute to their society. Workers who had participated in Old Regime corporations (or guilds) held a firm sense of morality. They believed that hard work should be paid fairly and that everyone should work to support himself or herself and his or her family. They considered it immoral for anyone to make more money than was needed to support a family, since such hoarders were gaining at the expense of others. Because urban workers shared difficult lives with others engaged in the same trade, they were always ready to help out their fellow artisans. Workers' morality thus demanded each and every person should work hard, should help others, and should be self-sufficient; they called this morality *virtue*. Many Parisian workers believed that hard work, self-sufficiency, and patriotism were what the entire country needed to solve its problems. Moreover, many Parisian workers were sure that these values had made the Revolution possible and were what it would need to succeed. For this reason, Parisian workers saw themselves as patriots, the backbone of the Revolution, who sought to advance the cause of the people. To symbolize that they had nothing personally to gain from the Revolution, Parisian workers referred to themselves as sansculottes, meaning they did not wear stylish clothing such as britches. Patriots admired the sansculottes, because they were not fancy-pants lawyers or merchants but instead ordinary people with nothing personally to gain from their civic activism.

For urban workers, neighborhood assemblies, known as *sections*, were the place to build the Revolution, by voting for office, debating news of the day, and signing petitions to influence the city and national governments. Simply by going to section meetings, Parisian workers showed their willingness to work hard and sacrifice for their fellow citizens, especially in moments of crisis when the Revolution and the country seemed to be in danger. Along with other patriots, sansculottes generally believed that aristocrats (including both former nobles and wealthy non-nobles) were a great threat to the Revolution. So sansculottes stood ready to do anything they could to prevent the Revolution from being taken over by others less self-sacrificing, less hard working, and less patriotic than themselves. This passage from a pro-Revolutionary newspaper, printed during the intense political crisis of May 1793, describes how sansculottes saw themselves and wanted others to see (and be inspired by) them.

## DOCUMENT 9: WHAT IS A *SANS-CULOTTE*?

"What is a *sans-culotte?* He is a being who always travels on foot rather than in a carriage...and who lives simply with his wife and children...on the [top] floor [where the smaller, less expensive apartments were found].... He knows how to work a field, how to force, go saw, to file, to cover a roof, make shoes [and other useful skills].......Since he is a worker, he will never be seen in the [expensive cafés] where people gamble and conspiracies are hatched, or at the theater when they are performing [counter-revolutionary] plays, such as "Friend of the Laws."

In the evening, he goes around to the *section* meeting, not wearing powdered wigs or perfumes or boots, not hoping to be seen by the citizenesses, but to show his support for good policies [that will help the Nation.] Besides, [he] always has his sword ready to cut off the ears of those who speak ill [of the Nation.]...and at the first call to duty, he will be ready to leave for the [countryside] to fight in the Army."

[Source: *Père Duchesne* (May 1793).]

***

## THE REVOLUTION IN THE COUNTRYSIDE

Like urban workers, peasants (whom we might think of as family farmers) lived very hard lives and struggled each year to feed their families and not be overwhelmed by debt. Each year, farming families had to pay dues and obligations to the lord, not only for possession of a plot of land (as one might rent land today) but also for the use of that land: to plant, farm, harvest, or produce anything of value on the land. This might be best thought of as a sharecropping arrangement, and it resulted in constant tension between lords and peasants in the countryside. This tension often took the form of lawsuits. But unfortunately for the peasants, these suits were heard in courts presided over by the lord. (This form of seigneurial justice is discussed in Chapter 5.)

To pay their dues, peasants offered borrowed money, from each other or from merchants in the cities. Consequently, peasants generally resented the nearby cities. Moreover, peasant culture was very traditional, and any change was feared as dangerous. For all of these reasons, news of the outbreak of the Revolution in Paris was not welcomed in the countryside, and many peasants feared the violence would spread from the cities. They especially feared that bands of robbers, or brigands, would come to steal their crops from the fields, which they had yet to harvest. To lose a crop in the field meant that the debts could not be paid that year, and the land would be lost. To defend themselves against such threats, peasants traditionally had organized themselves into informal militias; in the summer of 1789, peasants organized such militias in many regions of the French countryside. These peasant militias marched against the lords' castles to fend off what they were certain would be attacks by brigands from the cities, supported by the lords.

These documents are from two different regions of France and describe the Great Fear, the conflict of the French peasants against their perceived enemies. In the first document, the mayor of the village of Arpajon, in the Essonne just south of Paris, writes to villagers from a neighboring town; in the second, a soldier records events in the Dauphiné in the Alps.

## DOCUMENT 10: THE GREAT FEAR IN THE ESSONNE

"[W]e learned yesterday of the help you have been kind enough to give us... The alarm proved to be false. It began in Limours, three leagues away and spread successively... At two in the afternoon, the rumor spread that seven to eight hundred soldiers were pillaging, burning, and sacking the nearby villages and that the women of the villages were running into the woods to hide, with their children in their arms... We sounded the tocsin and formed our militia....

It appears that what had in fact happened was that a detachment of the Parisian militia had come in the morning to [two nearby villages] to requisition [soldiers]. The mayor of one of the villagers sent his domestic [servant] to find out what was going, and the [Parisian] soldiers chased after him, arrested him, and brought him back. It is said he was hit on the head with a sabre, so hard that his chapeau was cut.... Another version has it that the vicar of [one of the towns] had been asked by the [Parisian] soldiers to serve as their guide, but he had refused and he himself began to sound the tocsin...We were able to restore calm among the soldiers only by promising to send the vicar to City Hall in Paris to be interrogated."

[Source: Translated from "La Grande Peur en Paris et l'Ile de France," *Mémoires publiés par la Fédération des sociétés historiques et archéologiques de Paris et de l'Ile de France* (Paris: 1967–68) 18–19.]

## DOCUMENT 11: THE GREAT FEAR IN THE DAUPHINÉ

"We were told by different persons...of a troop of soldiers...who were burning piles of wheat in the fields and in the silos...to try to keep order amidst such reports, we formed up our regiment of the town militia and went, first to Mass to sing the *Te Deum* and pray for the preservation of France from such bad acts, and then joined up with musketeers and cannons. We were told of 800 brigands setting fires in the countryside.

About half an hour past noon, a cavalier came from a neighboring village to tell us of a great chase of brigands on horseback, which alarmed us enough to sound the tocsin such that the villagers fled...and a good part of the town returned with their arms. The militia commander placed sentries to defend the town...

The rumors spread not only here but in nearby villages, where it was said that 20,000 in Savoy [a neighboring region] were exchanging fire with the brigands...The most frightening was to hear the cries of the women and children, the infirm and the aged, leaving their homes to flee into the woods with their animals and whatever furniture they could carry...while their men ran off to prepare for combat across the border in Savoy. What worried us the most was the lack of munitions and above all of food. We sent orders to all the butchers and bakers of the town to send us provisions for the brave patriots. We also ordered that all citizens must close their doors, extinguish their fires, and hide in their homes all night.

We learned the next day . . . that two regiments had chased 1800 brigands into the forest . . . and that 1200 brigands had ravaged [another nearby town] and demanded to be quartered. Again, we sent a delegation to verify the report and sounded the tocsin. Then we formed up and prepared our arms. . . . We began to march out with precipitation, when we encountered one of our scouts who told us that the report was false, and there had only been a couple of unknown travelers who had come to the town . . . but that a large troop of peasants had burned and pillaged nearby *châteaux*."

[Source: Pierre Conard, *La Grande Peur en Dauphiné* (Paris: 1902).]

***

Although these mobilizations had begun in response to false rumors, they led to direct armed attacks by peasants on the property of landowning nobles. These attacks did not target the nobles themselves or even their property but the symbols of their power under the seigneurial system. These symbols included scales for weighing grain, mills for grinding the grain, ovens for baking bread, and presses for crushing olives into oil or grapes into wine. Only lords could have such equipment, and peasants had to pay dues for its use Peasants also attacked the walls and roads around lords' *châteaux* (which peasant labor had generally built and maintained). In some cases, peasants broke into the lords' houses to burn the land titles that provided the legal basis for the dues that peasants owed to the lords. But the peasants did not seize land outright.

In late July, in response to these rural protests, as well as to the wave of urban protests that had followed the taking of the Bastille, the National Assembly began debating what changes it could make right away. It wanted to show it could reform the privileges enjoyed by nobles, clergy, landowners, and corporations and make everyone equal under the law. To this end, on August 4, 1789, the National Assembly decreed the end of all privileges—those of landlords over peasants, of nobles over commoners, and of certain cities and regions. To underscore how broad they intended this change to be, the deputies began the decree by stating "the National Assembly abolishes the feudal system entirely."[1] Since most deputies to the Assembly had been nobles, clergy, landholders, or members of *corporations* (such as the legal bar), this measure represented a great sacrifice of personal interest for the greater good.

By this decree, the Assembly intended to abolish privileges, hierarchies, and corporations all across French society and replace them with equality under the law. This equality would mean the end of special laws for nobles and the clergy, and for cities, towns, and regions that enjoyed special powers granted by the king, such as lower tax rates. The goal of the National Assembly's deputies, who were strongly influenced by the political and economic theories of John Locke and other Enlightenment authors, was to create what we would call today a civil society. A civil society is one in which people associate with each other based on their own choice, rather than tradition, and based on shared economic interests, such as defense of private property. In such a society, individuals who owned property were entirely free to do what they wanted to it (sell it, rent it out, farm it, or mine it). This idea held great appeal in cities, especially among the better-educated people who had economically useful property, such as businesses that they owned themselves, rather than in common with anyone else (such as a lord or other members of a guild).

The situation in the countryside was much more complicated. Peasants were more traditional and worried about change; moreover, most rural property was owned in common, between lords and peasants. Peasants paid the lord rent to occupy the land and also dues to use land, but for most people, these payments were indistinct. By its decree of August 4, the National Assembly intended that the land would not be redistributed, nor would rents owed by tenants for the right to occupy land (rather than the right to use it) be abolished. Nor would tithes (owed to the church rather than the landowner) or taxes (owed to the government rather than the landowner) be abolished. But again, most peasants did not distinguish one payment owed from another, and they expected the decree would free them from all obligations to pay.

As a result, response to this decree in the countryside was mixed. Landowners asserted that since the decree abolished only privileges (such as the privilege of harvesting on the land) but not ownership (such as the power to rent out the land for others to farm and harvest), peasants should continue to pay for use of the land. Peasant responses varied from region to region, depending on the particular conditions of land ownership. In the region of Brittany, for example, where much land was held in mixed ownership between peasants and lords, lords and peasants alike worried about the consequences of such a great change, as we see in the following petitions to the National Assembly in September 1789 from peasant farmers of that region.

## DOCUMENT 12: PEASANTS FOR THE ABOLITION OF FEUDALISM

"Although we were very attacked, like all other Bretons to the particular privileges enjoyed by our region, when we consider the general sacrifice, made by all the Orders of the country and by other provinces of their privileges, for the general good, we become persuaded that [the loss of] our particular advantages [in this region] will be amply compensated by the advantages that will result from a perfect equality [under the law] of all people in the kingdom. We have therefore taken the opinion that we should consent to the abolition of our supposed privileges...

...In consideration of current events, when we are trying to...establish a uniform government under which all French people will have civil liberties and civil rights...there is no district or province, no city and group of people, who should seek to preserve their privileges rather than sacrifice them for the general good. Based on these considerations, we should support the decrees taken...by vote of the National Assembly...for the greater good...because [under the new government] there will be no new tax created...without the consent of the Nation..."

[Source: Translated from Jean-Pierre Hirsch, ed., *La Nuit du 4 Août* (Paris: Gallimard, 1978) 238–42; reprinted from National Archives (AN) 8 AQ 11 and 8 AQ 14.]

## DOCUMENT 13: PEASANTS AGAINST THE ABOLITION OF FEUDALISM

"We must consider that the privileges of Brittany are its very heart and that if they are suppressed, the result will be a dangerous discouragement [in the economy:] first in agriculture, then in commerce, and then in manufacturing. This will lead to the ruin of all property...Everyone knows that in general, the soil of this province is neither as good nor as fertile as the rest of France...and so we should not pay the same taxes...which are for this region a very heavy burden.

The dues [owed to landowners by those who would use the land] are indeed real property and very important to truly patriotic Bretons, so they cannot be given up for the good of the rest of the kingdom without some equivalent indemnity [to compensate landowners in this region.]"

[Source: Translated from Jean-Pierre Hirsch, ed., *La Nuit du 4 Août* (Paris: Gallimard, 1978) 238–42; reprinted from National Archives (AN) 8 AQ 11 and 8 AQ 14.]

***

On the one hand, supporters of reform and the Revolution wanted to convert the land to private property on which tenants would pay rent while eliminating seigneurial dues to be paid for the right to work on the land. On the other hand, no one could clearly distinguish between rent paid for possession of land and dues paid for the right to use it. In the fall of 1789, most French people considered themselves patriots and were willing to make personal sacrifices—such as seigneurial privileges—for the greater good of the country. But at the same time, everyone was very worried about the economic hardship that might result. Consequently, there was general support for and acceptance of the decree of August 4—but at the same time there was the hope and expectation that the National Assembly would answer more directly the question of what kind of private property ownership would be considered a sacred and violable right. In a petition published in a pro-revolutionary Parisian newspaper in September 1789, the author calls for such reforms as the Assembly made on August 4, to put an end to the privileges of the Old Regime. At the same time, he argues against allowing landowners simply to live off the work of others, by claiming their private property rights in the name of liberty.

## DOCUMENT 14: LET US APPRECIATE FULLY... THE SACRIFICES OF THE NATION

"If the general welfare requires that we make sacrifices, [the National Assembly] was a bit late to make them. Its only in the light of the flames of the burning *châteaux* that [landowning deputies in the Assembly] found enough patriotic spirit to give liberties to a people that had already started to take them with arms in hand!

The true cause of the troubles of France are the grain shortage, bad government... that costs the public, the rapacity of monopolists [who charge too much for goods], the firing of employees, the conspiracies against the homeland, exploitation of ordinary people by those who have had privileges; these troubles will not be relieved by the sacrifice [called for the decree of August 4.]... [A]ll... personal privileges would be revoked by a general law [of equal rights]; why then should we celebrate this as a grand sacrifice.

Let's understand what really needs to be done. It's evident that an awful faction, those aristocrats, who are opposed to a new constitution [with equal rights for all]...are fighting against the Nation through the illusion by claiming [the abolition of privilege to be a] sacrifice."

[Source: Translated from Hirsch, 249–50; reprinted from *L'Ami du peuple* XI (21 September 1789).]

***

## THE SLAVE TRADE IN THE FRENCH COLONIES: PRIVILEGE OR PROPERTY

The August 4 abolition of feudalism and the Declaration of Rights of Man and Citizen of September 1789 declared the goals of the National Assembly: to replace the Old Regime's three orders, hierarchy and privilege, corporations, and traditions with a new society of individuals at liberty to pursue their own individual economic, political, and cultural goals. Though there remained much work to do in putting those ideals into practice, in the fall of 1789 nearly everyone expected that the two goals of replacing privilege with private property and of assuring individual liberty and equality under law would be mutually reinforcing and would not conflict. However, very quickly, as they began to debate slave labor in French Caribbean colonies, the revolutionaries began to argue about whether property and liberty were always the same thing. The English woman Helena Maria Williams was living in Paris in 1789. She was greatly influenced by the Enlightenment idea that all individuals must be free and equal under the law. So she believed that slavery clearly violated the principle of liberty and should be brought to an end by the Revolution. She understood the Revolution to be first and foremost about putting into place the Enlightenment idea that for a country to break out of the traditions and hierarchies of the Old Regime, it had to define each and every individual in terms of their free will and personal liberty. In this letter, written from Paris to an English friend, she makes this case by calling for an end to slavery as contrary to liberty:

### DOCUMENT 15: HUMANISTIC ARGUMENT FOR THE ABOLITION OF SLAVERY

"The loss of external commerce is a never-ending topic of complaint; the planter [land-owner and farmer in the colonies, who was neither a lord nor a peasant] looks back with stern regret to the prosperous and halcyon days of Negro slavery. But the friend of humanity, when he has less colonial [sugar or tobacco] to consume, he knows that France is no longer covered with the infamy that hangs so heavily over other countries and that . . . the rights of man [are for both the] European [and the] African [who also] finds liberty a substantial blessing. . . . Those changes [liberation of slaves] will indeed be effected with the imprudent precipitation that characterizes all revolutionary acts and will produce much intermediate calamity. [Williams refers to the potential loss of revenue from the slave trade and to the potential for slave revolts that might result from abolition.] We can find consolation . . . that these temporary evils will terminate in a permanent good and will have removed evils that were far more terrible. That change must open the whole have been favorable to humanity [and will] have relieved miseries that were intolerable . . . Sugar-canes and coffee-trees may . . . flourish in less abundance . . . but the [freed slave] will point to another tree, round which he will dance as a free citizen . . . the liberty tree [a popular symbol of the French Revolution].

I have often heard the assertion that the lot of [slaves] in the colonies is happier than that of the poor in Europe; if this were true, it would only prove that it is time the lot of the poor should change. It is for that unfortunate and extensive part of the family of mankind that revolutions ought to take place."

[Source: Helena Maria Williams, *Sketches of the State of Manners and Opinions in the French Republic* (London: 1801) 48–50.]

***

Williams' point of view was supported by a group of like-minded men and women known as the Society of Friends of Blacks. This group argued for the abolition of slavery in the French colonies as necessary for equality and liberty. Others, however, argued that ending the slave trade would bring hardship on slave-owners in the colonies and on those parts of France, such as the port city of Nantes, which traded with the colonies. This argument, like the abolitionist argument, framed the question in terms of defending the liberty and property of ordinary French people: that of slave-owners and slave traders. Their property, their supporters argued, would be lost if France were to abolish slavery. The decree of August 4 and the Declaration of Rights of Man, supporters of slavery argued, did not concern slaves, since slave-owners did not enjoy privileges; they were private property owners using their liberty to pursue their economic goals to the best of their abilities and for the good of the overall society. The following document, written by Monseron de l'Aunay, who represented the port city of Nantes in the National Assembly, makes this argument on behalf of businessmen engaged in the slave trade.

## DOCUMENT 16: ECONOMIC ARGUMENT AGAINST THE ABOLITION OF SLAVERY

"Only perverse men would abuse the purity of intention [of the leaders of the Revolution] by criminally interpreting the decrees of the National Assembly to serve their perfidious goal against the humanity, liberty and happiness of citizens in the other hemisphere [i.e., French colonists in the Caribbean]....in the name of this humanity...and in the name of the homeland, those who are the best citizens [of France] join in your concern for the Haitian islands [that is, French Caribbean colonies], for French landowning colonists [in the colonies], and for the many French citizens who live from commerce with the colonies. Consider that these colonies will determine the destiny of France; they support, through the sixty million [*livres*] of [colonial] products exported every year, the enormous weight of [our entire economy.]...Six million men make their living from this trade, including ninety thousand French who live there...Half of France would be plunged into destitution and misery [if the slave trade were to be abolished.]

Our eternal rival [Britain], whose ambitious policy is to sharpen their knives, smiles at our misfortune...and prepares its scepter to rule over the entire globe, which no human force will be able to stop. We must not wait, sirs, for news to confirm this unhappiness. [Soon]...the fire [of a slave revolt] will burn up everything; fifteen hundred leagues away, doubt [about the future policy of France] is more frightening than certitude [for the colonists]....[Soon,] their spirit of even the best of them will be lost, and work will be suspended. There will be a long delay in the contribution [of the colonies] to our fortune.

Let us all plead with the National Assembly to protect the life and the fortune of French people by issuing a solemn decree putting all the force of the executive power to ensure that there is no damage to the colonies [by the abolition of slavery or the slave trade.]"

[Source: *Chronique de Paris* (16 December 1789).]

***

## MEN AND WOMEN: GENDER AND FAMILY IN EVERYDAY LIFE

The Revolution brought changes in social relationships between nobles and commoners, between lords and peasants, and between owners and workers. It also brought changes in social relationships within families, between men and women. Under the Old Regime, some women had enjoyed privileges, as nobles or as members of a corporation, such as the seamstresses' guild. Some women had enjoyed substantial wealth in the form of family estates or modest wealth in the form of a workshop inherited from a husband. (Women had longer life expectancies in the eighteenth century [as they do today], and widows of workshop owners frequently continued to run the family business even if they remarried.) Other women supported themselves as domestic servants.

But many women also lived in dire poverty, as did many children. The most striking symbol of women and children in poverty in Old Regime France was the practice of wet-nursing, in which poor women suckled infants of other families for pay. This deprived their own children of their mother's milk. It also spread diseases among infants, helping contribute to the high rate of infant mortality. Only one in five children born in eighteenth-century France lived beyond their first year; only two in five lived to adulthood.

The Revolution, as we have seen, began as a protest, led by women, about the high price of food. However, the leaders of the Revolution did not consider the concerns of women or children to be different from those of France as a whole. Some of the most progressive thinkers, such as Marie Jean Antoine Nicolas Caritat (known as the Marquis de Condorcet), and Emmanuel Sièyes, an abbot who supported the Enlightenment, argued that women possessed the same potential as men to exercise reason and should be considered the same under law. Others, such as the pamphleteer Olympe de Gouges, who raised her son on her own, argued that women had different concerns from men and that women's distinct input on issues concerning family life must be considered for the new government to succeed.

Most men, including most leaders of the new government, did not agree with either of those views; they followed the traditional medical and religious view that men were better suited for government. Moreover, they believed that only men with property could use their reason fully in matters of public policy. So the National Assembly granted active citizenship rights only to adult males who owned some property.

Yet in many ways, the Revolution made great improvements in the lives of women, children, and the poor. Early on, the Revolution made men and women equally eligible to inherit property. Prior to 1789, many regions of France had followed the tradition of primogeniture, whereby only the oldest son inherited property. The Revolution also made another important change when it legalized divorce, so that women could leave unhappy marriages—and could have a right to part of the common property, too. For ordinary children, the Revolution made a significant change when it created a system of education to teach every girl and boy. The Revolutionary leaders hoped that public education would replace the traditional, and very limited, teaching by the Catholic clergy, so that all children would have opportunities to improve their minds, their job skills, and their morality. Ultimately, this project proved too expensive and had to be scaled back.

The documents in this section show how social relationships among ordinary men and women changed, and how poor children were affected by the Revolution, for better or worse.

Helena Maria Williams, the Englishwoman living in Paris during the French Revolution (whom we met earlier in this chapter), was an enthusiastic advocate of Enlightenment ideas. She supported the revolutionaries' basic goal of creating a society based on those ideas: individual liberty, equality under the law, and the use of reason to improve society. At the same time, she was critical of some of the Revolution's shortcomings, such as the National Assembly's decision in 1789 not to accord active citizenship (that is, voting rights) to women or the poor. In this letter, she answers a question sent to her by a friend in England—whether the Revolution had much effect on the lives of ordinary women.

## DOCUMENT 17: BENEFITS AND INJUSTICES TO WOMEN, BEFORE AND AFTER 1789

"The present equal division of hereditary property is certainly a great and substantial benefit conferred on women; as wealth, in all countries, is power, the real influence [of women] is considerably augmented [by this change in law]. The cruel tyranny of paternal authority can no longer be exercised, which has so often doomed the younger [daughters] of noble families to wither in the gloom of convents . . . without their consent. . . .

The question is not whether women have gained from the Revolution, but whether they have gained as much as they ought. . . . Of the injustice that has been or rather of the injustice that has been withheld from the female part of the country [of the right to vote] complaints have been made by some of the celebrated advocates of the Revolution, such as Condorcet and Sieyes [who also called for the abolition of slavery in the colonies.

When [Revolutionary] lawmakers establish public institutions where women may receive the blessings of a general education, when they shall have allowed for her whole mind [to be] enlightened by study and . . . [she gains] some honorable and dignified employment, then will she [embrace] with glowing enthusiasm . . . the hallowed name of liberty.

Political rights, she would observe, are no more affected by this union [i.e., marriage] than by any other civil association [that a woman might choose to make.] nor is it certain that the union of persons constitutes necessarily a union of wills . . . if civil liberty be the consequence of political liberty, it is not clear how from this union [of marriage] women can remain [legally] single and politically married; that if the representation must always by vested in one party [of the husband] since by nature they are constituted to exist together]."

[Source: Williams, 51–59.]

***

Nicolas-Edme Réstif de la Bretonne was one of the most prolific writers of the eighteenth century. He worked as a printer before he became a writer and was very interested in the lives of working people. He was also very interested in promoting social and moral reform through his writings, though he became increasingly skeptical about the chances of succeeding. In this passage from his book of anecdotes about daily and nightly life during the Revolution, *Parisian Nights,* he describes the dire poverty of some women and children that he encountered in a public garden.

## DOCUMENT 18: CHILD POVERTY

"Once inside the public garden where I often walked, I looked for the vices I was accustomed to see there. In almost every arcade I was invited by the most disreputable people to join in the gambling. Farther on, I saw a young girl, attractive though quite undeveloped, being escorted by a prostitute who intended to sacrifice the girl's youth and health. A moment later I saw an even greater horror: children of both sexes at the age of the sweetest innocence, provocatively dressed, entrusted to madams who profaned their childhood...Some prostitutes walk around with children simply to give themselves the respectable appearance of motherhood and titillate old bachelors. But others prostitute these tender victims for the depraved tastes of old libertine.

And who are these victims? Sometimes quite simply children of the greengrocer...or children stolen at a very young age; or foundlings; or children purchased from the poorest people on the outskirts of the city. These last are sold outright to the prostitute, who does with them as she wishes, without being accountable for their fate....

That evening, noticing two children—a girl and a boy—accompanied by a large woman of handsome enough countenance, I approached them. The woman asked if I wished to go up with them....it was easy to see that they were not really playing; rather, they seemed bored, tired, and pained....I replied that I...would pay her, but that I only wanted to know a few details about her business...."Fine, fine," she said. "You're more stupid than malicious....Well, I bought these two from a...woman who [procures them], then raises them on...goat's milk, and sells them to the rest of us when they are ripe. Often she gives money in advance to women who are concealing their pregnancies from their husbands and who come to her to give birth....There are others who buy children, by choosing the prettiest ones, from poor folk who can't afford them. "We're happy," she added, "if a pretty child isn't broken or crippled on us. It's only half bad if a libertine does no more than give them smallpox. We have people to treat them. If a child is delicate, we just cover up the symptoms to keep him going six months, a year, during which time he's used for all he's worth."

I did not wish, I could not bear, to hear more. I was feeling ill and about to faint. I walked out, and I was already on the stairs when I put a three-*livre* note in the woman's outstretched hand. I went away horribly ill."

[Source: Nicolas-Edme Restif de la Bretonne, *Les Nuits de Paris* (1793) (Paris: Hachette, 1960) 48–49.]

***

Réstif captured another aspect of both social change and family life in different passage from the same book. In the anecdote that follows, a *ci-devant* (former nobleman), whose title had been revoked, decides that he will demonstrate his patriotism by marrying a laundress. The anecdote, though fictional, shows the belief that many people had that those who had formerly enjoyed privileges under the Old Regime would be reformed in their views and become committed to equality.

## DOCUMENT 19: AN ARISTOCRAT MARRIES A LAUNDRESS

"A rich nobleman-when there still were some—who had not so far wished to marry, was alarmed at the threats being made to the aristocrats. He resolved to take a wife and to put himself under the protection of the sansculottes by allying himself with them. However, this way seemed difficult to him, for although they were not haughty, he didn't know how to approach them. While he was pondering the problem one day, as he walked along in the street, he noticed a young *sans-culotte* nymph passing by with her mother; she was dressed in red linen, but 'smart as a sou,' in the days when there were any. Quite apart from any other motive, he found her charming and felt that happiness would consist of being loved by her. In another time, had he been sufficiently enamored and the girl virtuous enough, he would have revealed his intentions immediately and offered his fortune. Today, however, the *ci-devant* keeps his status secret. Luckily he wore the uniform of the national guard [Parisian citizen milita]. He followed them to the doorstep of their little one-story house. There be greeted the mother pleasantly.

"You seem to know me, citizen," she said, "but I can't say that I know you."

"Perhaps I'm mistaken," replied the former noble. "I took you for . . . " He was about to mention a name when a laundress with a little basket on her arm came up to them, and assuming the right of any pretty girl to interrupt the conversation, she said, "Madame . . . here is your laundry . . . Good day, Marie Louise. Don't tell me you're interested in that . . . whatever-he-is . . . painter, engraver, draftsman?"

"No, no," answered the woman. "That would be a fine thing in these times. Who wants to die of hunger? I'd prefer a soldier with a good character. . . . "

"Madame, I am happy to know you," says the man. "Allow me to come in with you and we'll talk."

"Gladly, citizen! What's your name?"

"Gemonville, at your service. I lived for a long while in Nantes..."

"Well, I see you are a patriot and a good Breton.... I have always lived in Paris, where I was born."

"...Citizeness...well, here I am all of a sudden in love with your lovely daughter, whose hand in marriage I will ask as soon as you know me better."

"Heavens, Citizen Gemonville, I like the way you lead up to that! Isn't he a scream, Marie Louise?" Marie Louise blushed without answering. "Come, come, citizen—when we know each other....

"I propose marriage however you'd like it-performed before the municipality, or even in a church if you think it more binding, citizen."

"You know, Marie Louise, he's a handsome lad. Well, citizen, to begin the acquaintanceship: my daughter...is an only child; she'll get everything. We had a little property in Brittany...but we don't have it any longer. What do you have, citizen?"

"I, citizen? I have four houses in Lorient bringing in three thousand *livres* [per] year...I will prove it to you before the wedding, Citizenness."

...They dined gaily, that is to say, the suitor and [the mother], for the girl was a bit uneasy. Gemonville asked permission to return the next day with his papers, and asked the Citizenness to have someone present whom she trusted. She agreed, and he went away...Marie Louise agreed that he was pleasing, had wit, and wasn't self-seeking; her mother that he was handsome and polite. "And," she added, "he's very rich!"

He returned the next day and found Citizenness with her family, as well as a solicitor summoned to discuss business. Gemonville impressed everyone with his courtesy and candor-without speaking of his former status. He showed himself a good Breton, a patriot, and ready to sacrifice himself for it....Because he was pressing, Madame drew up a list of terms then and there. He offered the future bride even more than they had asked; in short, he showed such uprightness and good will towards Marie Louise that everyone congratulated her. Afterwards, there was a sumptuous dinner. Gemonville asked permission to contribute to it, and the rest of the day was spent joyfully. That evening, before parting, the mother allowed a moment for the couple [to be alone].

Gemonville used it well. He showed such tender, generous, decent feelings that he touched the heart that his good appearance had already disposed in his favor. He came by in the morning to invite the ladies to honor him with a visit. His lodgings were unpretentious, which was fitting for an aristocrat who wished to become a *sans-culotte*....

Gemonville saw his paramour every day and married her ten days later. Once married, it was even better. He developed the sensibility and taste of his wife, who had excellent natural aptitudes. Their happiness delighted [the mother]...She now had at her disposal a large garden in the Faubour Saint-Marcel, where she was charged with preparing a good dinner every Sunday for as many people as she wished to invite: Her son-in-law begged her not to worry over a few *sous* more or less. These dinners surrounded Gemonville with an imposing number of people, which reassured him. He was president of his delegation; be composed addresses to the Convention, heard them applauded, and his name was on everybody's lips. When it was a question of patriotic donations, his was always the first. "I owe my happiness to the Revolution," he used to say, "without it, I would have married my equal, and never would I have suspected the good qualities present in the hitherto lower stations. No, it's only in the middle class one finds a woman's heart like that of my wife, and a joyous and pleasant disposition like her mother's. But I never even knew of the kind of happiness these two women have brought me; it is too alien to the customs and the manners of the late aristocracy."

[Source: Restif, 337–42.]

## NOTE

1. Jean-Pierre Hirsch, *La nuit du 4 aout* (Paris: Gallimard, 1978), 147.

*Chapter 4*

# Ordinary People for and against the Revolution

After the initial and unexpected shock of 1789, when the Revolution began by tearing down the old society of three orders, everyone could see that the French would have to replace their old ways with new ones. As people of the time said, they had to "regenerate" their society. How was this to be accomplished? Who would decide what the new society should like look and what ideas and words should be used to describe it? What role would ordinary people have to play in this debate? Across France, there was what one historian called "an underlying democratic persuasion."[1] By this, he meant that Revolutionaries believed ordinary people should participate as much as possible.

On first glance, participation meant the right to vote. But it quickly became clear that for ordinary people, political participation would mean both more and less than getting the right to vote. Some would not be able to vote, because the new government restricted this right to those it considered most able to use it: property-owning men, who could be recognized as French by language and race. To us today, this seems a very weak and limited idea of democracy. But at the same time, contemporaries noted that many others, including the poor and women, succeeded in participating in other ways: by attending political clubs, by joining the army, by following news of the Revolution, or merely by using new names that the revolutionary government gave to places, seasons, and people.

This regeneration was not always smooth and was rarely predictable. In the storm of revolutionary politics, where the situation changed constantly, many men and women found themselves denounced for opposing the Revolution—even if they considered themselves supporters. Likewise, some who had only limited sympathy for the Revolution became its leaders. This turbulent experience is recorded in the documents of this chapter, which show us how ordinary people participated in politics, both for and against the Revolution.

## ORDINARY PEOPLE IN REVOLUTIONARY POLITICS

Until 1789, government remained an activity restricted to a very small portion of French society. Moreover, the basic idea of government's relationship to the people can be appreciated by remembering that French people were considered subjects—that is, subject to the authority of the king. The king's authority was presumed to be absolute and to derive directly from God rather than from the consent of the governed. But not all French people had believed this; during the decades and centuries preceding the Revolution, the divine right of kings had been contested by noble judges in the royal law courts. They argued that the king's power was only to represent the will of the nation, as expressed through its natural leaders, the nobles. The major change, then, brought by the Revolution was the idea that the entire French people, rather than just one small segment of nobility, should participate—either directly or indirectly—in government.

Leaving aside the questions of political theory, this section explores the experience of political participation in the Revolution. It follows several different individuals from various backgrounds through the political storm to their varied destinies. Their stories are told by two men—an eyewitness, a Swedish diplomat, John Adolphus, whose later service took him to Philadelphia, where he published his *Biographical Memoirs of the French Revolution;* and the writer Réstif de la Bretonne.

### DOCUMENT 1: SYLVAIN BAILLY, A SCIENTIST IN POLITICS

"Like many others, [Bailly] abandoned the safe and quiet shore of loyalty and obedience to adventure on the boisterous sea of [politics]...and was shipwrecked in his attempt to regain heaven.... Born in Paris, his father was a wine merchant, and.... some [of his] relations held places in the government [of the king before 1789]. He was at first intended for the church but on the death of an uncle who left him [an inheritance], he renounced his first intention and studied for the bar. This profession, however, was no more congenial to his taste and he devoted himself principally to the study of natural philosophy....

"At the assembling of the States General, he was [elected as a] member of the Third Estate....On 23 June, the day of the [king's] speech to the Estates General, Bailly was active .in his protests to the [royal ministers] against the indignity offered to the [deputies of the Third Estate] over which he presided, by detaining them...in a shower of rain while the superior orders took their seats....[Because of this opposition to nobility] the people assembled at his door and hailed him with shouts and acclamations...." After the murder of Flesselles [who held the post of "Provost of Markets" of Paris, killed by the crowd on 14 July], Bailly was elevated to the rank of...mayor of Paris...He is said to have owed this elevation to the intrigues of the [duke dé] Orleans and the [Count de] Mirabeau who were anxious to attach their party [supporters of a constitutional monarchy] to the men of letters [supporters of Enlightenment reforms]....

He, however, ascribed his new dignity to his own merit alone as a leader of the people. By virtue of his office, he was appointed to regulate the ceremony when the king entered the capital [on October 6, 1789]. Though it was [widely known] that the royal family [feared] the assassination of the king, Bailly would not allow [the king] the protection of his faithful bodyguards...who were replaced, at a certain distance from Paris, by a detachment of the National Guard.

[On 17 July 1791, after proclaiming martial law during the Festival of Federation] his popularity received a mortal wound when he read the proclamation, which authorized the soldiers to fire on the people; this ruined him in the eyes of the Parisians, and they turned all their esteem and friendship [for him] into disgust....Insignificant, degraded, and dispirited, he continued in the mayoralty till the dissolution of the constituent assembly [September 1791] and then...he resigned his office.

From the period of his resignation he lived in a state of privacy for nearly two years.... never interfering in politics except by his attendance at the Feuillant [Club]....When [a prominent patriot] denounced him.... he was snatched from his retreat and cast into the prison of the Conciergerie." [Bailly was finally executed during the Terror on July 11, 1793.]

[Source: John Adolphus, *Biographical Memoirs of the French Revolution* (London: Cadell, 1799) (2 vol.) I, 161–69.]

## DOCUMENT 2: NICOLAS GOBET, A PRIEST IN POLITICS

"Gobet . . . was born of plebeian parents at Porentrui, in the dominions of the prince bishop of Basel [in Switzerland]. That prelate had shown great kindness to . . . his family and by his assistance, Gobet was advanced to the bishopric of Lydda . . . [In 1789], he was [elected] a member of the [Estates General] for a canton of Alsace [on the eastern frontier of France]; he was one of the left side and a constant attendant at the Jacobin Club.

[After service in National Assembly, he returned in 1791 to Porentrui and then in 1792, upon the founding of the Republic] he was elected to the Convention. . . . On his return to Paris, he formed a connection with the Cordeliers and . . . was induced to make a formal and public renunciation of his religion. . . . He went to the bar of the convention and made a speech in which he averred that there ought to be no other worship but that of liberty and equality and renounced his functions as minister of the catholic Church . . . Clergy from all quarters of the republic made similar protestations . . .

[During the Terror], he applied to the abbot Barruel for advice . . . that he might be enabled to return to the bosom of the Church. . . . The Pope listened with kindness to his professions of penitence and promises of future fidelity [that] Gobet had written his retraction of errors in six letters . . . He was anxious to quit France that he might escape the fury of the Jacobins but his design became known . . . So it was that only five months after his abjuration of religion, Gobet was arrested, tried on charge of counter-revolutionary crimes and executed [in April 1794]."

[Source: Adolphus, II, 484–85.]

## DOCUMENT 3: MICHEL LEPELLETIER DE SAINT FARGEAU, AN ENLIGHTENED NOBLEMAN IN POLITICS

"The family of Lepelletier was originally of Mans . . . as far back as the year 1508. His father was a judge . . . Before the revolution, Lepelletier was remarkably unobtrusive; he forbore interfering in the disputes between his *corporation* [the Parliament of Paris] and the crown. He would not assume titles of nobility, though he possessed several counties in his own right; he principally employed himself in the improvement of the very large property he derived from his father.... He was a member of the Society of Friends of Blacks....

He was [elected] a member of the [Estates General] where.... from the beginning, he attached himself to the [party of liberal nobles who favored a constitutional monarchy, led by the Duke of] Orléans, and he never deserted his party.... He was president of the Assembly at that famous session [of August 4, 1789] when...the nobility and the clergy sacrificed all their rights and privileges and spoke...[for] the abolition of titles.

His principal labor was the formation of the penal code in the new constitution, which gave rise to many debates. His mind was by nature disposed to mercy and gentleness and [by applying] modern philosophy to...old jurisprudence, all his notions were derived from laudable sources, and many of them had an appearance of rectitude and propriety. He was for abolishing pains of death...this innovation was too great for him to carry, but he seceded in obtaining the suppression of all tortures.... He endeavored to obtain for malefactors a period of three days to appeal against their sentence...and he abolished whipping and branding of criminals...and that the crown should be deprived of the power of pardoning.

He was elected to the national convention for the department of Yonne.... He renewed his attachment to the party of [enlightened reformers, led by] Orléans by voting against the motion for a law against the instigators of murder, alleging...that it would be a restraint on the liberty of the press.

[In January 1793,] he voted for the sentence of death [for the king] and the next day, when he went to dine at a coffee-house...six persons came from an adjoining room and...plunged a saber into his body.... The wounded deputy...expired at one o'clock the next morning.... Ten days later his presumed assassin was discovered...He was a former guard of the King...."

[Source: Adolphus, II, 5–6.]

## DOCUMENT 4: PIERRE MANUEL, A STARVING STUDENT IN POLITICS

"Manuel was the son of a linen-draper at Montargis; he received a liberal [arts] education and early in life went to Paris without money and without recommendation to improve his fortune by the exercise of his abilities. He was hired [by] a banker, as a tutor to his children, for which he was paid 1000 *livres* a year. He was then retained by M. de Sartines [the Lieutenant-General of Police for Paris] as a spy for the police, in the department of publications...he wrote a pamphlet on the famous affair of the necklace [a scandal involving rumors of an affair between the Queen and the Cardinal de Rohan, a prominent nobleman and leading member of the clergy]...which occasioned his imprisonment....He was soon released and returned to Montargis where he supported himself by hawking prohibited and indecent books.

He was thus struggling against poverty when the Revolution commenced....After the destruction of the Bastille, he became a Jacobin and...was named provisionally to the administration of the police in Paris. In this situation he obtained access to many original papers and selected from them...to prepare for the press these papers. Within a year, he produced in two volumes the book *The Police of Paris revealed*. This work affords a copious collection of all the abuses of the old government....It had considerable success....

Manuel did not become opulent; he lived in a garret, at the house of Garnery the bookseller, where he employed himself in publishing another book [of the letters of Mirabeau]. But the creditors of Mirabeau, who considered themselves better entitled to the produce of this publication than any other person, obtained an order from an administrator of the police...to seize the original letters and prevent the publication." [It is thanks to Manuel that we know a great deal about the police of Paris under the Old Regime.]

[Source: Adolphus, II, 12–14.]

## DOCUMENT 5: FÉLICITÉ PRODIGUER, A COUNTRY GIRL IN PURSUIT OF A PATRIOTIC HUSBAND

"A young lady from Caen, a true patriot, but somewhat fanatic, came to Paris with the intention of atoning for the wrong done the Republic by the temporary deviation of her province.... She was a passionate brunette about twenty-six years old....She intended to bestow the pleasures of love on patriotic heroes. In pursuance of this noble project, she made inquiries. Then she wanted to see and learn....She was in the midst of these pursuits when I encountered her by chance....She approached me. I mistook her for a street prostitute who accosts me sometimes, and my reply was in keeping with this idea.

"I see that you misunderstand," she told me, "...Who are you?"

I told her about myself. The young lady reflected. "You are perhaps as good as another, but first of all I think I must ask your advice." She thereupon related to me how she had come to Paris to repair...the wrongs of her province. I listened attentively.

"I think, citizen," I finally said to her, "that it would be more appropriate to dedicate your pretty person and your considerable fortune to a young patriot whose happiness you would assure and who would assure yours, thus providing two good subjects for the State. What do you say? And to suit your purposes, I advise you to choose a Parisian who has already served with distinction." I explained to her what I meant by that. She begged me then to take her to a few public places such as the spectacles, the cafés, the neighborhood headquarters. I consented, and we left at once.

We entered a café, where she made her first observations. From there, we went to my office where she took great interest in a young man. We made an appointment for the next day. We went to the Italian theater, since the French theater had just been suppressed for having performed various plays in which elements of aristocratic taste appeared, and for having shown inclinations in keeping with it. Tuesday we went to the Opera. Each night to a different theater and finally Sunday we returned to my office, where she dropped her handkerchief in front of the young man. They met and were soon married,...and I believe they will be happy."

[Source: Nicolas-Edme Réstif de la Bretonne, *Les Nuits de Paris* (1793) (Paris: Hachette, 1960) 173.]

***

## VOTING: TAXPAYER RIGHTS OR POLL TAX

The essence of a democracy is the right of every individual to vote. And whether or not France should be a democracy became one of the crucial conflicts of the early years of the Revolution. Which offices should be chosen by election? Who should vote in these elections? How should voting take place? In 1789, France had twenty-six million people, larger than the population of most states in the United States today; it faced no easy task in developing a brand-new system for the massive number of elections that were needed to replace the entire Old Regime government, from town councils to the National Assembly.

At the same time, many people in the eighteenth-century—including some of the most ardent advocates of the Revolution—feared democracy. They knew that far fewer than half the people (most of these in the countryside) could read and that only a handful had experience governing. They worried that such a society might quickly fall apart if it made decisions too rapidly. So Revolutionaries sought a compromise between a voting system that would establish the total sovereignty (that is, power) of the people collectively and one that would ensure political, economic, and social stability. The solution they sought was to empower those most able to make use of reason to determine, through public debate, the good of the entire society. The early Revolutionaries sought give those with such an ability active citizenship—the power to hold office and vote in elections. At the same time, the Revolutionaries wanted all people to enjoy passive citizenship, or equal protection under the law.

The key to voting rights, in the early years of the Revolution, was property ownership. Property owners, the leaders of the Assembly thought, had a stake in French society and a natural desire both to preserve individual liberty (in the form of private property) and to promote the general interest (in the form of a stable society). Those without property, the leaders thought, would acquire it eventually and thus gain voting rights. This plan, the early leaders hoped, would lead to a gradual progress towards a society in which everyone would own a bit of property, but no one would own enough to control others or be so poor they would want to change society. At that point, they believed, democratic politics could function peacefully.

But property ownership was hard to measure. In the countryside, most peasants had some land, but whether or not they owned it remained uncertain (as we saw in the last chapter). Workers in cities owned their tools but no property. To them, a property requirement ignored their determination, self-sacrifice, and patriotism. Sansculottes leaders argued that even property-less workers should be entitled to vote, precisely because they would have a different point of view from property owners. The Assembly decided, after some debate, to grant active citizenship rights to those who paid a minimum level of taxes on their wealth, equal to three days' wages.

Prior to 1789, only those who owned property held any political power, which they used to defend their property and privileges from royal taxes and from challenges by those who worked on their land. The Revolution sought a practical alternative between two views of voting: the idea put forth by John Locke and the English Whigs that voting enabled taxpayers to defend their property from the government, and the idea put forth by Jean-Jacques Rousseau that elections provided a means for society to come together to resolve inequalities together.[2] This question became one of the central cultural conflicts of the Revolution, and it remains today a pressing question for democracies. In the following documents, we see two different points of view about the people who should be represented by the National Assembly.

## DOCUMENT 6: DECREE OF THE CONSTITUTIONAL COMMITTEE OF THE NATIONAL ASSEMBLY, 4 JANUARY 1790

"The direct contribution of 3 to 10 days of work that serve as the rule for being able to exercise the functions of an active citizen—voting and holding office—are to be based on the total tax payment by each citizen, either based on personal property or personal income.... One day's work is to be calculated based on the wage of an unskilled day worker...in any given place, be it in the city or the countryside..."

[Source: AN C 11, 156, no. 16; reprinted in Legg, 189.]

## DOCUMENT 7: PATRIOTIC NEWSPAPERS ATTACK THE POLL TAX AS A THREAT TO DEMOCRACY

"The requirement of three days of work means that two thirds of the citizens will be crossed off the lists of voters and those eligible for office. We see how dark will be the consequences fo[r] such an abuse; the choice of municipal officials will be left to a discussion of a very small number of individuals...such an attack on the rights of the people will certainly produce an insurrection by those who would be excluded by this decree."

[Source: *L'Ami du peuple* (17 January 1790) 3; reprinted in Legg, 190.]

"The condition of the *marc d'argent* [a coin used in some regions to calculate the value of one days' wages, and, thus, the required minimum tax contribution to be eligible to vote]...makes us fear that...an aristocracy of wealth will merely replace an aristocracy of birth....we insist that public confidence [that is, declarations of loyalty to the revolution] should be the first and only requirement of eligibility, because a monetary requirement will, by human nature, have too much influence on politics, unless the National Assembly prevents it."

[Source: *Courrier de Provence* (21 March 1790) 69; reprinted in Legg, 190.]

### DOCUMENT 8: DEFENSE OF TAXPAYER'S RIGHTS

"This decree, so much under attack by so-called patriots, is the . . . only way to liberty. . . . It is rare that a man who has nothing can be concerned with the prosperity of the country, no matter how susceptible to sentiments of patriotism."

[Source: *Courrier français* (10 February 1790) 324; reprinted in Legg, 190.]

***

## CONSCRIPTION: PATRIOTIC DUTY OR UNFAIR OBLIGATION

Along with voting rights, the Revolution also provided a new opportunity for ordinary French people to participate in their government through military service. Prior to 1789, military service was an obligation of peasants to a noble lord or of townspeople to a city militia. Once pressed into the royal army, soldiers served seven difficult years of scarce food, unhealthy conditions, poor pay, and high risk of illness, injury, or death. Military obligations fell on the poorest, since families that could afford to would pay a substitute to take their son's place.

The Revolution sought to change this situation, by creating an army of citizen-soldiers. Such an army, they hoped, would be a larger version of a citizen militia; citizens would serve out of a patriotic commitment to defend the ideals of the country. These citizen-soldiers would elect officers based on ability (rather than on birth), and they would enjoy other benefits of citizenship, including education and adequate pay (to be sent to their families in case of injury or death).

At the same time, military service still represented a great sacrifice, especially since calls to arms usually came in the spring, when farmland needed to be plowed and sown, and when workers in towns and cities had the most work to do. So poorer families tended not to view military service as a right of citizenship. This conflict comes across in the following document, in which a citizen of Paris, Edmond Biré, describes the scene in a poor neighborhood of Paris when citizens are called to arms.

## DOCUMENT 9: A VOLUNTEER ARMY: PATRIOTIC VOLUNTEERS OR JOBS FOR THE POOR

" '*Citizens, hasten to the aid of your country. The Republic is in danger... support it with your patriotism and your strength!*'

During the reading of the proclamation, many bystanders turned away and showed no desire to hear.... A fishwife answers... with an oath and the words, 'the devil take them; I won't let my man go!'... the bystanders break out into laugher and as soon as the municipal officers have gone, they speak more boldly. 'They ask for twenty thousand men,' says one, 'a little later they will ask for ten thousand more, and then for another five thousand, until at last there will be no one left. There are at least two thousand policemen in Paris; why don't they send them instead of disturbing peaceful citizens?'... The crowd meets this remark with approval.

On May 1, the Commune [the city government of Paris] issued a decree ordering the formation of an army corps of 12,000 men. Each section... was to furnish fourteen recruits... from among the unmarried men... This decree gave rise to serious disturbances in many of the *sections*.... On May 4, large rallies were held in several public parks to protest against thee decree, and groups of several hundred young men swore not to obey it.... These continued for several days.

[Two weeks later,] the most absolute form of anarchy reigned in the *sections*. A few have obeyed the decree; others have demanded that the conscripts draw lots [to determine who should serve], while the majority has pronounced in favor of voluntary service. Unfortunately, there seems to be little zeal to volunteer.... Patriots declare that their presence in Paris is more necessary than ever; that it is their duty to stay and prevent [moderate politicians] from sinking the republic. One section demanded that instead, they should off the priests... At least, the [leaders of] the *sections* opened their eyes to the fact that with regard to both men and ammunition, money was the sinews of war and if volunteers were wanted, they would have to be paid. This principle being accepted, the recruitment proceeded in a much more satisfactory manner....

The sentiment which animates the bulk of the population of Paris not belonging to any political club... may be summed up, 'If the [enemy forces] come to Paris, we are ready for them... If, however, we go and meet them in the provinces, we are sure to perish. By staying in Paris, we risk being plundered but we shall certainly save our lives.'"

[Source: Edmond Biré, *Diary of a Citizen of Paris During the Terror,* 2nd ed., trans. John de Villiers (London: Chatto and Windus, 1896), 1:228.]

***

## POLITICAL CLUBS: CIVIC ACTIVISM OR FACTIONAL POLITICS

Ordinary people found in political clubs yet another new way to enter into politics during the Revolution. Clubs were of two different forms. Some began as gatherings of deputies to the National Assembly, who met outside of the assembly hall to debate their positions on issues and then had printed pamphlets and newspapers explaining their positions to others. These clubs eventually began to attract more people who participated in the debates, though they were not deputies to the Assembly. The most important of these clubs was the Society of Friends of the Constitution, known as the Jacobins, because it met in a former Jacobin monastery.

Other clubs formed at the opposite end of the political spectrum, among ordinary people who gathered in neighborhood assemblies to elect representatives and to debate how they wanted their representatives to vote on leading issues of the day. The neighborhood electoral assemblies were known as *sections,* and these gatherings attracted the sort of political activists known as sansculottes who considered it their responsibility to keep an eye on the elected deputies and ensure the deputies followed the will of the ordinary people who had voted for them. Some considered these gatherings to be places where newcomers to politics could acquire political ideas, learn how to debate, sign petitions, organize protests, hear and even give speeches, read and write newspaper articles or pamphlets, volunteer for militia or military service, and generally help the Revolution to defeat its enemies. Indeed, deputies from the National Assembly, especially Jacobins, often appealed to the *sections* to demonstrate on behalf of a certain position, to show that the people supported their views. To encourage ordinary citizens to participate in the *sections,* the Jacobin leader Georges Danton proposed a daily stipend for attendees.

Others considered those who attended the *sections* to be rabble-rousers. Critics charged that at moments of great political tension, such as during the wars of 1793–94, the *sections* prevented the country from achieving stability in the economy or politics. Some revolutionaries, who considered individual liberty more important than the political participation of ordinary people, regarded the *sections* as dangerous, because their demonstrations sometimes involved threats of force against elected representatives who did not enact what the *sections* demanded. Even some Jacobins eventually came to this conclusion.

The deputy Le Chapelier was a strong supporter of individual liberties and equality under the law, which he considered a more important goal than providing opportunities for ordinary citizens to participate in politics or fostering patriotism to create a sense of unity. In the following speech to the National Assembly, he argued that since the Old Regime had been brought to an end, there was no longer a need for ordinary citizens to be involved in politics through popular societies. He spoke in September 1791, just after the completion of the new constitution, when he and many others believed the Revolution had achieved its goals. He now wanted France to return to stability and order.

## DOCUMENT 10: A CALL FOR AN END TO POLITICAL ACTIVISM

"Enthusiasm for liberty has led the people, in this time of the establishment [of liberty] but also of storms [that threaten it], to form these societies, which have produced a positive effect on people's spirits and helped them form centers of common opinion, to help them learn that only a minority opposes an enormous majority that seeks the destruction of the abuses [of the Old Regime, such as noble privileges], the reversal of traditional prejudices and the establishment of a free constitution. But...these spontaneous institutions, formed from the purest of motives, soon go past that goal...and take on a sort of political existence that they should not have.

So long as the Revolution continued, they...were more useful than harmful. [They allowed] each citizen to be a lawmaker: to deliberate...on public affairs....But since the Revolution has finished with the completion of the new constitution, since a new [government] has been put in place, we must return to the most stable and orderly way, in which nothing blocks the new government from using its power...to preserve the rights of every citizen. The influence of some must need exceed the influence of others. [Le Chapelier supported the distinction between active and passive citizens so that only those of property could vote or hold office, but he feared that the popular societies, which included many poor workers, would be able to exert pressure on the elected government.]

All citizens must be permitted to assembly peacefully. In a free country...the dear and profound sentiment [of patriotism] creates a desire, even a need, in each person to be involved in public affairs...and thereby to contribute to the society. But...from this point on, the most important show of patriotism is to want to put an end to the [civic activism] of the Revolution. The time for the destruction [of the Old Regime] has passed.... we must now defend the liberty and equality we have constructed...by cherishing the new order rather than...degrading the [newly] established authorities. So...we must guard against some of the [popular] societies taking too active a role in public affairs and becoming...detractors and even despotic over those who serve in the government....

The Nation now expects that we [in the new government] restore peace and affirm order; this is the honorable task of those elected under the new constitution. There is no longer a need for public opinion to be heard through petitions or demonstrations [organized by political clubs]; the French now want only to enjoy the benefits of liberty and equality...to restore commerce, agriculture and industry...to restore prosperity....

Since we have now moved from one form of government to another, the [newly established] constitution calls for the disappearance of those *corporations* and will only recognize...individuals. As a consequence,...it must be forbidden to circulate petition or posters that speak in a collective name. [All political speech must] be in the name of individual, [active] citizens who are the only ones to have their political existence recognized by the constitution."

[Source: Le Chapelier, *Rapport sur les sociétés populaires* (Paris: 1791) 62–63.]

***

In response to Le Chapelier, the Jacobin leader Maximilien Robespierre argued that for the Revolution to achieve true liberty in France, it must continue beyond the constitution of 1791 and broaden political participation by ordinary people.

## DOCUMENT 11: THE REVOLUTION MUST CONTINUE

"Even if the [new constitution] is finished...is it any less necessary to promote knowledge and...public spirit for the constitution to survive? Is it any less useful for citizens to assemble and discuss, in common, their interests and those of the homeland?...The constitution must be continually re-affirmed, because [the risk of] the collapse...of the constitution means the Revolution must continue. This means only that the Nation must continue to make efforts to conserve [its] liberty. How can we propose now that the most necessary part of the Revolution so far, the movements of the people, are now without influence?

I see that with the birth of the constitution, there are still interior and exterior enemies....I see intrigue, deception...by the leaders of opposing political factions [in the National Assembly] who want to dominate the power...and who want to prescribe blind obedience [for everyone else] in the name of liberty. They want to kill public spirit and restore the prejudices...that kept us in slavery to despotism and tyrants [before 1789]....So they want to be able to destroy the [patriotism of ordinary citizens] to impose their personal ambition over the will of the Nation.

...Would it really be so bad, in current circumstances, for public opinion to develop.... for some men, after having served the country so well [by starting the Revolution], to be a little bit more audacious...and to remain good, active citizens...in patriotic societies.... These [societies] have never had any other goal than allowing citizens to instruct and enlighten each other,...to expand Enlightenment...and knowledge of the laws. To destroy, paralyze, entirely eliminate such useful institutions, [as Le Chapelier had proposed]...is this not to do a favor to the enemies of liberty?"

[Source: Maximilien Robespierre, *Oeuvres de Robespierre* (Paris: Société des études Robespierristes, 1879) 67–68.]

***

Popular societies continued to meet, and the revolutionary government, both to hear the voice of the people and to keep tabs on upcoming demonstrations, went to great lengths to monitor what was said in these club and *section* meetings. Here news of the neighborhood, of the nation, and of the world was discussed, from the scarcity of food in the local market to the course the Revolution should take. Indeed, the police developed a Bureau of Public Spirit, which monitored attitudes of ordinary people. These police reports describe the scene in several different popular societies, as the *sections* became known in 1794.

## DOCUMENT 12: MONITORING PUBLIC SPIRIT IN THE CLUBS

"The popular assembly of the *sections*... are extremely numerous and there are many women. At the assemblies, different decrees from the Committee of Public Safety are read... many are pre-occupied with the issuance of certificates of civic virtue [to designate citizens of good, patriotic standing, who can then serve on juries of revolutionary tribunals.]... At another reading, a speech by Robespierre is read... for over an hour and a half. At each line, he was warmly applauded. Then, there was a discussion of how to provide proper meals for the sick... there was much noise throughout the debate.... At [a different] *section*, there was a lot of time given to the awarding of certificates of civic virtue and discussion of how to plant potatoes and vegetables in uncultivated spots near public buildings... for good and patriotic reasons [of producing more food in the city of Paris.]

There was discussion of a woman with a fruit stand who had several pounds of butter and eggs [rarities in the city, during these difficult years.] This caused a great commotion among the women, who were about to strangle her for having hoarded these goods. Much was taken from her and if not for the intervention of several good citizens, she would have been the victim of an attack. There was discussion of another event in the market, at half past nine in the morning, when three citizens charged with keeping order were insulted by fish-wives, under the pretext that one of them had two pounds of butter... A fight broke out among the women, and several lost their bonnets until all were taken away by the militia.

One section sent a deputation to the other popular societies to announce the rumor that tunnels had been found to the prison in which livestock were being smuggled. The deputation had a petition to the National Assembly to stop this abuse.... Finally, there were announcements of several [taverns] in the neighborhood where several small groups were going to drink and [eat] horsemeat.

[At another meeting] attendance was very high, and many ordinary working people. There was a long discussion about the decree... to make the churches into 'national goods' to be sold [to pay off the public debt.]... One strong sansculotte asked, 'how can we sell this church, which has become thanks to our efforts a temple of reason where we hold our meetings? Brothers and friends! At this time, the people need a gathering place and tell me where else is large enough for us to gather?... Now more than ever, we must be able to keep up with current events, and share our ideas, so don't worry, . . . no one will think it unpatriotic if we keep this place."

[Source: Charles-Aimé Dauban, *Paris en 1794 et en 1795* (Paris: 1869) 79–80.]

***

## THE PEOPLE AND THE KING

We tend today to presume that democracy is the opposite of monarchy. But in the early years of the Revolution, many French people viewed the king as the one person who could ensure the success of the Revolution. Only the king, after all, could unify the entire country by eliminating the privileges and special powers of the nobles and clergy. Moreover, the king alone could restore credibility to government, by dismissing those despotic ministers who sought to abuse royal power. So when the National Assembly created a constitutional monarchy, it gave the king veto power over laws passed by the National Assembly.

While a veto might seem to us today an important check on the power of the legislature, many revolutionaries in 1789 regarded it as an obstacle to the will of the people. This humorous engraving shows the uncertainty about the question of the royal veto, as evident in the title "You've got to try it." Even though some worried that the veto required the king to be a patriot (that is, a supporter of the Revolution) for the new constitution to work, ordinary people generally trusted the king to use his veto to ensure all laws would be fair to the entire country, active and passive citizens alike.

This situation changed in June 1791, when the king and his family tried unsuccessfully to escape France and join with former nobles to plan a counter-attack. In July 1791, demonstrators at the Festival of Unity called for the king's removal, leading royal soldiers to fire on the demonstration, and the city government briefly declared martial law in Paris. From this point on, the constitutional monarchy and the king became a matter of conflict.

The political club known as the Girondons sought to preserve what they considered a new regime of individual liberties, notably the sacred and inviolable right of private property; the Girondins continued to favor the constitutional monarchy, even after the king was opposed to it. To support their case, this group pointed out that under the constitution of 1791, the king was inviolable, or not subject to arrest or removal from office. Other clubs, such as the Cordeliers and some of the Jacobins, argued that since the king had betrayed the

The text reads, "You've got to give it a try." The scales suggest that the National Assembly was trying to find the appropriate balance between the power of legislature to pass laws and the king to veto them. Courtesy of the Library of Congress, Department of Prints and Photographs, PP 1789.37.

Revolution, no true change could occur until France once again revised its constitution and became a republic. So at the center of the question of whether the Revolution should preserve order, individual liberty, and private property, or try to unify the country and better the lives of poor people, was the question of the executive power of the king: Should the king preserve order by preventing further change, or should the king be removed to make possible farther-reaching change? This is the question that was debated by elected officials and ordinary people across France in late 1791 and 1792, as we see in the next document—the proceedings of a meeting of the Jacobin club recorded by the British diplomat, Earl Gower.

### DOCUMENT 13: THE FATE OF THE KING IN THE HANDS OF THE PEOPLE

"In the evening, I went to a meeting of the Jacobins Club... It was extremely full, not less than 1000 persons. The question to be debated was, can the King be tried? Who should try him? On what charge and how should be tried? Two speeches took up the whole time.

The first... spoke for the King's... absolute inviolability... an argument not well suited to the temper of the present times. He was heard or rather not heard with... indignation and tumult.... After him, another read a speech very violent and inflammatory to prove that the king's person was inviolable only for those acts of government transacted through his ministers, but that this was a case in which he is personally answerable and that he ought to be tried for his conduct like any other, ordinary citizen..."

[Source: Oscar Browning, ed. *Dispatches of Earl Gower* (Cambridge: Cambridge University Press, 1885), 287–8.]

***

## POLITICS IN THE STREETS

Political conflicts affected ordinary people throughout the Revolution in more mundane ways as well. Because the Revolution's leaders wanted to replace everything old about the Old Regime, they proposed changes in all forms of everyday life—including the systems of weights and measures (by creating the metric system), the calendar, and the names of regions, towns, and even streets. While these laws passed readily, their application in the lives of ordinary people became occasions for cultural conflict; those who supported the Revolution were sure to use the new systems, while those who wanted the Revolution to come to an end resisted the new systems. For instance, the new calendar involved 10-day weeks. While this system was more rational than the seven-day week (it allowed everyone to know easily what days of the week a given date fell on), it meant that ordinary activities such as religious services, market days, and days off from work occurred less frequently—every tenth, rather than every seventh, day. The intensity of this political question is evident in the following document, in which an ordinary citizen writes to a friend abroad about the renaming of Parisian city streets.

### DOCUMENT 14: RENAMING CITY STREETS

"It is the aim of the Revolution [to change]...all things and even their names. To establish a republic in a country that has existed for fourteen centuries with a monarchy...a clean sweep must be made of the past, and every trace of it removed. France must become a nation without ancestors, a people without a history; a pitiless hand must be laid upon the statues of our [Old Regime] heroes and upon any thing that might conjure up old recollections. And that is why our streets, our public squares, and our gardens, are losing those old names that were [known]...to the citizens of Paris.... The city...must become a new city, dating from 14 July and 10 August [1792, the date of the overthrow of the monarchy]....[But this] a foolish attempt, for though they may pull down a statue or a church, they cannot efface history, nor tear from the soil and the heart of the Nation the deeds and memories of its great men."

[Source: Biré, 121.]

***

## WHO WERE THE COUNTER-REVOLUTIONARIES?

If those who participated in the Revolution came from all walks of life and found many different ways to participate in the great conflict of their times, what about those who were supposedly on the other side? What can be said of the so-called counter-revolutionaries? What motivated them to take up arms against the new government? Was it because they did not want individual liberty and equality for all? For some, perhaps it was, since they considered these ideas contrary to the traditions of the Church and traditional morality. Was it because they did not want to see greater participation in politics by ordinary people? For some, yes, because they considered the king, the nobles, and the clergy to be chosen by God as the only legitimate form of authority—without which society would fall into anarchy.

But many of those who became involved in what the new government saw as counter-revolution movements did not oppose the Revolution. They were, however, disappointed with the course of the Revolution, because they saw the departure of respected clergymen, local landowners, or military officers, due to such laws as the Civil Constitution of the Clergy (1790), the decrees against seigneurialism (1790), or the amalgam (1792). Others considered the personal sacrifices being asked of them—such as military service, the patriotic contribution of taxes, or adherence wage and price maximums—to exceed what they might gain. Many were disappointed with what they considered too much centralization of power in Paris and called for decentralization to the provincial cities or countryside. Others hoped to gain land from the sale of confiscated noble or church estates, but did not—and became bitterly disappointed.

In any change of regime, whether elected or revolutionary, those who make up the rank and file have to decide if they are going to follow the new leadership. This decision is particularly important in the case of those who serve in the military, since they are usually the best organized and best armed part of society and therefore possess the force to either resist the new regime or enforce its authority over others. In the case of the French military, this choice had to be made by nearly all soldiers and sailors, because the old officer corps—made up exclusively of nobles—quickly dissolved. Some helped reorganize the army, even serving as officers themselves. Others refused to recognize their new superiors and mutinied. In the following document, we read about a mutiny of some ordinary soldiers in August 1790 in the city of Nancy—near the French border with German-speaking Europe and close to where emigrant nobles were gathering to oppose the new regime. These soldiers sought to restore what they considered legitimate authority in the army, but their actions left the new government little choice but to consider them traitors against the Revolution.

## DOCUMENT 15: THE LOYALTY OF SOLDIERS AND SAILORS: MILITARY INSUBORDINATION

"France cannot exist without soldiers, but it may soon be unable to exist with them. While . . . [we are] daily discovering fresh causes of alarm from abroad, a universal relaxation of discipline and a want of discipline and a want of energy are forming dangers at home.

A most alarming insurrection of the garrison of Nancy has obliged the National Assembly to give to the king the full power of the sword...Three regiments, in short the whole garrison of Nancy, have risen against their officers, broken open the military chest, and divided the money contained in it. The Assembly have unanimously decreed that the instigators of this rebellion...are guilty of the crime of *lèze-Nation* [treason]...and shall be punished accordingly....

[September 3, 1790] By the activity of [a patriot military officer], the insurrection.... is suppressed but not without considerable slaughter. On the first day of this month, he appeared before the town with all the troops and Gardes Nationales [local citizen militia] he could collect...who volunteered to be in the front ranks, in hopes that their appearance might prevent the seditious soldiers [who would recognize them] from firing, but unfortunately this did not have the desired effect.... had the insurrection not been suppressed, it would probably have been the beginning of a civil war."

[Source: Gower, 25–31.]

***

In the early months of the Revolution, most of France—including many members of the upper orders—supported greater individual liberties (especially defense of private property) and the use of reason to reform abuses in the government (such as exemptions from taxation for nobles.) However, in June 1790, two important changes created a conflict between the new culture of the Revolution and the old ways of the Old Regime: the abolition of seigneurialism and noble titles, and the Civil Constitution of the Clergy, which required priests to swear an oath of loyalty to the nation. Some nobles believed that this was too much change and decided to emigrate from France to Prussia. Likewise, about half of the clergy abandoned their pulpits rather than take the oath. Though these emigrant nobles (or non-juring or refractory) clergy did not necessarily want to bring back the Old Regime, the leaders of the Revolution considered them aristocrats and blamed them for the continuing difficulties of patriotic, ordinary men and women. Moreover, the National Assembly ruled that such resisters must be considered outside the protection of the law and could be stripped of their offices and large estates (in the case of nobles) or their standing in the clergy. As a result, the emigrants and refractory clergy became even more fervent in their resistance, since they now had to see the end of the Revolution to regain their former positions and property.

In these letters from Earl Gower, the English diplomat, written in the winter of 1790–91, we see how French patriots responded to the first open resistance to the Revolution from emigrant nobles and refractory clergy.

## DOCUMENT 16: EMIGRANT NOBLES AND REFRACTORY CLERGY

"[December 17, 1790] The aristocratic party expresses openly in public their [*sic*] hopes of a speedy counter-revolution. Three people have been lately taken up and sent to the prison . . . on account of the discovery of a treasonably plot; and between hope and fear, many people attached to the [Old Regime] are leaving Paris daily.

[December 31, 1790] There has been considerable dissension among the French . . . aristocratic party at Turin [in Italy, where some emigrant nobles gathered]. Because their leader, the Prince of Condé, has spoken disrespectfully of the King of Sardinia [for not invading France to suppress the Revolution] he has been obliged to leave [his place of exile] and many expect him to return to France [to fight against the Revolution].

A serious . . . [and] certain . . . plan for a counter-revolution has been discovered at Lyons [the second largest city in France]. . . . A number of men arrived there from the [surrounding countryside] with horses, which they left [rather than turn them in for military service, as ordered by the revolutionary government] and then returned home. . . .

[January 14, 1791] All the bishops except four have refused to take the oath [of allegiance, known as the Civil Constitution of the Clergy]. The greater number of parish priests of Paris have taken the oath; some, however, have asked for another week to consider the question and declined to take it at this time. Meanwhile, no official answer has arrived from Rome [with instructions from the Pope about what priests should do.] These priests [in Paris] who refused to take the oath have been permitted to go home without bloodshed, but not without insult from the populace. In the provinces though some cruelties have taken place and in one place, a mob cut off the priest's head and placed it on the altar, then sprinkled it in derision with holy water."

[Source: Gower, 46–49.]

***

In September 1792, when a republic replaced the constitutional monarchy, France faced not only invasion from emigrant nobles and foreign armies (from Prussia, Austria, and Britain) but also deep internal divisions. Some, including the Girondins, considered the Revolution to have achieved its basic goals and called for a damping down of political activism. Others, notably the sansculottes and clubs such as the Cordeliers and the Jacobins felt the Revolution had to be pushed forward through more aggressive politics to help small shop owners, workers in the cities, slaves in the colonies, and ordinary citizens.

The Jacobins in the National Assembly and sansculottes in the *sections* of Paris and other large cities sought to force the issue in the summer of 1793 through repeated demonstrations, some of them violent. By the fall of 1793, under pressure from the sansculottes, the Jacobins in the National Assembly declared revolutionary government, or a suspension of the constitution, to allow for mandatory requisition of all able-bodied men and property for the army, in the interest of saving a country in danger. To help alleviate the still-catastrophic economic situation, the legislature, led by the Jacobins after June 1793, issued more paper money, known as *assignats,* and established price controls for bread and other basic commodities, known as the Maximum. The Jacobins also enacted a system of trials by revolutionary tribunals—jury trials for treason—of those suspected of undermining the homeland in a time of war. By the spring of 1794, although the situation was less dangerous on the home front, thousands of people were being denounced each week as suspects and tried by the Revolutionary tribunal in what was known as the Great Terror.

In this letter from an ordinary citizen to a friend, Edmund Biré describes the statement by the public prosecutor calling for all patriotic citizens to keep an eye out for politically suspicious behavior by their neighbors and to denounce it as suspect to a government official. From this letter, we get a sense of how, on the one hand, not all suspects were necessarily former nobles, clergy, or royalists, and on the other, how susceptible ordinary people were to being arrested and tried in a political system that had suspended basic liberties, such as rights of the accused to defend themselves in an open trial.

## DOCUMENT 17: WHO ARE SUSPECTS AND BY WHAT SIGNS THEY MIGHT BE KNOWN

"The day before yesterday, the [public prosecutor for Paris], Chaumette, explained to the [city government] who were suspects and by what signs they might be recognized [by patriotic citizens].... The following are suspects and should therefore be arrested:

1. Those who in public assemblies attempt to stem the people's will by cunning speeches [that are] seditious [against government policy].
2. who...speak mysteriously of the misfortunes of the republic, lament the fate of the people [for having started the revolution] and are always ready to spread bad news....
3. Those who...loudly inveigh against the least faults of the patriots and in order to appear republican, affect a studied austerity [with respect to] moderates or aristocrats.
4. Those who pity the avaricious farmers and merchants against whom the law [of the Maximum] is obliged to take measures....
6. Those who take no active part in the Revolution and who instead of doing so [through military service or attendance at political meetings] make payment of contributions of patriotic gifts and by so doing have a substitute serve for them in the National Guard....
9. Those who do not attend sectional meetings and who excuse themselves on the ground that.... their business holds them back.
10. Those who speak with contempt of the constituted authorities...of the political clubs, and of the defenders of liberty [in the army].
11. Those who have signed counter-revolutionary petitions....

It is not however only the big merchants and *aristocratic shopkeepers* [a term used in a patriotic newspaper to denounce those who were suspected of charging prices above the maximum, to increase their profits] who can be suspects. The poorest artisan and even the water-carriers [the lowest paid job in Paris, often filled by young girls] are included...even chimney-sweepers can be suspects...Especially are those who have clean hands, neatly kept hair, and well-shod feet. Those, especially women, who do not wear a tricolor cockade [a cloth ribbon] in their caps....Those who have retained any furniture or dishes bearing the proscribed emblem of the lily [the symbol of the Bourbon dynasty of kings, including Louis XVI.]"

[Source: Biré, 321–23.]

***

The most overt cultural conflict between the Republic and its domestic opponents took place in the western region of the Vendée, one of the most rural and agrarian in France. Prior to 1789, this region had featured the highest ratio of clergy and nobles to ordinary people; after 1790, it saw the highest rate of refusal by clergy to the oath, leaving many villages without their priests. It also saw the departure of many nobles to emigration, leaving sharecropping farmers without the means to take their produce to the marketplace. In this region, the government auctioned off a great deal of land confiscated from the Church, but very little of this land came into the hands of the peasants. The final straw for the frustrated peasants of this region came in the spring of 1793, when the new Republic sought to draft all able-bodied young men for military duty, at the height of the ploughing season, when farmhands were needed in the fields.

In response, the peasants of western France revolted in the city of Nantes against the Republic, seizing the tax collectors of the region. This eyewitness account by a government witness describes the scene in March 1793, as a crowd of young men forms to protest against the draft and bloodshed results:

## DOCUMENT 18: THE VENDÉENS: DEFENDERS OF THE FAITH OR COUNTER-REVOLUTIONARIES

"A considerable group is formed . . . and after about two hours . . . the municipal officials orders a contingent of National Guardsmen to keep the peace. Since the morning, small groups have been forming in the inns and taverns . . . at about two in the afternoon, they gather in great number at one inn . . . The second commander of the National Guard orders them to disperse, but after he speaks, someone charges at him furiously, grabs his saber, and seriously wounds him on the leg and the head. Shots are fired from a pistol, and the National Guard is forced to return fire. Three men are killed, and the rest disperse."

[Source: Translated from Claude Petitfrère, *La Vendée et les Vendéens* (Paris: Gallimard, 1981) 20; reprinted from Departmental archives of Maine-et-Loire, 1 L 757 (4 March 1793).]

***

From there, the movement quickly spread across the west of France, in the form of both an organized army and guerilla units. The guerillas had a great advantage in this region, because many fields were divided by thick hedgerows, known as *bocages*. Being from the region, peasant guerillas knew how to move around *bocages;* the government troops, generally from other regions, did not and grew frustrated with the hostile terrain, as evident in this letter by a government officer:

## DOCUMENT 19: GUERILLA FIGHTERS IN WESTERN FRANCE

"Their attack is . . . subtle, often improvised, because it is very difficult in the Vendée to see for any distance, resulting in a guarantee of surprise. . . . They form into small lines [of soldiers], who provide cover for their best snipers . . . Before you know it, you're blown away under heavy fire, and our guns are not comparatively very effective. They do not form battalions or platoons . . . they almost never use a cavalry. They disperse themselves and escape us across the fields, through the woods and bushes. They know the paths through the forests and gorges, so they can cut [our units] in two and when we retreat, they pursue us with incredible speed."

[Source: Louis-Marie Turreau de Garambouville, *Mémoires pour servir à l'histoire de la guerre de la Vendée* (Evreux: 1795) 22–23; reprinted in Petitfrère, 25–26.]

***

To suppress this rebellion, the republican government sent both regular and irregular army units. In some cases, these units resorted to brutal force that wiped out entire villages of French citizens. The soldiers, mostly volunteers from Paris or from the eastern part of France, could not understand why their fellow Frenchmen in the western villages fought so hard against them. Nor could they understand the guerilla tactics employed by the peasant fighters; these tactics made every encounter, on or off the battlefield, dangerous for the republican soldiers. Their frustration became evident, as we see in this letter by a republican deputy, Léquinio, sent to report on the fighting.

## DOCUMENT 20: BRUTALITY IN WESTERN FRANCE

"The [war] crimes were not merely the ordinary pillage [of a town by soldiers seeking food]; rape and extreme barbarity were present in every town. We saw republican soldiers rape rebel women on the rocks along the road, then shoot or stab them . . . We saw others carrying children on the end of their bayonets . . . Also, wives and daughters of patriots [i.e., supporters of the republic, rather than the rebels] were often requisitioned by the soldiers.... All this horror hardened spirits on both sides and increased the number who were miserable, which only made more common the massacres..."

[Source: Joseph-Marie Lequino de Kerblay, *Geurre de la Vendée et des Chouans* (Paris: 1795) 14–15; reprinted in Petitfrère, 56–57.]

***

Was this force a necessary precaution against traitors in a time of war, or an excessive desire for unity by the new government? Were the opponents of the Parisian government fighting to defend regional traditions or fighting against individual liberty and equality for all? These two views are evident in the following documents, in which participants on the republican and the rebel side, respectively, try to explain the motivations of ordinary soldiers on the other side of the conflict.

## DOCUMENT 21: THE REPUBLICAN VIEW OF THE VENDÉE REBELS

"It would be an error to view this uprising as a spontaneous revolt of the inhabitants of the region that came about accidentally; there was a powerful force behind it all, which knew the countryside well and which opposed the principles of the Revolution: [it was]...the priests and the nobles....The priests are able to use the promise of heaven or the threat of hell, and the nobles had no less powerful a menace...to control the independent character of the people here....What else could have given this impulse to the inhabitants of the countryside to be so furious and bloodthirsty?...They have had their imaginations inflamed by fanaticism....The inhabitants of this countryside, kept in the deepest ignorance and deprived of all communication [with the rest of France], have remained the servants of the nobles and the priests, while the rest of France has been freed."

[Source: Jean-Julien Michel Savary, *Guerre des Vendéens et des Chouans contre la République française* (Paris: 1824) I, 32; reprinted in Petitfrère, 71–72.]

***

By contrast, the rebel point of view emphasized the discontent of the peasants with the Republic.

## DOCUMENT 22: VENDÉEN VIEW OF THE WESTERN REBELLION

"At the beginning of the insurrection, I didn't know who was organizing it other than a guy named Catelineau. I went with him to gather with men from four or five other parishes which had refused to supply the number of men demanded by the [republican government] for the draft...it was not, as they saw, organized by the nobles and the priests.

The unhappy peasants had been so badly hurt by the heavy demands made on them [by the republican officials, for taxation and conscripts] could no longer support it and revolted, guided by local men who had their trust and affection.... [They] never were enemies of the cause [of the Revolution] which these peasants had even supported and marched for with such courage; but no reasonable person could ever have imagined that a handful of poor people, with no arms or money, could defeat the entire force of [the republic.]...We never had that goal, not or even really hoped, but after the first success [against republican forces at Nantes], we went on an attack...without either a plan or much intelligence. All the people just rose up at once...

The fathers [of the Vendée peasants] had been happy and tranquil under the Old Regime, in the shadow of the pulpit and the throne, and they did not have any reason to support a bloody republic.... The noble *chateaux* in the region were built and furnished without magnificence...Gentlemen in the region lived simply, and their only amusement was hunting....The relations between the lords and the peasants did not resemble what they appear to have been [elsewhere in France]; there was a sort of union unknown elsewhere. They shared the produce from the land due to sharecropping, so each day they had common interests and confidence and good faith [in each other]. The lords...treated them paternally, visited them often on their farms, chatted with them about their land...and animals...they even went to the weddings of peasant children and drank to their good health. On Sundays, they danced together in the courtyard of the lord's *chateau*...When they hunted [together]...each one brought his own rifle.... so naturally, [when the uprising took place] they fought together...the peasants here never shared the [immoral] opinions that dominated the rest of France. Their conscience never allowed them to renounce [the Catholic] religion of their fathers, and never did their hearts turn against the charitable lords who ensured that they

This engraving from 1792 suggests the domestic forces arrayed against the Revolution, including the archbishop of Paris; formerly noble military officers, royal officials, and courtiers; a group of Capuchin monks; and several former royal police officers from the corps of the Bastille. The banner they carry reads "Pastoral letter" (the official document used to appoint clergy to the pulpit) and "Long live the nobility and the clergy!" Courtesy of the Library of Congress, Department of Prints and Photographs, PC-1792.4b.

had enough to eat, nor against the charitable pastors who supported them through difficult times. Instead, these good people remained friends of the throne, of the pulpit, and of the *châteaux* [i.e., of the king, the clergy and the nobility.]"

[Source: *Mémoires du comte de Cxxx* (Hambourg: 1801) 95, 129; reprinted in Petitfrère, 80–82.]

***

To many, the conflict of 1793–94 pitted those seeking to take a heroic step forward towards liberty, equality, and patriotism against those who had formed a single movement combining all the powers of the Old Regime: nobles, clergy, royalists, and enemies of the Enlightenment. In this humorous engraving, we see one patriot's imagination of the counter-revolution as a single cultural movement at conflict with everything he hoped the Revolution would stand for: constitutional democratic rule, individual freedom of belief, and, above all, progress forward rather than blind faith in tradition.

## NOTES

1. Isser Woloch, *The New Regime* (New York: W.W. Norton, 1994).
2. John Locke, *Second Treatise on Civil Government* (London: 1690); (Irvington: Irvington Publishers, 1979); Jean-Jacques Rousseau, "On the Social Contract," in *The Basic Political Writing*, Donald A. Cress, trans. (Indianapolis: Hackett, 1987), 141–227.

*Chapter 5*

# Law and Order in Everyday Life during the Revolution: Violence, Public Order, and Collective Action

Ordinary people in eighteenth-century France experienced violence on a daily basis well before 1789; violence was a common event at home, in the streets, at the workplace, and in the tavern. Under the Old Regime, nobles regularly threatened and inflicted violence on commoners with impunity: Lords enforced the collecting of peasants' dues with violence; nobles demonstrated their right to commit violence by wearing swords; and the king could have his soldiers arrest and imprison anyone, anytime, for any reason.

At the same time, people in the eighteenth century greatly feared collective violence. Any crowd that might gather in a public place such as a market, a theater, or even a field could quickly turn violent. People expected the government to prevent violence from happening—that is, to preserve public order. The government was supposed to use violence legitimately—arrest and imprisonment, for example—to prevent illegitimate and dangerous violence, such as a riot. Under the Old Regime, violence by nobles and the king was considered legitimate; most other violence was not. After they abolished the special status of the nobility, the leaders of the French Revolution sought to find a new way to preserve public order, without empowering some in society to use violence on others arbitrarily.

For this purpose, they created a new judicial system. Under the Old Regime, the king and the nobles literally owned the judicial system. Only nobles could be judges, and nobles owned their seats on royal and regional courts, which they could sell or pass on to heirs as property. To replace this system, the French revolutionaries sought to create a new judicial system. The new system included such innovations as trial by jury (for criminal cases), justices of the peace to resolve petty disputes without the need for expensive lawsuits, and a police force of ordinary citizens motivated by patriotism and a desire to enforce the law equally, rather than by pay or power.

This goal of a fair and impartial police force that defends the rights of every individual (including private property for those individuals who had any) seemed to many Revolutionaries as the essence of liberty and equality. At the same time, many ordinary people who supported the Revolution wanted the police force and judicial system to do more than merely preserve the peace. They worried that if the police force only acted to defend public order, it would prevent ordinary people, especially those without property (and thus without the right to vote), from participating in politics through demonstrations and protests (as discussed in chapter 4). They worried that if the police and courts defended only public order, they would defend, in effect, the authority of property owners to coerce those who worked on their property, such as farm hands or artisans.

Sansculottes expressed these concerns in section meetings, and other patriots made the same points in Jacobin political clubs. They argued that collective action—such as daylong protests known as *journées*—did not violate public order, since this action enabled the people to defend their liberty. That such protests might lead to violence, they argued, was a good thing, since violent protests allowed patriots to take action, to fight actively against the Revolution's enemies, especially those enemies who had hidden among the people to await their chance to end the people's freedom.

As the tension grew, due to invasions, civil wars, and continuing shortages, revolutionaries from the more activist political movements, such as the Jacobins, wanted the judicial system not only to defend law and order, but also to enforce the need for patriotism. They felt that in a time of war, with the homeland in danger, anyone whose beliefs or behavior might diminish national unity should be considered a traitor—and be arrested, tried, and if convicted, subject to the death penalty.

So one of the crucial cultural conflicts of the French Revolution was between those who saw collective action as the most important part of the Revolution (the people, unified and active, enacting change by any means necessary) and those who saw collective action as the greatest threat to public order (mob rule).

## LAW COURTS, JUDGES, AND JURIES

Under the Old Regime, the power to maintain law and order belonged to the nobles. In the countryside, seigneurs held, as one of their privileges the power to settle any legal question, criminal or civil, on their fief. The lord's manor therefore served as the local court of each village. Likewise, the lord, or those he chose, performed the functions of the police and of the prosecutor. Most cases that came before these seigneurial courts involved legal challenges by peasants against the privileges of the lord; since the lord owned the court, the overwhelming majority of rulings went against the peasants.

In this document, from the transcript of a seigneurial court on the land of the Marquis de la Perrière in the region of Burgundy, we see how these courts influenced the lives of ordinary people in the countryside:

### DOCUMENT 1: A SESSION OF A SEIGNEURIAL COURT

"Jean Joliclerc, prosecutor and bailiff...summons [several local villagers] to appear before the court and an oath [of loyalty to the lord] is sworn...[The cases are heard and the judgments are rendered:]

By order of the court, it is forbidden for any inhabitant of this land belonging to the Marquis to hunt or to bear arms or to keep arms at home...or to carry firebrands in the streets...

[The court] also orders that the inhabitants...should not be given wine at any time, including Church services [preventing them from taking Holy Communion] and that they are not to go to taverns...

[The court also] orders that inhabitants are not to graze their animals anywhere but the common land [the small, uncultivated part of the lord's lands that belong to all the villagers, rather than the lord.]...and are not to allow their pigs onto the meadows.... Inhabitants shall not keep goats [which are likely to wander onto the lord's land to graze].

...Those who work as threshers are not to have lighted pipes in the barn..."

[Source: Translated from Pierre de Saint-Jacob, *Documents rélatifs à la communauté villageoise en Bourgogne* (Dijon: 1962) 60–62.]

***

Starting in the seventeenth century, the Bourbon kings of France tried to reform this system, which allowed each lord to set an entirely different set of laws on each fief. But the king did not have any legal basis, or the brute power, to force the lords to give up this power. The best that Louis XIV and Louis XV could do was to create special courts to deal with cases that arose on parts of the countryside traditionally considered the property of the king, such as roadways, rivers, and forests. The courts that ruled over rivers and forests provide us with a good example of how the royal judicial system worked for ordinary people, as described with mocking humor by the writer Louis-Sébastien Mercier:

## DOCUMENT 2: HUNTING AND FISHING COURT UNDER THE OLD REGIME

"This tribunal is still known by its old name of the 'captaincy,' [because the judges were originally chosen from among captains in the army, who were all nobles]. Its function is to make judge and to send to the galleys anyone convicted of feloniously slaying partridges and hares. [It is absurd that by law,] a hare may eat a peasant's cabbages, and pigeons may descend in swarms upon his ripening corn; in the river bordering his field, fish may swim in shoals, but by this same law, [the peasant] may not interfere with the hare or the pigeon's proclivities nor set a line for the fish. [This is because only lords have the right to hunt or fish on royal lands.]

If [the peasant] kills [an animal that is eating his crops], he is hung. And that is the end of him. Because of his hideous, barbarous [punishment], such crime is rare... but this court only hears such cases and does not punish [more serious crimes such as murder or] parricide.

It is strange that this court was created by the best of kings... Henri IV [who ended the Wars of Religion and unified the kingdom during his reign from 1589 to 1610. As part of his popular reforms, designed to limit the power of the nobility, he created] the first law that attached the death penalty to the crime of poaching. The statutes [from the years of Henri IV's reign] which this tribunal administers are... totally unrelated to our time and to the rest of our laws. We have plenty of these barbarities [outdated laws], that ordinary citizens, in the course of their regular daily work and without knowing it, are continually breaking, which keeps this unnecessary court in business."

[Source: Louis-Sébastien Mercier, *Tableau de Paris* XCIV, I, 277–78.]

***

Judges who heard these cases were not paid directly by the king. As nobles, they were expected to work out of a sense of duty rather than for pay. Yet as laws became more complicated, nobles often hired experienced lawyers to sit on the courts and advise them on the way to decide. These lawyers expected to be paid for their work. Since they received no pay from the government, they collected fees, known as *spices,* from those who came before the court. While many judges considered it fair for those who went to court to pay these fees as compensation for the judge's work, others saw spices as bribes.

The debate over whether judges should be paid or not illustrates one of the key cultural conflicts of the Old Regime: between a traditional idea of power as the prerogative of nobles serving out of a sense of duty, and a newer idea of authority based on the effective use of reason. The Revolution clearly sought the latter, which meant that those who exercised power, such as judges, would have to be trained and paid by the government to best serve the people. In this document, the popular playwright, Pierre-Augustin Caron de Beaumarchais (who himself served as a judge in a Hunting and Fishing Court), mocks the idea of spices. The following document is an excerpt of a legal brief Beaumarchais prepared for a celebrated court case in 1773 over a large sum of money he owed to a count. Beaumarchais explains that the wife of the judge, Goëzmann, demanded 15 gold *louis* just so he could meet with the judge to argue his case.

## DOCUMENT 3: MONEY AND JUSTICE

"In the days before the trial, I tried three times to see him . . . until finally the porter, tired of seeing me, sent me away. . . . The next morning, when I went for a fourth time, he told me to come back again; that afternoon, the same response. . . . So you can understand my concern. . . . why couldn't the judge simply open his curtain, and he would have seen through his window the unhappy man waiting outside his door? . . . Not knowing what to do next, I went to my sister's to get advice and calm down . . . There, a man named Airolles, who was staying at my sister's house, remembered that a bookseller named Lejay was close to Mister Goëzmann and could perhaps arrange for me the meeting I sought. . . . He explained that Madame Goëzmann often went to his bookstore to receive the royalties for her husband's books that he sold, and she had taken up a friendship with Madame Lejay. . . .

[Airolles made the inquiry and then informed Beaumarchais that it would cost him] 200 *louis.* I couldn't believe the sum, but it was absolutely necessary that I have a meeting with the judge. I knew this because when I had been involved in a lawsuit [at a different court], I had to pay not only to see my lawyer but even his secretary, so it went without saying for a judge....

So I tried to borrow the money, which I didn't have, from my sister....She suggested we [send Airolles back to offer] 50 *louis* ...but soon Airolles was back for another roll [of coins], and my sister.... sadly give him another 50...Several hours later, Airolles told my sister that Madame Goëzmann, once she had the 100 *louis* in her hot little hands, had at last promised a meeting that evening. The instructions passed along to me where to 'go this evening to the door of Mr. Goëzmann. They'll tell you he's already left, but protest a lot and ask for the lackey of his wife. Give him this letter...and you'll be certain to be admitted.'

So I went that evening, with my lawyer...All that was promised happened, until when I gave the letter to the lackey, he told me, with a haughty air, that I could not see the judge, 'because he is in his office with his wife.' I insisted and the lackey...soon told me 'to go up to the [judge's] office...by the back staircase that led to [his wife's] chambers.' [Finally] at half past nine, I was admitted to the office,...and I saw the table being set for dinner. I excused myself for delaying their dinner.... and was about to talk about the evidence, when...he told me that he knew enough already to judge the case...As he spoke, I saw a misleading smile on his face which alarmed me greatly....

The following Sunday, the day before the trial, I asked Airolles to find out if there was any hope left for me.... We negotiated again, because Madame Goëzmann insisted that a second meeting would require a second sacrifice, and instead of 100 *louis* that I didn't have, she would accept a diamond watch. [Beaumarchais, before becoming a writer, had been a watchmaker.] I got it to her through the sister of Airolles who gave it to Lejay....But then, Airolles told me that this woman had added another demand, 15 more *louis* for her husband's secretary....The money was carried over, and the meeting set for seven o'clock. But it was again in vain.... If the reader is at this point tired of reading about all these vain promises, imagine how much more outraged I was to receive them....

The next day, I lost the case. Mr. Goëzmann, on leaving the courtroom, said out loud to my lawyer, before several people, 'that he had taken his arguments under consideration.' but it would have been better if [his client] had come to see him to discuss the case...What cruelty...."

[Source: Pierre-Augustin Beaumarchais, "Mémoire à consulter pour Pierre-Augustin Caron de Beaumarchais," in *Oeuvres,* ed. Pierre Larthomas (Paris: Gallimard, 1988) 677–89.]

***

Prior to 1789, the highest law courts in France were known as *parlements* (from the Latin for "discuss," the same root as the English Parliament). The judges on these 13 courts—one for each of the 12 provinces of France, plus the most important, the *Parlement* of Paris—were nobles who owned their seats and so could not be removed. Though technically these judges served by the approval of the king, most inherited their seats from their families or bought them as a means of ascending into the nobility. Known as magistrates, these men took their tasks very seriously; not only did they hear civil and criminal cases, they also approved all royal laws that applied to their region. Most magistrates were highly educated and had been influenced by Enlightenment ideas. The most important example of such a judge was the Baron de Montesquieu. Montesquieu wrote an important book called *The Spirit of the Laws,* which advocated the separation of legislative, executive, and judicial power in the government.

When the revolutionaries, in 1789, abolished all noble privileges, they had to replace all those courts and judges. Everyone agreed that the new judges should have no personal interest in the cases they heard and should apply the law equally. Some believed the best way to assure this outcome was for the one person who best understood what was best for all the people, the king, to select judges, based on their proper training and knowledge of the law. Others feared giving this much power to the king and argued that the people should choose directly, by electing judges. They did not worry that elected judges would decide cases based on what was most popular, and this argument carried the day in the spring of 1790. The National Assembly voted that under the new constitution, judges would be elected. An article from the pro-monarchist *Courrier de Provence* in May 1790 discusses how this issue divided supporters of the Revolution into two different sides, depending on whether they considered reason (that is, the fair application of the law) or democracy (that is, the participation of the people in all exercises of power) to be more important.

## DOCUMENT 4: THE SELECTION OF JUDGES

"We have seen a great agitation...about this question of what should be the role of the king in the selection of judges.... Is the decision of the National Assembly to exclude the king from this role a triumph for the cause of the people? Or is it [a threat to] reason? If the fears inspired by royal involvement are justified and if there was no way to reconcile those fears with the good of the people, then the Assembly should have followed the constitutional principles to which it has sworn itself previously....

With respect to the separation of powers, very much discussed by the Assembly, the theory of Montesquieu, while well founded, has never been examined [in practice]. Those who invoke it on this occasion [to argue that the king should have no role in the choice of judges]...should be careful.... To make the law and to execute it are two different things; the first is the role of the elected representatives of the people [in the legislature], and the latter is the role of the king [as the executive]. Since the making of law is always a matter of general principle and the application of the law is always a matter of the particular case, there must be power in between [the legislative and the executive]....

Let us agree then that any constitution that divides the powers of legislative and executive [meaning a constitutional monarchy] confides in the [king] the power to judge. But since it is also impossible for the king to judge himself each case,...it is clear that others must be named to hold this power and judge in his name, with his authority....All this is for the individual liberty and tranquility of the citizens....

The [decision of the National Assembly has been that the] determination of facts [in a case] should be reserved to the people itself, in juries drawn from the people while the application of the law to these facts, once known, should be confided in elected judges. This is based on what they imagine to be the most careful choice being made [by the voters] in the election of judges....But this power of choosing judges should not be left with the ordinary people....It will tend to establish a judiciary aristocracy [who will rule to preserve their own power by being re-elected, rather than choose judges best trained in the application of law]....Only one power can choose judges properly, it's the supreme...representative of the Nation. We are not suggesting that the king best knows each individual person who is best suited to be a judge in his kingdom, or even that his ministers can best make this choice, but it cannot be left open [to election] without threatening liberty. . . ."

[Source: Translated from *Courrier de Provence* CXLI (9 May 1790) 141; reprinted in Legg, 219–223.]

***

The nation received this decision very favorably. Patriots who sought to enhance the power of ordinary people particularly applauded the idea of electing judges. We see this point of view in the newspaper, *Mother Duchêne,* that offered political commentary in the voice of a market woman—full of expletives, contempt for the former nobles, and celebrations of the goodness of the ordinary people.

## DOCUMENT 5: CONGRATULATIONS TO THE NEW JUDGES

"Now, justice is no longer decided by the weight of gold. Judges no longer leave the poor pitifully dying outside the courtroom door. . . . Damn, they saw that everything goes smoothly in your courtrooms now and things are calm, even respectful. I'm happy about that; there is really nothing surprising about it. Religion is more respected now, and government ministers do their work regularly and properly. It wasn't like that before. God dammit! The cries, the shouting, the trickery all chased justice out of the courtroom. The bailiffs kept having to shout: 'Quiet!' . . . Women can no longer be shooed away; they can see everything!

Despite the reforms in justice, I am still worried. Will not the old lawyers come back as prosecutors? . . . Excuse-me, gentlemen, for speaking so directly; but I fear seriously this return. . . .

In a trial that I was in before [the Revolution], I had the biggest loudmouth in the world as a lawyer. Once he got going, it never stopped. He complicated things for the judges, until they were half-asleep. . . . for goodness sakes! Despite the eloquent verbiage of M. Chatterbox [her lawyer], I lost my suit, and I was obliged to pay five or six hundred *livres* to a judge who . . . wasn't worth two sawbucks. Damn it all, damn an injustice so unjust and all those clever schemers who stocked away their privileges!. . . . Now it will be a pleasure to be in court, instead. . . . The Nation's new judges will be disgusted by 'spices' . . . Now we toss away everything that isn't good for healthy politics, based on sound reason; everything is like new in France; we have new judges, new defense lawyers, and soon we'll have a new legal code and a new criminal code...."

[Source: *La Mère Duchêne* no. 4 (1790) 1–5.]

***

The National Assembly set out to create those new legal codes in 1790–91, as it drafted the new Constitution. It quickly found issues concerning law and order to be highly controversial, beginning with the death penalty. Prior to 1789, torture of those accused of crimes had been a common technique in trials; tactics for eliciting confessions included being broken on the wheel (tied to a stone wheel and spun, while being pounded with a hammer), being dunked in water, being burned at the stake, and being drawn and quartered (being pulled apart, as each limb was tied to a horse sent off in different directions). These tortures are visible in this engraved woodcut, which shows the fate of Robert Damiens, who was accused in 1759 of attempting to murder the king.

Many revolutionaries wanted to replace these techniques of torture with a judicial system based on equal rights for all accused on the use of reason to prove guilt, by demonstration of evidence. As discussed previously, the new system also included jury trials for criminal cases. Those influenced by Enlightenment ideas of liberty and reason further believed that the penal system should try to reform criminals and return them to society, rather than punish them merely as acts of vengeance. To this end, many revolutionaries believed it would be an important step forward for humanity to abolish the death penalty. The patriot newspaper, the *Revolutions of Paris,* called for the end of the death penalty. The following article argues that a society in which some citizens sentenced others to die would never be fair or unified and thus would never be truly patriotic or free.

## DOCUMENT 6: DEBATE OVER THE NECESSITY AND UTILITY OF THE DEATH PENALTY

"On what basis was founded the power of a king [under the Old Regime] to inflict the death penalty on his subjects? I suppose it was based on the idea that to be in a society, one had to consent to lose one's life for the good of that society.... But it is a philosophical trick

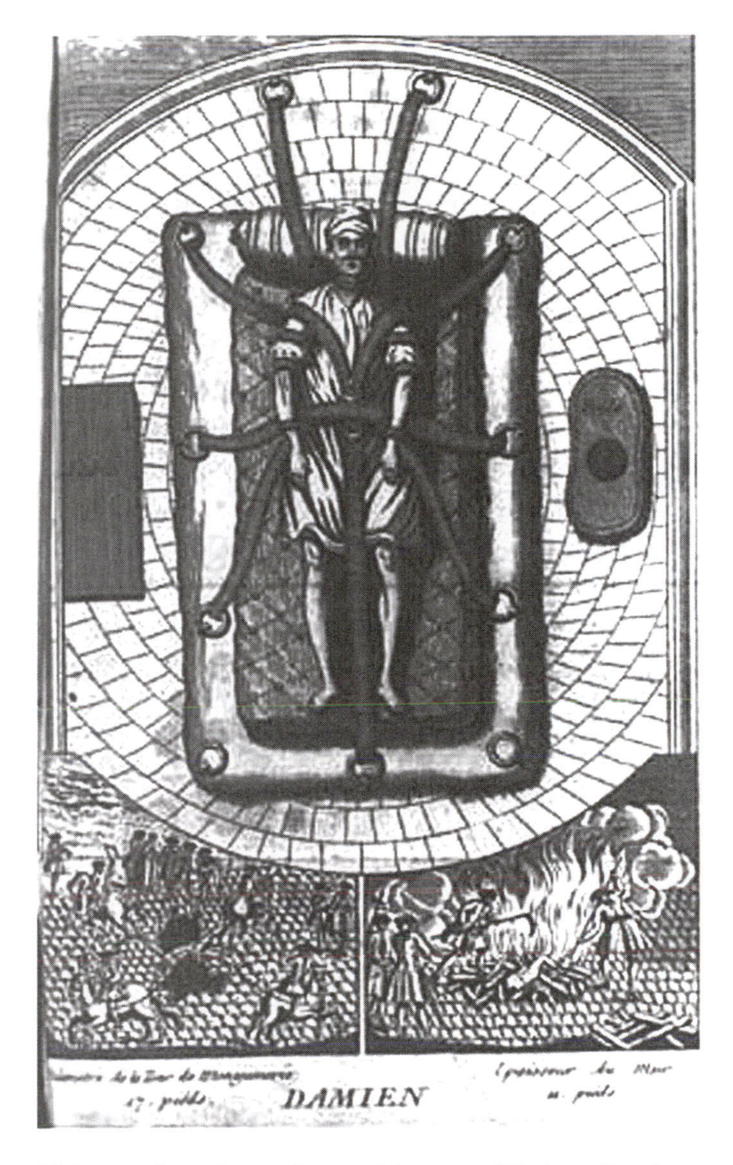


This woodcut shows the punishment of Robert Damiens, who had been convicted of attempting to assassinate King Louis XV in 1759. In the large central frame, Damiens is about to be broken on the wheel, meaning he would be spun around while the executioner hammers at his limbs. In the lower left, he is shown being drawn and quartered, meaning his limbs were tied to four different horses, then pulled apart. Finally, in the lower right, his remains are burned, a common treatment for the body of a heretic under the Old Regime. Courtesy of the Library of Congress, Department of Prints and Photographs.

to compare [the sacrifice made by] a criminal condemned to death to a soldier who marches to combat....

To send citizens to combat is based on the collective responsibility of all citizens to defend the homeland when it is attacked; that is part of the idea of the *Social Contract* of Jean-Jacques Rousseau.[1] ... But for a citizen to die must be against the will of any [government.] Especially for a citizen to be put to death by his own government, which ought to protect him against all threats... Moreover, death sentences... are executed neither by necessity nor by utility."

[Source: *Révolutions de Paris* XXIV (26 December 1789) 8; reprinted in Legg, 186–87.]

***

Others argued for the death penalty as necessary for a fair system of justice. Supporters of the death penalty believed that the Revolution would reform the courts to ensure justice would be based on reason and equality, so that the death penalty would be administered fairly and humanely. As a sign of this reform, they introduced a new, scientific, and humane form of capital punishment, the guillotine. This reform led to a cultural conflict between those who favored a society based on the greatest possible use of reason to defend individual liberty (opponents of capital punishment) and those who favored the use of patriotism to promote the greatest equality possible (proponents of capital punishment). In the National Assembly, supporters of a reformed death penalty, following a jury trial and enacted by the more humane method of the guillotine, won the debate in 1791 over those who argued it would create division within society. This issue of whether a democratic society can by right kill one of its own members as punishment remained a deeply divisive, cultural conflict across the Revolution. (It remained so in France until, in 1981, a newly elected government ended the death penalty to show that, at last, France had become a truly modern country of liberty and reason.)

By 1793, after the founding of the Republic and the outbreak of both foreign and civil wars, the judicial system was again reorganized. The Republic, seeking an even more democratic means of meting out justice, put both trials and punishments in the hands of juries made up of patriotic citizens who possessed certificates of civic spirit. These were known as revolutionary tribunals, and they heard cases of common crime. They also heard crimes of treason. In the fall of 1793, the meaning of treason was expanded to include any act that put the Revolution in jeopardy including armed resistance to the republican government, as in the west and south, or implicit criticism of the government (as discussed in chapter 4). Patriots considered this aggressive pursuit of treason absolutely essential to the survival of the Revolution and everything it stood for, including individual liberty.

Robespierre and Antoine Saint-Just, two provincial lawyers who sat on the legislature's executive committee, known as the Committee of Public Safety, defended the revolutionary tribunals, and especially sentences of death for treason, as the only moral choice the country could make given the continued attacks on France; Robespierre called it "the very principle of democracy applied to the country's most urgent need." Robespierre and others among the left wing of the Jacobins believed that if the only republic in the world were to survive and preserve liberty, equality, and democracy (rather than return to the Old Regime), it would have to ensure that all patriots were unified against their common foe. France's opponents, Robespierre suggested, were tyrants, who had shown, by invading, that they were willing to use deadly force. Against an invasion, how could France defend itself with only philosophical arguments of liberty? "Tyranny kills," he warned, "while liberty argues."[2]

Others considered the revolutionary tribunals to be a dangerous form of intimidation and a renunciation of the revolutionary ideals of liberty and equality. Critics argued that this system of justice did not respect rights of the accused to defend themselves and that revolutionary tribunals amounted to little more than political persecutions. This argument became much more convincing—but also harder to make—in the spring of 1794 when a new law prevented suspects from defending themselves before the tribunal. These critics included even many Jacobins, who agreed that the Revolution had eliminated aristocrats but worried that through continued violence, it now risked falling under a small group of Robespierre's followers, known as "Incorruptibles"—the opposite of equality and democracy.

To get a sense of the drama of attending a trial of a suspect by the revolutionary tribunal, we turn to a fictional source: Emmuska Orzcy's novel, *I Will Repay.* Orzcy, born an Austrian baroness in 1865, grew up obsessed with the French Revolution and with the end of the nobility in France and across Europe. She wrote very popular novels that romanticized the nobility as having heroic values that would be lost in a democracy. In this scene from *I Will Repay,* based on historical documents, she paints a vivid picture of the revolutionary tribunal of Paris.

## DOCUMENT 7: A SUSPECT FACES THE REVOLUTIONARY TRIBUNAL

"It is all indelibly placed on record in the *Bulletin de Tribunal Révolutionnaire,* under date 25 Fructidor, year II of the Revolution. Anyone who cares may read [it] in the National Archives . . . of Paris. . . . The day had been an unusually busy one. Five and thirty prisoners . . . had been tried in the last eight hours. And Citizen-Deputy Foucquier-Tinville, the Public Prosecutor . . . seemed indefatigable.

Each of these five and thirty prisoners had been arraigned for treason against the Republic, for conspiracy with her enemies, and all [required] irrefutable proof of their guilt to be brought before the [court]. . . . Sometimes a few letters, written to friends abroad, and seized at the frontier; a word of condemnation of the measures of the extremists; an expression of horror at the massacres on the Place de la Révolution, where the guillotine creaked incessantly—these were irrefutable proofs; or else perhaps a couple of pistols, or an old family sword seized in the house of a peaceful citizen, would be brought against a prisoner, as an irrefutable proof of his warlike dispositions against the Republic.

The day's work was not yet done. The political [trials] had been disposed of, and there had been such an accumulation of them recently that it was difficult to keep pace with the arrests. And in the meanwhile, the criminal record of the great city had not diminished. [Just] because men butchered one another in the name of Equality, there were none the fewer . . . thieves and petty pilferers . . . ordinary cutthroats and public wantons. And these too had to be dealt with by law . . . [by] an elaborate administration of justice. There were citizen judges and citizen advocates and the crowd, who came in to listen to the trials [and] acted as honorary jury.

The afternoon of this hot August day, one of the last of glorious Fructidor, had begun to wane and the shades of evening to slowly creep into the long, bare room. . . . The Citizen-President sat at the extreme end of the room, on a rough wooden bench, with a desk in front of him littered with papers. Just above him, on the bare, whitewashed wall, the words: *La République: une et indivisible* and below them the device *Liberté, Egalité, Fraternité!* To the right and left of the Citizen-President, four clerks were busy making entries in a ponderous ledger . . . no one is speaking, and the grating of the clerks' quill pens against the paper is the only sound which disturbs the silence of the hall. In front of the President, on a bench lower than his, sits Citizen Foucquier-Tinville, rested and refreshed, ready to take up his occupation for as many hours as his country demands it of him.

In the center of the room a platform surrounded by an iron railing is ready for the accused. Just in front of it, from the tall, raftered ceiling above, there hangs a small brass lamp, with a green [shade]. On each side of the long, whitewashed walls there are three rows of benches—beautiful, old, carved oak pews—snatched from Nôtre Dame and from the churches of St. Eustache and St. Germain l'Auxerrois. Instead of the pious worshipers of medieval times, they now accommodate the onlookers of the grim spectacle of unfortunates....

The front row of these benches is reserved for those citizen-deputies who desire to be present at the debates of the *Tribunal Révolutionnaire*. It is their privilège, almost their duty, as representatives of the people, to see that the sittings are properly conducted. The Citizen-President impatiently rings his hand-bell again. "Bring forth the accused!" he commands in stentorian tones....

One by one, the accused had been brought forth, escorted by two men of the National Guard in ragged, stained uniforms of red, white, and blue; they were then conducted to the small, raised platform in the center of the hall and made to listen to the charge brought against them by Citizen Foucquier-Tinville, the Public Prosecutor.

They were petty charges mostly: pilfering, fraud, theft, occasionally arson or manslaughter. One man, however, was arraigned for murder with highway robbery and a woman for the most ignoble traffic which evil feminine ingenuity could invent.

These two were condemned to the guillotine, the others sent to the galleys...the forger along with the petty thief, the housebreaker with the absconding clerk. There was no room in the prisons for ordinary offenses against the criminal code; they were overfilled already with [those convicted as] traitors against the Republic."

[Source: Emmuska Orzcy, *I Will Repay* (Philadelphia: Lippincott, 1906).]

***

Some suspects were brought before the revolutionary tribunal for actions prior to 1789—having served as royal officers or having been nobles or members of the clergy. In this document, Simon Guillaume Gabriel Bruté, who would grow up to be the very conservative Bishop of Vincennes in the 1820s, remembers the profound effect of attending the revolution trials as a boy.

## DOCUMENT 8: TRIALS OF PRIESTS

"In 1793, being a boy of fourteen years of age, I was often sent by my family to attend the tribunals...to witness and bring back information in regard to the trials of our priests. On account of the excessive terror which prevailed and the fear of betraying themselves to danger, by manifesting their feelings amid the savage mob which generally attended them, grown-up people dared not go....There were at this time three tribunals...the regular Criminal Court, to which generally the Priests were sent; the Revolutionary Tribunal which took cognizance chiefly of the so-called political conspirators, and...the Military Commission where those taken in arms or about the place of some [military] encounter were judged."

[Source: James Roosevelt Bayley, ed., *Memoirs of the Right Reverend Simon Wm. Gabriel Bruté*, (New York: Saldier, 1861) 95.]

***

Such trials of people who had committed no overt crime against the republic divided the country further. The Terror made it impossible to be a moderate. These trials created a cultural conflict that would divide France from the rest of the world for generations. This association of the Revolution with violence is evident in this haunting engraving entitled "The Executioner."

Under the Terror, any opposition to the government was considered a threat to the rule of law and an attempt to bring back the Old Regime. Or so it seemed until July 27, 1794, (9 Thermidor of the Year II, according to the revolutionary calendar). On that day, so many of the remaining members of the National Assembly (a large number had having already been arrested) feared that revolutionary justice had gotten out of control that they voted to arrest Robespierre and to declare a return to justice as the order of the day.

## FACES IN THE CROWD: DEMONSTRATIONS AND RIOTS

The fall of Robespierre in July 1794 represented a turning point in the Revolution. After that date, the Revolution's leaders no longer sought to push forward for more changes; they sought instead merely to consolidate the changes that had already taken place. For many

This engraving from 1792 is entitled, "The executioner." It depicts a guillotine, adopted by the revolutionaries in 1789 as a more rational and humane form of punishment than those used under the Old Regime. The guillotine, though, came to symbolize the excessive violence of the Terror. The executioner pictured here wears a tri-colored cockade, a symbol of support for the Revolution. The reed feather in his cap resembles a Phrygian cap, supposedly worn by freed slaves in ancient Rome and adopted by French patriots as a symbol of their own liberation during the Revolution. Courtesy of the Library of Congress, Department of Prints and Photographs PC 9201.

patriots, especially sansculottes and the left wing of the Jacobins, this meant the end of the Revolution. Though not necessarily supporters of the revolutionary tribunals, patriots supported the more activist, Jacobin ideal of direct citizen action—demonstrations and, when necessary, riots.

Patriots, from the beginning, had seen the essence the Revolution in its day-long demonstrations known as *journées* (French for "the experience of a day"). In these events, crowds of ordinary people, drawn from all walks of life, gathered, signed petitions, sang and danced, marched, and, in some cases, fought with soldiers or counter-demonstrators. Participants considered such demonstrations as signs that the French people were unified, strong, and willing to take to the streets to defend their ideals from attack. Whenever ordinary people became frustrated with politics as usual, they took to the streets.

*Journées* drew on a tradition of early modern protest in which the people, acting collectively, held great moral authority. When market women, artisanal workers, peasants or even reasonably well-off shopkeepers gathered to manifest their discontent—whether over food prices, rates of taxation, opposition to military service, or other obligations—they believed the authorities (the king, the city government, the local noble lord) had a moral responsibility to respond to their concerns. Such demonstrations had been a regular part of life across Europe under the Old Regime, yet they became less common in Paris during the eighteenth century. Whether due to fewer shortages, a larger and better police force, a diminished sense of community in the fast-growing city, or a growing belief in the power of reasonable debate over crowd action, such protests seemed less effective in the years leading up to 1789. At least that's what the writer Mercier thought in 1784, as we see in the following article.

## DOCUMENT 9: RIOTS BEFORE 1789

"Dangerous rioting has become a moral impossibility in Paris. The ever more watchful police, two regiments of [soldiers] in barracks nearby, the royal bodyguards, the garrisons outside the capital, plus countless individuals whose interest leads them to remain loyal to the government; all these factors make the chance of any serious rising seem altogether remote.

During the past fifty years there have only been two such riots [in 1750, protests over rumors that the royal soldiers were stealing children from Paris and shipping them to the French colonies; and in 1775, over bread shortages, which were blamed on government policies deregulating the grain market] and both were quelled at once.

Paris has had more than a century of peace since the time of the Fronde [an uprising of Parisian artisans and high-ranking nobles in 1648, that nearly overthrew King Louis XIV]. We now have mounted police and troops stationed all around the capital, so there is no place to hold a rally....

There is a law against peasant gatherings, but even if the peasants did assemble, where could they go? And what...could they do? They would have to reckon first with the police, then with regiments, and finally with an army or two. It is even worse for the Parisians. Even if they are more inclined to uprisings, were they to attempt anything, they would find the gates of the [city]...promptly shut;...no food would be allowed to reach them; and empty bellies would soon bring them to their knees....

We are not practiced rioters, we Parisians, and possibly for that very reason an outbreak (if such a thing were ever to occur) would quickly become out of control. Still, if it should happen, and if the authorities were to respond right away with prudence and moderation, and to avoid spilling blood, the people's malaise would dissipate on its own. [If] this course were to be adopted by the magistrates, their firm reason would prevent the spread of any discontent....

[Finally, Mercier concludes, there is the question of public opinion towards protestors in Paris, which is divided between two views: they are seen as either] good fighting men...of energy and courage...who defend their civic pride and freedom against authority...[or] insolents [who threaten] the peace of all citizens...We have not resolved this problem yet,...nor have we settled in our minds the difference between disturbance and revolution."

[Source: Louis-Sébastien Mercier, *New City of Paris* (London: 1880); translation of *Le Nouveau Paris* (Paris: 1798–99).]

***

No one exactly knew what to make of the large demonstration that broke out in Paris on July 12, 1789, and continued for several days. The protest combined a traditional protest against rising bread prices, usually staged by women, with a political protest against the king's dismissal of the popular finance minister, Jacques Necker. As the demonstrations grew among the ordinary people of Paris (who would soon call themselves sansculottes), rumors spread that the royal government in Versailles would soon send soldiers to dissolve the recently seated National Assembly and to suppress by force the demonstrations in Paris. This news only further angered the Parisians, even many who had not supported the initial actions, since it suggested that the king was not listening to his people and that the city was in imminent danger of being invaded.

The crowd demanded that the mayor and city council organize the militia to defend the city against the royal soldiers. Then on the morning of July 14, the crowd took matters into its own hands. A large crowd assembled and charged, first on the cannons and powder stored at the military hospital known as the Invalides and on the military depot known as the Arsenal, and next on the fortress that served as a prison, the Bastille, and finally on Paris City Hall. The crowd overtook all these buildings, freeing the Bastille's few prisoners and killing its commander, then ejecting the Old Regime city government and killing the mayor of Paris. This demonstration-turned-riot showed definitively to the Parisian people, the royal government, and the entire country that patriots were willing to take to the streets and fight for change. Some observers considered July 14 to be the day on which occurred a desperate act by starving people who could not afford bread to eat. Others saw it as the day of political protest against royal despotism, symbolized by the Bastille. Still others viewed it as the day of dangerous crowd violence, symbolized by the murder of two government officials whose heads were paraded around town on pikes. Whatever one's interpretation, the taking of the Bastille represented a new type of cultural conflict, in which ordinary people took direct action.

This event set the tone for the way cultural conflicts would be fought during the Revolution. Two months later, after the National Assembly had issued its August 4 decree abolishing privilege and the Declaration of Rights of Man and Citizen, ordinary people in Paris continued to suffer from shortages, high prices, and frustration with the gradual pace of change in the National Assembly. On October 5, drawing on another tradition of popular protest in which women from the marketplace brought their complaints directly to the king and queen, the market women of Paris began to march to the royal palace at Versailles.

Joined by Parisian National Guard units, the women arrived at Versailles and stormed the royal residence. The women appealed to the king and queen to return to Paris, to unify its people in this time of crisis. Prompted by the commander of the National Guard, the Mar-

Women who worked in the Parisian fish market were well-known social types. They were known for speaking plainly and for their fairness. However, when not treated fairly, they were known to use rough, everyday language to make their point directly. By tradition, these women would occasionally protest by sending representatives, on behalf of the people, to explain to the king and queen what they considered unfair. One such protest, on October 5, 1789, became a turning point during the Revolution, as depicted in this German engraving from the same year. The woman on the right holds a Phrygian cap above her head, and the other two women carry pikes; both of which were often associated with sansculottes. Courtesy of the Library of Congress, Department of Prints and Photographs, 1789.

quis de Lafayette, the king agreed, and the next morning, the royal family returned to Paris, with the National Assembly. This event demonstrated how the ordinary people—and their culture of protest in the streets—could push forward the National Assembly and its culture of reasonable debates.

Thereafter, patriots considered street protests to be their most reliable, and exciting, tactic for pushing the Revolution forward. Liberals, by contrast, feared street protests as a threat to their goal of gradual change towards greater individual liberty, including private property rights, and reasoned debate (among property owners). This cultural conflict, between those who called for popular demonstrations to push the Revolution along and those who opposed them as a sign the Revolution was veering off course, became one of, if not *the,* central issue of the Revolution. Should ordinary people take an interest in politics and be able, even morally obligated, to participate through direct action in the streets? Or should they listen passively and learn from their wealthier, better-educated, fellow citizens until they were ready to participate in reasonable debate?

For the leading patriotic journalist of the day, Jean-Paul Marat, the choice was clear, as evident in this article from his newspaper, *Friend of the People,* from July 1790. Marat argued that for the Revolution to continue against powerful enemies, ordinary people had to get involved through protests and, if necessary, by fighting in the streets:

## DOCUMENT 10: MARAT CALLS FOR POPULAR DEMONSTRATIONS

"Citizens, the enemies are at our gates, and the government is ready to open the barriers to them, on the pretext that everyone should have the liberty to travel through the territory. Perhaps at this very moment, they are marching on us, and the King, he is preparing to welcome them or even go join them in Austria! Soon, everyone who is unhappy [about the Revolution] will be at his sides.... already, one of our government ministers has been denounced as a conspirator and has fled from France, and the others will certainly soon follow his example.

To keep from worrying [the people] about these dangers, [the government] is trying to distract you with festivals and to get you drunk [Marat here disparages the Festival of Federation, scheduled for 14 July 1790, to celebrate the first anniversary of the taking of the Bastille].

...And to defend you, the Parisian militia is only a bunch of vain and blind men who have no love for the homeland...

Citizens of all ages and rank, the National Assembly cannot save you from perishing. It's up to you from here on; if you do not take up arms, if you do not recover your heroic valor from 14 July and 5 of October [demonstrations in 1789] which twice saved France [by defending the Revolution], if you not take over for yourselves...the responsibility [of defense] by taking up arms,...then the cannons will be taken from each district and [the king will issue] dangerous decrees against the people. Run, run, while there is still time, for soon there will be legions of enemies descending on you. Soon, the privileged orders and despotism will be back, stronger than ever.

Five or six hundred heads knocked off will assure your liberty and happiness;...if not, it will cost a million of your fellow citizens [whose] blood will flow...and your enemies will triumph in an instant. They will slit your throats without pity; they will violate your wives, their bloody hands will seek the hearts of your children, and they will kill forever your love of liberty."

[Source: *L'Ami du peuple* (July 1790); translated from Legg, 250–51.]

***

Though many leaders of the constitutional monarchy were shocked by Marat's call for violence, his appeals gained popularity as the Revolution advanced and the situation became more tense in France. In 1791, the king openly declared his opposition to the Revolution by attempting to flee the country, and the emigrant nobles across the border in Germany were preparing to invade. Leaders of Parisian sections sought to act on Marat's call for ordinary people to take forceful and immediate action. Seeking to force action by the Assembly and the king, sansculottes held a demonstration at the Tuileries Palace, where the royal family had been installed in Paris. The official newspaper, *Mercure de France,* described the action taken by ordinary people seeking to put pressure on their leaders to defend the country from what they feared to be imminent attack.

## DOCUMENT 11: DEMONSTRATION AT THE TUILERIES PALACE

"That day, an immense crowd filled the gardens of the Tuileries between four and five o'clock in the afternoon; this crowd was made up mostly of women from the ordinary people, of prostitutes from the nearby streets, and men in disguise...The National Guard diligently took up its positions and closed the gates to the palace. The first platoons...were not enough to hold off the crowd and were ordered to raise their bayonets...The cannons were brought in and their fuses were lit...to threaten the demonstrators. Three hundred privates were sent to defend the king and queen in the palace, in case of danger. The mayor and city councilors told the crowd to disperse, but the crowd mocked them and demanded to see the king. The mayor made the mistake of opening the gates to receive a deputation of women...without realizing what the consequences would be....[The crowd rushed in to the courtyard and the soldiers advance on them]....

The demonstration did not appear sufficiently peaceful...and the National Guard was ready for anything to happen....The rumor was that the king and queen were trying to escape through the underground tunnels of the palace dungeon. Based on this [rumor], large groups of people set off for the dungeon until the soldiers dispersed them and arrested 60 of them.

Finally, all the agitation wore out some of the people who became disillusioned with the idea of a protest and began to say instead that the people should not openly violate the law [by attacking the palace]."

[Source: *Mercure de France* (12 March 1791) 147; reprinted in Legg, 332–33.]

***

## RIOTS DURING THE REVOLUTION

Popular demonstrations at the royal palace occurred several times over the next year. Then on August 10, 1792, the crowd overran the soldiers guarding the king's residence. Acting in the name of the nation, the crowd put the royal family under arrest. In this way, the people—or at least a crowd claiming to represent the people—forced the Assembly to depose the king from power. Patriots celebrated this event as the second French Revolution, the day when the people overthrew the monarchy.

This engraving shows the scene in front of the Tuileries, as a crowd of sansculottes fights with the Swiss Guard, the royal bodyguards. To some, such an image shows the intensity and heroism of the ordinary citizens, willing to brave such dangers for their cause. To others, the scene suggests the disorder and mob violence that necessarily resulted from continual calls for activism by Marat and the Jacobins.

Journée du 10 Aout 1792.

This engraving, part of a series depicting great moments during the Revolution, gives a romanticized view of the demonstration of August 10, 1792, which overthrew the monarchy. Courtesy of Department of Special Collections, Lied Library, University of Nevada, Las Vegas.

Several weeks later, after more pressure from the sansculottes, the Assembly voted to revise the constitution to create a republic instead of a constitutional monarchy. To found this new republic, new elections were held for a constitutional convention. But before the new body could meet, the Prussian army began the long-feared invasion of France. Terrified without a government in place, and having lost many experienced military officers due to the emigration of many nobles, many in Paris expected to be overrun quickly by the superior Prussian forces. Already suffering from continuing food shortages, Parisians feared that the invaders would besiege their city and starve its people. Patriot leaders, such as the journalist Marat, called upon the people to take direct action to preserve their endangered liberty (see his article earlier in this chapter).

Patriots were worried enough about the Prussians, but Marat warned they had even more to fear from those conspiring with the invaders to bring back the king and the Old Regime—such as members of the clergy who had refused to swear an oath of loyalty to France. In this tense atmosphere, the need to act urgently to save the country led to an outbreak of violence in Paris. Groups of sansculottes broke into the prisons where former clergy who had not sworn oaths of loyalty were being held. The ensuing mayhem became known as the September Massacres. The writer Réstif de la Bretonne, an early supporter of the Revolution who became increasingly worried about the course of events, described what he saw in Paris during the first few days of September 1792:

## DOCUMENT 12: THE SEPTEMBER MASSACRES

"On Sunday [September 3, 1792] at six or seven o'clock I went out, unaware as usual of what was happening. I set off for... the beloved island of Saint-Louis. In this tranquil refuge,... I heard nothing except for a domestic who was saying to another through the window: "... that sounds like the alarm ringing! Is something else happening?" Catherine answered, "I guess so. Master says to lock up." I moved on, without seeming to listen. I did not walk around the island completely; I left by the Pont Marie.... In the streets, people were dancing, and I found that reassuring. When I reached [a nearby] restaurant... I saw more dancing. But just then a passer-by exclaimed, "Will you stop your dancing! There are big doings going on elsewhere in town!" The dancing stopped. I went on, following the river... until

I reached a [café] in the Théâtre-Français *section* [one of the more politically active districts of Paris, where demonstrations were common during the Revolution].

In that neighborhood, I knew an old man, of Swiss extraction but born in Paris, who always knew what was going on around there . . . He told me, "The crowd is killing people in the prisons. . . . It started yesterday when a man in the stocks said he 'didn't give a damn for the nation' and hoped it was invaded. . . . People got excited and took him to the Hôtel de Ville, where he was condemned to be hanged. He said that the prisons were full of people who thought like him, and that they'd get their chance soon enough, that they had weapons, and that they would [use them against the people] in Paris when the volunteers went off to the front [to fight the invaders]. . . . Then, crowds gathered in front of the prisons, forced open the doors, and began killing everyone who was in there for anything other than debt." I became very upset and frightened as I listened to little old Swiss man [and decided to get out of that part of town].

We set out together. . . . We went as far as the prison gate without difficulty. There we found a group of spectators in a circle; they were watching a crowd inside the gate. Inside the guardroom [in the courtyard of the prison] the prisoners were being brought in to be judged. . . . They were asked their names. Then the record of each one was studied. The nature of the charge against them decided their fate. . . .

A tall man, cool and sober in manner, was brought before them; he was accused of hostility [to the Revolution] and of aristocracy. They asked him whether he was guilty. "No, I have done nothing; . . . in the three months I have been in prison they have found nothing against me." At his words, the judges inclined toward clemency, but a voice cried in the Provençal accent, "An aristocrat! Off with him. . . ."

The man who had shouted shoved him outside through the fatal gateway. Here, he was astonished by the first sword-thrust [from the crowd], but then he dropped his hands and let himself be killed without a gesture of protest . . .

I was shaking! I felt I was getting weak and threw myself to one side. A shrill scream from a prisoner more sensitive to death than the others instilled me with a wholesome rage, which strengthened my legs enough to leave the place. I did not see the rest . . . I went home to bed. . . .

But that was not all. Toward two o'clock I heard a bunch of savages pass beneath my window, none of whom seemed to speak with a

Parisian accent; they all sounded unfamiliar to me. They were singing, roaring, and bowling. In the midst of it all, I heard: "Let's go to the Bernardins! Let's go to Saint-Firmin!" [Saint-Firmin was a residence for priests; Bernardins was a former convent where those condemned to the galleys were held.].... Some shouted, "Long live the nation!" One...shouted furiously: "Long live death!".... They meant to kill both the convicts and the priests.

[At Saint-Firmin, the crowd interrogates an abbot, who is asked] "Why did you retract your oath [of allegiance to the Revolution]?" The man [who had posed the question] turned his back on the priest,...and gave a signal to his companions. The abbot was not stabbed, he was granted a kinder death; they threw him out of the window. His brain splattered, but he did not suffer....

Do not think for a moment that I am taking the side of the fanatic priests just because I have related this moving incident! They are my sworn enemies—in my eyes the most despicable beings. No, no, I do not grieve for them! They have done too much harm to the country; earlier, by their scandalous behavior which removed all restraint from the people; later, by scheming [against the Revolution.]

The priests believe that their [loyalty to the Church and the People] is essential, but they are wrong. What is essential [in religion] is fraternal love. [The Priests] violate it, even when saying mass.

After this, I prepared to make my way home when I was struck by another scene. I saw two women come out: one [was] Mademoiselle de Saint-Brice, lady in waiting to the former crown prince; the other was a young woman of sixteen, Mlle. de Tourzel. They were led into the Saint-Antoine church. I followed them. I looked at them closely, as much as their veils would allow. [One] was weeping, and [the other] was comforting her. They were kept prisoner there. I left after a while; I could not go back...

There was a pause in the slaughter: something was happening inside...I talked myself into thinking that it was finished. Then a woman appeared, white as a sheet, supported by a doorkeeper. Brusquely she was told: "Shout 'Vive la nation' "No! No!" she said. She was forced up onto a pile of corpses. One of the killers seized the doorkeeper and pulled him away. "Please," the pitiable woman cried, "don't hurt him!" She was told again to shout "Vive la nation!" She refused with disdain. With that, [someone from the crowd] grabbed her, tore off her dress, and slit her belly open. She fell and was finished off by the others. Never in my life had I imagined such atrocity....I fainted. When I came to, I saw the head soaked in blood [and] mounted on the point of a pike.... That unlucky woman was Mademoiselle de Lamballe [a young aristocratic woman and friend of Queen Marie Antoinette].

It is too painful to remember those atrocious deeds, carried out in cold blood, without the knowledge of the mayor or the minister of justice.... [Those who carried them out] are in hiding [and] dare not show themselves. If they believe that what they did was right, then they should come forward and state their reasons! We will lament...perhaps enlighten them [on the need for proper trials for a republic to be governed by the rule of law.]

What were the real motives for this butchery? Many think it was carried out to show support for the volunteers, so that when they set out for the frontiers, they would not worry that their wives and children would be at the mercy of criminals if the courts were to acquit and release them. But I think that the only purpose was to wipe out the non-juring priests. Some even wanted to eliminate all priests. They worried about religious fanaticism [that might diminish support for the Revolution.]"

[Source: Nicolas-Edme Réstif de la Bretonne, *Les Nuits de Paris* (1793) (Paris: Hachette, 1960) 247–54.]

***

The English diplomat Earl Gower, like many progressive-minded thinkers, had supported the early reforms of the Revolution. But in 1792, he feared that the replacement of a constitutional monarchy with a republic would lead to chaos. As he witnessed the September Massacres, he now thought his fears were being realized:

## DOCUMENT 13: ANOTHER WITNESS TO THE SEPTEMBER MASSACRES

"[Paris, September 3, 1792]. A messenger arrived yesterday with the news that the Prussians [had past] Verdun [a town near the border between France and Prussia]. Upon hearing this news, the National Assembly decreed...a universal alarm...to prepare for defense. As a consequence of the sounding of the tocsin in Paris, and by the firing of the alarm cannons, the people were in a panic and assembled in large crowds...at about seven o'clock, they surrounded the Church of the Carmelites, where about 160 non-juring priests [who had refused to swear the oath of allegiance] had been arrested since 10 August. These unfortunates fell victim to the fury of the enraged populace and were massacred.... The mob next went to the Abbey Church and, after demanding from the jailors a list of prisoners who had been confined only for debts, pulled to pieces most of the others. The same cruelties were committed during the night and have continued this morning in other prisons.... Their vengeance is principally directed against the refractory priests [again, those who refused to swear allegiance].... The Assembly sent some of its most popular and most eloquent members to try to bring the people to reason and a sense of duty. These gentlemen were not themselves attacked, but they were none the more listened to."

[Source: Oscar Browning, ed. *Dispatches of Earl Gower* (Cambridge: Cambridge University Press, 1885).]

***

Few popular demonstrations were as violent, or as pointless, as the September Massacres. Most were well-organized actions on a specific political or economic issue—most commonly, over the high price of food. In the fall of 1792, sansculottes hoped that the new, republican government would be less concerned with protecting individual property (of farmers, factory-owners, or shopkeepers) and be more concerned with assuring all citizens the right of subsistence. They demonstrated for a guarantee to each citizen of at least a minimal income and a maximum on prices, to assure that everyone could afford food. After yet another harsh winter of 1792–93, widespread food protests broke out in Paris, led by clubs such as the Cordeliers and a new group known as the *Enragés* (or Mad Dogs). These groups asserted that liberty, equality, and fraternity meant that no citizen should starve to death; they argued against the more narrow definition of liberty and equality, or defense of private property and equality under the law, favored by many of the better-educated leaders of the Girondin party that controlled the legislature. A Parisian citizen, Edmond Biré, describes this conflict of cultures during the food riots of February 1793:

## DOCUMENT 14: FOOD RIOTS OF FEBRUARY 1793

"The riots we have long expected broke out on Monday. The general destitution is so great that the only surprise is that they did not break out before. The scarcity of food continues to increase, and the supply of bread may end at any moment. Every evening, this question is discussed in the *sections* and there is a general uproar. Every night, crowds gather at the doors of the bakers' shops... in the snow and rain.... to wait until nine on the morning for the small amount of bread that will be for sale, and many are turned away every day hungry... No wonder they listen to those who tell them that all this is due to [grain hoarders in the countryside, who monopolize the grain to drive up the price].

A week ago Monday... a deputation from most of the *sections* of Paris petitioned [the National Assembly] to supply food by ruling that 'no farmer or merchant should be allowed to charge more than 1 *livre* per 10 pounds of wheat... under pain of death.' 'The people must have bread or they will die,' said the spokesman who presented this petition at the Assembly. 'Where there is no bread, there is neither law, nor liberty, nor a republic.'...

Last Friday, the washerwoman went to the [city government] to complain about the high price of soap. Chaumette, the public prosecutor [at the revolutionary tribunal, where he was well-known for demanding the death penalty], supported their cause by stating, 'We have destroyed the nobles and the [king]; there remains an aristocracy to overthrow—that of the rich... who monopolize the food.... death to the monopolizers!'... Such incitement was not without effect.

On Sunday of this week, the washerwomen marched to the riverfront, where several boats were arriving with soap. They compelled the [soap] to be given to them... almost for nothing.... After that, a group from the Revolutionary Citizenesses [a political club of female patriots allied with the Jacobins] led a... tumultuous crowd of people yelling 'bread and soap'... From that moment, the evidence that a riot was inevitable became more abundant, but the [Committee of Public Safety, twelve representatives to the Assembly responsible for keeping order, most of whom were Jacobins] did not trouble themselves to stop it.

The next morning, Marat [the patriot journalist] published an article in which he incited the mob to riot against monopolizers.... By eight o'clock in the morning, a few men began... they say to the grocers '... let us have... sugar or coffee or soap.... at the prices we set, or else look out for the rope [that is, threatened to be hung].' A few moments later, all the shops are besieged and invaded [by] women wearing pistols in their belts and men dressed as women—though, in many cases, they have not bothered to shave off their beards. [By tra-

This hand-colored engraving of a drawing, by the popular eighteenth-century English cartoonist James Gilray, gives a comical, yet critical, view of the French Revolution, mocking the idea that the French have become more free than the British. It depicts a sansculotte on the left, praising the National Assembly for liberating him from slavery by abolishing taxes while gnawing on a root. On the right, a well-fed Briton dines on a thick roast beef while complaining that the government, by collecting taxes, is starving him. Courtesy of the Library of Congress, Department of Prints and Photographs, PC1-8145.

dition, women participated in protests over the high price of food which, while not legal, were generally tolerated by the police and supported by many people, because it was presumed the women were protesting on behalf of their starving children. By dressing as women, the sansculottes men were not seeking to disguise themselves (note that they do not shave) but to gain the same moral support for their cause, to be considered as acting on behalf of children and the poor.]

. . . By ten o'clock, all the shops in the street were completely sacked, in this neighborhood and in other quarters of the city. In Saint-Jacques street, a grocer armed himself with a knife and attempted to defend his store; he would have [been killed] had his wife and children not been there to plead [with the crowd] for mercy. He got off with his life, but lost his goods. . . .

At five o'clock [in the afternoon] the role of a drum is at last heard, and soldiers begin to patrol the streets. They were everywhere, but the pillage continues. In a few places, the officers attempt to do their duty and disperse the crowds, but they are abandoned by their soldiers and . . . resisted by the crowds. Several of the officers were wounded. . . . Were not the [soldiers] also husbands and fathers of the women . . . who were sacking the shops?"

[Source: Edmond Biré, *Diary of a Citizen of Paris During the Terror,* 2nd ed., trans. John de Villiers (London: Chatto and Windus, 1896), 1:337–43.]

***

Not all were as sympathetic as Biré. In this engraving, the popular English cartoonist James Gilray mocks the idea that the Revolution brought liberty to the French people. On the left, the engraving depicts a French sansculotte wearing a liberty cap but no shoes, gnawing on roots while praising the National Assembly for liberating him from slavery. On the right, a robust, well-clothed Englishman, shown under the symbol of the monarchy, complains about royal taxation while eating heartily a large piece of beef. Gilray clearly intended his viewers to ask if the British people were not better off with less liberty and more government. The French, he implied, had overthrown their government but had suffered a great loss of standard of living.

## MOB RULE OR "WHIFF OF GRAPESHOT": WHICH VIOLENCE TO PRESERVE LIBERTY?

One could view the Revolution, as discussed previously, as a conflict between justice and protest (that is, between making a new set of laws and judicial system on the one hand and protesting outside the legal and judicial system on the other). If so, then the central issue would be *which* violence, that of the government or that of the people, was necessary to preserve liberty? Did the Revolution need to preserve order fairly by creating a new and equal legal and judicial system that could arrest and punish anyone who violated the law, or did the people need to force changes by protesting until everyone was provided for equally and securely from outside threats to their liberty?

This question came to define the final phase of the Revolution, following the fall of Robespierre in the summer of 1794. During this phase, the revolutionary leaders sought to consolidate what they considered the principal changes—individual liberties, equality under the law, and a limited democracy—while preventing the return to either the Old Regime or the Terror. To pursue this politics of balance, the third constitution of the Revolution was put into place in the fall of 1795. Some patriots considered that constitution an end of liberty, because it restored the distinction between active (voting) and passive (non-voting) citizens based on property and because it removed the right to subsistence. Others considered it the restoration of liberty because it eliminated the Revolutionary tribunal and emphasized individual rights, especially the rights of private property.

Under this constitution, the government took measures to protect private property and order by suppressing popular demonstrations. When a group of royalists held a demonstration against the Revolution as the cause of the continuing high bread prices, the government turned to a popular and effective military general, Napoleon Bonaparte, to restore order. Bonaparte proclaimed that he would give the demonstrators a whiff of grapeshot (cannon powder). This use of force made him popular among supporters of the Revolution, and also among those, known as revisionists, who thought France needed to put an end to demonstrations and stabilize the Revolution by tamping down the political temperature.

For four years, the Directory balanced between support for individual liberty and suppressing demonstrations of protest. On two occasions, the Directory also annulled elections when the results threatened to undermine the Republic, thereby giving greater credibility for those who called for a revision to the constitution. Finally, in late 1799, these revisionists made their move to restore order once and for all. They enacted a *coup d'étât* (literally, a blow by the state), which is a change of government through the use of force by those already within the government (rather than by demonstrators in the streets). To gain support for this move, which involved arresting the legislature and revising the constitution to remove most individual liberties and rights to vote, they placed Bonaparte at the head of this new government.

Bonaparte's newly revised constitution, adopted by a plebiscite in December 1799, began with the word *citizens* to suggest he would not restore the monarchy, under which people were subjects. It went on to announce that the new government would be based on the principles on which [the Revolution] was begun, such as the end of privilege and equality under the law, although not the right to subsistence or the right to vote. It then asserted that these questions would no longer be open to debate or conflict: The French Revolution is over. This coup, known as Brumaire (because it began, by the revolutionary calendar, on 18 Brumaire, Year VIII), signaled to some the restoration of order and a government that could at last preserve basic rights (especially private property). Others regretted the end of political participation or patriotism.

The Englishwoman Helena Maria Williams comments on this event as a conflict between two ideals of liberty—freedom to protest versus freedom from intimidation.

## DOCUMENT 15: THE COUP D'ÉTAT OF 18 BRUMAIRE

"On returning [from horse-back riding in a park in Paris], we entered a garden where... we beheld through the trees, deputies of the [Assembly] moving along in flowing robes, like tragic heroes in a play... The events of the preceding day, 18 Brumaire, seemed to threaten the public safety, but from the way the proceedings were reported in Paris, everyone imagined that those at St. Cloud [the suburb where Napoleon had carried out his coup d'étât] would be calm.... The transfer of power had been decreed... before the Parisians knew that any such thing was going on. The garden was open, and the citizens were taking their usual morning walks, without any suspicion of what had passed....

The scene, however, suddenly changed when the orders of Bonaparte were put into [action]. The gardens filled with troops who ordered everyone to remain where they were.... Such appearances of force were seen throughout the day in Paris.... after more than an hour, many placards were posted on the walls informing the city and the good citizens of Paris that they were under the protection of Bonaparte.

[Williams goes to Saint Cloud to see the new legislature, appointed by Bonaparte, sworn in.] I found the ceremony... very patriotic, and extremely dull, notwithstanding the occasional utterances of protest against... tyranny and statements of fidelity to the constitution of the year three [which Bonaparte had annulled.]... Then Bonaparte himself... traveled, without arms, to the Orangery [a building in Paris, near where the legislature had met before the coup].... He was no doubt prepared to meet with opposition, but scarcely expected the reception he met, when a hundred voices issued from men who jumped from their seats on his entrance without allowing him to speak and began to thunder out threats and protests, 'Down with the dictator'...'no usurpers of the law'...'kill him'...In vain he tried to tell them that such a disorderly debate would not advance the business they had to do and he turned and left the hall....

A strong conflict must have arisen in his heart, between his obedience as a soldier [to the government of the republic, that he had just overthrown] and his regard as a citizen for the safety of the state [which he feared the old legislature had endangered by being too tolerant of protests].... Can we be surprised that he felt discomfort at being compelled to commit an act abhorrent to every idea of freedom [that of overthrowing an elected government] but one he considered to be strongly necessitated for its preservation [that of an orderly government]....

Can we be surprised at the humiliation that every friend of liberty must feel at this event [Williams includes herself here, since she had supported the Revolution at the outset and hoped it would create greater individual liberty and a greater degree of participation for all citizens. She then poses a question that has become a difficult moral question in European history for supporters of progress towards greater liberty and democracy: Must one always defend those are the most forceful advocates of liberty and democracy when they lead revolutions, since revolutions involve violence and, sometimes, repression of fellow citizens?]...It is an event that we may regret but...for the moment, it is a mistake to believe that the...existence of liberty in Europe is fixed on the fate of the French Republic. [That is, she believes that after the Terror, even those who supported the goals of the Revolution had to wonder if the Revolution was the best way to achieve those goals.] Raised to believe in liberty and abhorrent of tyranny...I must [depart] from the principle...that every friend of freedom...must defend [the Revolution]...in the present circumstances...."

[Source: Williams, II, 2–22.]

***

This engraving illustrates the conflict inherent in Napoleon's coup, showing Napoleon ushering symbols of the Revolution off the stage. On the one hand, it is the exit of liberty. On the other, it suggests that

This hand-colored English engraving depicts Napoleon's coup of 18 Brumaire. The text reads, "The exit of French liberty, of Napoleon closing the French farce." The delegates fleeing the Legislative Body chamber as the soldiers advance are wearing the tunic and cap designed to make the legislators of the Directory resemble Roman senators—the idea is mocked in the engraving because it shows how terrified the legislators are. Courtesy of the Library of Congress, Department of Prints and Photographs, PC1-526.

the liberty brought by the Revolution was not real, but only a farce (a comic play). The men in flowing robes and blue hats are the representatives of the Assembly, in the uniform created by the Directory to resemble the dress of senators in ancient Rome.

Bonaparte himself symbolized the conflict many ordinary people faced as participants in the Revolution. He himself had supported the Revolution's leaders, including the radical Jacobin party, in part because he believed that men of talent, such as himself, would benefit from a society that eliminated noble privileges (such as the privilege of serving as high-ranking military officers!). Thus, in this engraving, he regards with love the Phrygian cap, a red bonnet that had been worn in ancient Rome by freed slaves and a symbol in the Revolution of liberation from the Old Regime. He also holds a pike, the symbolic

The text reads, "We always return to our first loves." In his imperial uniform, standing on a throne, Napoleon nevertheless gazes lovingly at a Phrygian cap which he holds aloft on a pike—symbols of the sansculottes. The engraving, produced in 1819 after Napoleon had fallen from power, mocks Bonaparte by showing him as both the emperor who ended the Republic, and as still in thrall to the Jacobins he had supported earlier. Courtesy of the Library of Congress, Department of Prints and Photographs, PP1819.1.

weapon of sansculottes, since they were too poor to afford rifles. Yet he also sits on a throne and wears royal robes, suggesting his love for order and authority. The legend states "One always returns to one's first loves," leaving open the question of which he loves more, liberty or order.

## NOTES

1. Jean-Jacques Rousseau, *The Social Contract* (France, 1759). *The Social Contract* is one of the most famous in the history of philosophy; it was first published in 1759. Before the Revolution, it was not widely read, but from 1789 on, this and other writings by Rousseau were frequently invoked by revolutionaries as sources of ideas about how to achieve a society of true liberty and true virtue, in which citizens were both free from oppression and good towards each other.

2. Maximilien Robespierre, *Report on the Principles of Political Morality* (Philadelphia: 1794); reprinted in Keith Michael Baker, ed., *The Old Regime and the French Revolution* (Chicago: University of Chicago Press, 1987) 368–83.

*Chapter 6*

# Money and Economy: Work and Consumption during the Revolution

The greatest struggle that most people faced during the French Revolution was the one for food. Ordinary people in the eighteenth century lived with constant hunger and malnutrition; people commonly fell ill or even died due to starvation. This problem was particularly acute in the cities, where a constant supply of food had to be imported from the countryside. In an age without refrigeration, when it took several days for a cart to travel a few dozen miles, importing food to the cities was slow, difficult, and dangerous.

Under the Old Regime, ordinary people considered royal and city governments morally responsible for assuring they would have enough to eat at an affordable price. When the price of bread or other necessary food items increased sharply, working people commonly demonstrated against farmers and merchants in the countryside whom they suspected of hoarding grain to drive up the price of bread. The demonstrators believed that an ordinary working person should always be able to afford enough to eat; a fair day's work should earn enough to feed a family. The outrageous food costs must be due to immorality by farmers in the countryside or wholesale grain merchants, whom city workers thought did not work as hard or adhere to the same moral values.

In the late 1780s, a series of harsh winters brought an economic recession. As a result, ordinary people in Paris had even greater difficulty finding jobs and affording bread for their families. This food shortage led to demonstrations, which in turn contributed to the outbreak of the Revolution. Yet the Revolution, in its early years, brought no more bread to the city. The continuing cold weather, the shortage of currency, the ongoing political conflicts, the wars, and the difficulty of transportation all contributed to chronic shortages of food and sharp inflation, which hit hardest on working families.

Parisian workers, especially those active in political clubs and sections, signed petitions and held demonstrations that called on the Revolutionary government to find and punish those who were hoarding grain or speculating on the wholesale market for profit, while patriotic citizens starved! The sections demanded, for instance, price controls, so that ordinary citizens could afford bread and other necessities. They further demanded that the government punish those traitors who violated the price maximum!

One remedy for shortages under the Old Regime had been poor relief provided by the Catholic Church to those it considered the deserving poor. But because of the church's revolutionary reforms, it could no longer exercise this role. Instead, the people themselves, through their elected government, would look after their own well-being, particularly the well-being of those well-intentioned and hard-working citizens unable to support themselves. But how could a government still running a deficit and fighting a war afford to provide for the poor? Some suggested that it put to use workshops, factories, and farms whose owners had shut them down. But weren't those owners merely following the rules by using their private property as they saw fit; if their land or workshop was not profitable, did they not have the right to shut it down rather than lose money? Would not the government be encroaching on liberty to confiscate this property for the greater good?

The following documents reveal a conflict of two cultures. The culture of urban workers presumed a moral economy—that hard-working patriots should not suffer at the hands of their fellow citizens. This conflicted with another culture, the belief in an unregulated market economy in which people use their property to gain the most they can. This second belief also had a moral component—that the poor needed to learn new moral values such as self-reliance, thrift, and respect for those who had more wealth, rather than a belief in the shared virtue of all citizens.

## SHORTAGES AND FAMINE

In Old Regime Europe, food shortages and famines occurred in a regular pattern about every thirty years. A series of bad winters, an outbreak of disease, a war, or some other external factor would cause food production to drop, creating a shortage, which in turn led to more disease, deaths, and a decline in marriage and birth rates. The

English economist Thomas Malthus studied this cycle and concluded that nothing could ever break it.[1] During the course of the eighteenth century, a variety of factors—better transportation and communication, less warfare, improvements in sanitation, and hardier crops (such as potatoes)—diminished the frequency of shortages and famines.

The most evident result of a shortage was a sharp rise in wheat prices. At times of greatest shortage, such as the late 1740s, the mid-1770s, and the late 1780s, wheat prices shot up. Daily bread became unaffordable for ordinary Parisians. In fact, according to the research of the famous economic historian Ernest Labrousse, the month of July 1789 brought the highest wheat prices of the century in France.[2] This led to widespread shortages and famine across the country, especially in Paris, where ordinary people began to protest, and then to riot. These protests continued after July 14, so the new city government (installed immediately after the taking of the Bastille) had to address this problem. No clear solution presented itself.

Many early leaders of the Revolution believed strongly in the free market. They wanted the Revolution to tear down obstacles to free trade in the name of liberty. To them, liberty meant private property, unrestricted by guilds or traditions such as those of the moral economy. Other revolutionary leaders, however, argued that the new government needed to improve the lives of hardworking and law-abiding people of Paris; they argued that liberty could not exist if some citizens were starving while the fields were full of wheat ready to be harvested. This report of July 1789 from the official newspaper, *Mercure de France,* describes the efforts made, and difficulties encountered, to provision Paris.

## DOCUMENT 1: FAMINE IN PARIS IN THE SUMMER OF 1789

"For the last four days, bread has been very rare and before ten o'clock in the morning, most of the bakers' shops are empty for the day. Even in the middle of frozen winters, we have not seen such a shortage. The many convoys of grain from the countryside during the first 15 days of the Revolution [after July 14, the new city government had sent militia units out to assure these convoys would reach the capital] and the near completion of the harvests made us think that subsistence would get easier. In effect, much more grain has been harvested but little wheat has been ground, because the water supply in the rivers has run low, and the mills have not been in action, slowing up the convoys of grain to Paris. The next step is to try to build hand-powered mills in the countryside....

The fears we have had about the collection of the tithe [the obligation to give 10 percent of what was harvested off the land to the church] this year are coming true in many places, where the landowners, using the decrees of the National Assembly [to send all available grain to Paris] to their advantage, have dispensed with paying what they owe to the church, including the amount owed for the maintenance of the village priests. Many of the most committed village priests are in urgent distress...which was not at all the intent of the legislature."

[Source: *Mercure de France* (29 August 1789) 387, 394; reprinted in Legg, 117.]

***

Food shortages remained constant for ordinary people in Paris during the Revolution. They devoted much of their daily life—at work, at home, at the *section* meetings or at demonstrations—to this problem. Many Parisians saw the entire Revolution as a conflict between those who had enough, or even too much to eat (whom they called aristocrats even after the nobility was abolished) and those who worked hard but went hungry (symbolized by the imagery of the sansculottes as near-skeletons without pants or shoes, gnawing on roots).

This cultural conflict between luxury and poverty took a new turn after the founding of the Republic in 1792. The Republic's desire to reward patriotic citizens and punish those unwilling to sacrifice is evident in this sardonic, though serious, description from the diary of Edmund Biré of several proposals made in February 1793 during one of the worst months of shortage and famine of the entire decade:

## DOCUMENT 2: WAR ON CATS AND SPARROWS

"Leaving to others the fighting against enemies from across the border, General Santerre [the commander of the Paris National Guard] has taken upon himself to destroy enemies within France who are the most feared. I expect that you are thinking I mean those incorrigible aristocrats, those crazy moderates who conspire against the Republic [as described in chapter 4, on the revolutionary tribunal]. You have not guessed it. I must tell you that the real enemies...are...the dogs and cats of Paris! Santerre...will have the honor of counteracting their plots against Liberty....

He has just posted an order on the walls of the capital: '...the high price of food may serve the aims of the enemies. Our armies are on the frontiers, and many of the farmers believe Paris is about to be overrun. The decline in value of the *assignat* [revolutionary paper money] and the...high prices are brought about by the tactics of the aristocracy...I have two remedies to propose: first, all well-to-do citizens.... should substitute rice and potatoes for bread at least two days a week; this would cut down on the consumption...by about fifteen hundred sacks of flour...The second remedy is that all citizens should at once rid themselves of useless pets. In Paris, there are enough cats and dogs right now to eat the food of fifteen hundred men, which means ten sacks of flour wasted every day.'

Others have followed Santerre in this way...The editor of the [patriot newspaper] *Revolutions de Paris*...remarks that there was never so much noise at the mill for ten sacks of flour...[He proposes] to suppress the bread of the Sacrifice [that is, the bread of communion at Catholic Mass] in order to economize thirty million pounds of bread across the country annually; this would be a meritorious and patriotic action....

But these ideas are poor compared to the patriotic scheme of a citizen [published in the daily newspaper] the *Chronique de Paris:*

'Sparrows are pretty little creatures. They cheer me up in the morning when I hear them through...my chimney...But I place my love of country above all other considerations. Everyone knows that there is nothing more voracious than a sparrow...I therefore move that all the sparrows in Paris be killed....The harm these creatures do the nation by making grain more expensive is too evident...A sparrow eats from twelve to fifteen grains per day...this would make a loss of as many as ten million pounds of corn...enough to feed one hundred thousand men for seventy days.... But I must warn my fellow citizens not to eat [them] since this meat brings on epilepsy. I might therefore given them advice...that would be profitable to the Republic, of giving the sparrows to the cats...in order to kill the cats....'"

[Source: Biré, 334–36.]

***

Despite the famine, one of the interesting changes of the Revolution was the growth in the number of restaurants in Paris. This circumstance arose because many chefs who had previously been employed in the private kitchens of wealthy aristocrats now opened restaurants to support themselves. So even as many people starved, dining out in a restaurant became a more common activity for the middle classes of Paris. This difference created an obvious cultural conflict between those who viewed the spread of restaurant dining as a democratic advance from the Old Regime when the best cooking was in the private kitchens of aristocratic homes and those who viewed it with disdain as a sign that some ate gluttonously while their fellow citizens starved. This conflict is brought out in the following discussion of new restaurants, written by a Parisian in the fall of 1793, at the height of political and social conflict:

## DOCUMENT 3: RESTAURANTS IN REVOLUTIONARY PARIS

"Famine has now reached a terrible stage. There is an almost entire absence of certain commodities, such as sugar and soap, and it is more difficult every day to obtain bread. The crowds now begin to gather at bakers' shops at four in the morning and the people wait six or seven hours to be served. Sometimes, mothers with large families waiting their turn are sent away without a morsel, having wasted their time. [For those who are served,] two ounces for each person in the family per day is the maximum allowance. . . . As famine increases, and bread gets scarcer, fashionable restaurants are full of delicacies such as fine wines and costly liqueurs. The cellars of the former nobles have been auctioned off; what good patriots have not drunk has been snapped up by keepers of restaurants and taverns. Thrown out of employment by the ruin of their former masters, the chefs of the former aristocracy have moved from serving princes and nobles . . . to the public. The gain resulting from the Revolution might in the end prove to be the abolition of the monopoly of [tasty food] . . . by anyone except the [aristocrats]."

[Source: Biré, 332–33.]

***

In the sections of Paris, sansculottes debated what to do about the famine. They wanted the government to take forceful action against hoarders and speculators, who were seeking to profit from the high price of grain and bread. Since the sections not only debated but frequently organized protests which on occasion led to riots, the government kept close tabs, through the police, on these debates in *section* meetings. This document is from a police report filed in February 1794, yet another month of intense shortage for the ordinary people of Paris:

## DOCUMENT 4: PATRIOTIC CRITICISM OF BUTCHERS

"The meeting of the *section* of the Lombards [a neighborhood in Paris] was extremely crowded. One member read a long memorandum in which he developed all sorts of silly arguments against the butchers. And after a lengthy discussion...it was concluded that butchers, by selfishness, earn about 300 percent for the meat they sell in their shops, which amounts to killing off sansculottes....if in fact there were only good patriots [as butchers] then the people would not lack for things to eat....

The butchers are generally objects of public opprobrium. Most of the shops have been without meat for at least two days, and there are no vegetables to be had. Many workers complain that they cannot find anything to eat at mealtimes and they want the city government to do something about the shortages or else there will be more demonstrations. If this continues, they say, we are going to be killing one another for survival...."

[Source: Dauban, 82–83.]

***

The sansculottes believed strongly in the moral economy—that the availability of essential goods like bread was a matter of morality. They considered shortages therefore the result of immoral behavior. They called for the government to defend their right to subsistence by assuring that food prices would be affordable for workers. This differed from the theory of the free market, a theory holding that private property should be considered the basic right of the individual. Believers in this theory, such as the Girondins and some Jacobins, did not consider the availability of goods a matter of morality but merely of supply and money. In this police report from the year 1794, sansculottes discuss the abuse of markets by some citizens at the expense of others.

## DOCUMENT 5: SHORTAGE IN THE MARKETPLACE

"Some poorly intentioned people continue to stop the arrival of foodstuffs in Paris and take by force the deliverers to sell the goods at whatever price they demand. If the deliverers refuse to sell the goods, they are injured, sometimes beaten, and forced to return to the countryside without having made any money from their goods. They resolve never to run that risk again in Paris. This only contributes to the shortage of food.... What is even more pernicious than the stealing of grain is to steal goods from the marketplaces in Paris, such as eggs, butter, vegetables...and other usual goods. Then by violence and invectives, they force the other citizens to buy from them at raised prices...There are women who claim to be good citizens but are not.... They observe strictly the [government-mandated] price maximum when they buy but not when they resell. They take their goods to the homes of poor citizens whom they force to pay double or even triple what it cost them."

[Source: Dauban, 160–61.]

***

One of the greatest problems for workers in obtaining enough to eat was that their wages did not rise with the cost of food. Even though food prices had increased substantially in the final decades of the Old Regime, average wages had not. During the Revolution, as food prices spiked upwards, rising unemployment kept wages down. This chart, based on the research of economic historian Ernest Labrousse shows the consequences of static wages and rising food prices.

## DOCUMENT 6: WORKERS' WAGES AND THE PRICE OF BREAD IN 1789

| Occupation | Average daily wage (in *sous*) | Percentage of average daily wage spent on bread (July 1789) |
|---|---|---|
| Unskilled laborer | 15 | 97 |
| Construction worker | 18 | 80 |
| Mason | 24 | 60 |
| Locksmith | 30 | 48 |
| Goldsmith | 60 | 24 |

[*Sous,* the French equivalent of shillings, were worth one-twentieth of a *livre* (pound).]

[Source: Labrousse.]

***

We get an even better sense of the daily hardship faced by ordinary Parisian consumers by considering the following discussion of food prices described in the following police report from the winter of 1793. (Compare these prices with the daily wages indicated in the previous chart. Remember that by 1793, a much larger number of workers were unemployed and the guilds had been abolished, causing a drastic cut in daily wages.) The policeman who filed this report, named Perrière, also speculates on the causes of these high prices and tries to encourage the government to seek out those whose immorality leads them to increase prices by scaring patriotic consumers:

## DOCUMENT 7: SCARCITY IN THE MARKETPLACE

"Rice costs 24 sous per pound and is not easily found; a mother of a family seeking to buy six pounds of rice at a market was told by the grocer that he didn't even have that quantity to sell. Flour costs 24 sous per *litron* [an older measure, equal to about half a pound] and used to be only 7 or 8 sous. They are even making wheat from dried peas and selling it for 24 sous, which is causing a ridiculous increase in the price of that common vegetable. Raisins and dried prunes, which used to be 9 *sous* now cost 25 . . . [no quantity is given, but presumably a very small amount since such fruits were luxury goods]. . . . I mention these prices only because pretty well off citizens are substituting them for meat [which was strictly rationed in 1793, when available at all, because of the war effort.]

But these [better-off] people do not come to the market; they have their groceries bought for them [presumably on the black market] and they eat at home. [They do not see]. . . the great unhappiness than the lives of the poor who cannot have meat, fish, beans, or butter and yet who give the greatest support to the Revolution.

Is it the scarcity or the bad faith of the merchants that accounts for these high prices? Some [merchants] seek to exaggerate the fears of. . . a famine. . . so that as soon as food appears in the market, already at raised prices, everyone tries to get enough for their own needs. . . The crowds of consumers that form and the large amounts they seek to buy make the grocers arbitrarily increase their prices. . . "

[Shortages were not only in the city, though. Peasants were consumers as well as sellers, and peasants also struggled with shortages in the market of necessary goods. The same police report includes a discussion of what a group of peasants who had traveled to Paris to sell their produce were overheard discussing in a café:]

"The people from the countryside were saying... that there was no wheat to buy in any of the towns along the Rhône river valley, and that their women and children were crying from hunger. That the woodcutters [whom peasants might hire to clear land so more wheat could be planted] were not working at all in that region, since no one could assure them that as they did their work, they would be able to buy bread. It's impossible to get people to undertake a job when the people in the region themselves are so badly lacking...."

[Source: Dauban, 93–94.]

***

While sansculottes suspected that peasants were hoarding food for their own gain, peasant families also faced their own hardships. Peasants had always struggled to pay their debts, and the Revolution had increased peasant debt by requiring them to buy themselves out of their obligations to their lords. Moreover, the harsh winters hurt peasants even more than people in cities, since peasants kept very little of what they grew, so they could sell as much as possible.

To alleviate the problem of high food prices, which hurt people in the cities and towns alike, in 1790 the National Assembly began to issue paper money, known as *assignats*. Originally, assignats were to be backed by the value of land nationalized from the church. However, their value soon became inflated, leading to even higher prices. Throughout the Revolution, the issue of paper money also became a topic of controversy between those who believed that the highest priority should be to help poor citizens afford food (by giving them money and capping prices) and those who believed that the new government could best preserve liberty and private property by stabilizing the economy (by lowering the amount of money in circulation and letting prices float freely).

The intense debate between free money advocates and supporters of a tight currency policy is evident in this letter written by Edmund Biré to a friend abroad:

## DOCUMENT 8: THE HIGH PRICE OF MONEY

"A fresh issue of assignats is necessary; one hundred million in bills of five *livres* have already been decreed, and six hundred million more are expected. A new copper coin is also being decreed.... [Supporters of the paper money] say that the national lands [lands confiscated from the church] will amount to three thousand million [in revenue for the national treasury], but a third is already sold [and the national debt continues to grow]....No taxes have been collected yet, except the stamps on patents, and no land tax will be collected until autumn. The high price of money, which increases daily,...is not only a problem for individuals but also the government; the treasury was obliged to [borrow] ten million *livres* last month of which they have only seven hundred thousand in revenue [with which to repay the loan]....The public funds as a result have fallen considerably."

[Source: Biré, 88–89.]

***

The worsening national debt only heightened the inflation. The press widely discussed the distressing effects on ordinary people. Patriot newspapers called on sansculottes to seek out the cause for economic difficulties among those of bad faith, who were profiting at the expense of their fellow citizens:

## DOCUMENT 9: INFLATION HURTS ORDINARY PARISIANS

"Everyone talks about it the high price of money because everyone suffers from it. It cannot be denied that the shortage of currency is a result of the difficult circumstances, but at the same time, we must note that speculators and their agents abuse these circumstances to rip off the public! Parisians, you want a [revolution] but can you put up with what it takes to make one? You have sworn to obey the laws that protect the property of all citizens, so are you willing as well to dirty your hands with the hands of those who violate the laws?"

[Source: *Babillard* XV (18 June 1791) 3; reprinted in Legg, 39.]

***

The sansculottes' vision of a moral economy, therefore, often led them into conflict with those who sought a solution to the shortage in the free market. Ordinary Parisians regarded the market with suspicion, because they feared that it would allow large property owners, grain hoarders, financial speculators, or others of ill-will to ignore the need for patriotism in a time of crisis and instead to profit at the expense of their fellow citizens. The issues of the price maximum and the assignats were particularly controversial. Merchants wanted to be able to sell their goods for more than the established maximum price and to refuse payments in paper money (which was constantly losing value); sansculottes charged that this attitude was not only unpatriotic and immoral, but treasonous. What sort of person would turn a profit by refusing to accept the money that the freely elected government had decreed? Should not all those who supported the ideas of liberty and equality be willing to sacrifice personal interest for the greater good by selling at established prices? Should not all citizens accept the national currency as a way to support their country in a time of danger?

Sansculottes made many complaints in their sections about such behavior and about those people who engaged in such behavior, as we can read in the following excerpts from police reports in the harsh winter of 1793.

## DOCUMENT 10: SUSPICION OF PEASANTS AND MERCHANTS

"The city is calm since yesterday, free from menace and agitation . . . though still, the complaints and murmurs begin again, always as a result of the shortage of bread and the exorbitant prices for everything . . . Some have remarked that in many stores, the merchants continue to refuse to . . . take large bills of assignats. This reaction is caused here by the refusal of people in the country to exchange their goods for any paper money; all of this generates a great deal of discontent.

While we complain about the rapacity of the peasants, all those who have observed the effects of the French Revolution notice the tremendous amelioration in the condition of people in the countryside. . . . The Revolution seems to have been made for the peasants. While the clergy, the nobility, the property owners all have been ruined and while commerce. . . . has been interrupted by the continual political conflict, the farmer has been emancipated of all his feudal obligations and from his personal service to the lord, discharged of all onerous duties. . . . and released from the vampires of government taxation which sucked him dry . . . the farmer more than anyone else has reason to celebrate his liberty. . . . The lords' *châteaux* have been set to flames . . . and nearly all large land holdings broken up. . . . While the cities have been filled with horrible executions [a reference to the Terror], the countryside has not seen them.

During this long period of depreciation of paper money, the farmer pays off with one week's work his obligations for the entire year. This economic disorder allows [the peasants] to become owners of lands that they have only been able to rent previously... Selfish enough to recognize their advantage under the present circumstances, the peasant farmers sell their goods only for hard money [rather than *assignats*] while their former creditors [those who were formerly lords and urban merchants] are forced to sell their furniture to buy grain grown on their own lands in order to feed their families.... Farmer peasants now form a well-off class... and their wives, who used to go around barefoot, now proudly show off their new shoes with lace and large golden buckles, which display their vanity more than their faith or their patriotism."

[Source: Dauban, 563–64.]

***

The issue of poverty cut both ways in the cultural conflicts of the French Revolution. As noted previously, sansculottes expected the National Assembly and city government to intervene on behalf of poor but patriotic citizens. At the same time, they only believed that those who worked hard and sacrificed for the greater good deserved the benefits of such government action. While ordinary workers blamed those who supplied food and other goods for causing the shortages and misery, they also worried that not everyone in the city deserved their fair share of the limited food supply, because not everyone was willing to work. The following article, from the patriotic newspaper *Mother Duchêne*—written in the voice of an ordinary woman whose language included the vulgarity common in the streets—describes this attitude. It calls both for charity to alleviate poverty and for punishment of those who sought help without contributing to the nation's well-being.

## DOCUMENT 11: POVERTY AND CHARITY

"For the nation to be regenerated, and to reform all abuses what is more important... than for establishments to be created... to raise abandoned children. Must we treat these innocent creatures as the refuse of nature? Seven million times damn! Must they die for faults they have not committed? Have they not already been defamed enough with the stigma [of illegitimacy] attached to their birth giving them a burden of misery and misfortune? No, dammit, no; this must not be. I cannot stomach such mistreatment. It is the former *seigneurs* who must be responsible for their upkeep. I think in the past they were more concerned with the upkeep of their geese and ducks than with hospitals for the poor. But now the Nation can replace their authority with establishments that will take a new form.... We must find the necessary funds to support the most indigent... that is the sacrifice the homeland must make for its fellow citizens.... What torment for me to see so many beggars in the capital. This would not have been tolerated under the Old Regime.

I am impatiently waiting for the definitive work of the [Assembly's] Committee on Poverty. The government must hasten to stop the abuse of the poor.... Today, so many eyes are turned to the government, so nothing is easy. Every department, every neighborhood council must build a barrier against this problem of all these damned vagabonds in our cities and countryside... So many individuals without a home within our Nation... These damn weaklings are a plague on our country; they live off of us without working... They enjoy the fruit of the earth that they do not work with their sweat... those who are so lazy and useless, we should take the skin off their ass... there is no excuse for begging today.

I have recently visited some... public works and charity workshops [government agencies which hire the poor]. I was very unhappy with the workers there.... What do they do for their damn 20 sous [1 *livre]* per day?... Before too long, we will see there bad company who don't know what better to do and we'll have to find a way to make them useful."

[Source: *Mère Duchesne,* no. 13, 113–17.]

## NOTES

1. Thomas Malthus, *Essay on the Principle of Population* (London: 1798).

2. Ernest Labrousse, *La crise de l'économie française à la fin de l'ancien régime et au début de la révolution* (Paris: Presses universitaires de France, 1944).

*Chapter 7*

# Religion and Culture: The Ideas and Beliefs of Ordinary People

Prior to 1789, religion was the most important aspect of life for everyone in France. From the most devout clergy to the most Enlightened Philosophers, and from the poorest peasants to the wealthiest aristocrats, life revolved around religion. The overwhelming majority of French adhered to the Gallican Roman Catholic Church. Minorities of Calvinists, Lutherans, and Jews made up only a few percent of the population. Moreover, since King Louis XIV had revoked the Edict of Nantes in 1685, ending the official policy of religious toleration for the Calvinist minority, no one but a Catholic could hold public office or swear the oath necessary for membership in any guild or professional corporation.

As an economic entity, the Catholic Church was by far the largest single landowner and employer in Old Regime France. Roughly 10 percent of the cultivated land belonged directly to the church, in plots that were awarded to higher-ranking clergy as benefits from which they drew seigneurial dues from the peasants. The church also collected the tithe—10 percent of anything grown—on nearly all the land in the kingdom. With this money, the church operated several thousand parish church buildings, nearly a hundred cathedrals, and nearly all the universities, hospitals, and poor houses in France.

For most ordinary French people, the church's presence in their lives took the form of the local parish priest. Parish priests provided moral guidance and also performed important civic functions. They recorded births, marriages, and deaths (when they performed baptisms, weddings, and burials), and they recorded property ownership (when they collected the tithe). Parish priests were often the only literate ones in rural areas, so they provided peasants their only source of news from the world beyond the village.

Townspeople had a more direct relationship to the church. Most artisanal guilds and professional corporations had their own chapels, patron saints, and prayer groups known as confraternities. Townspeople were also more likely to have some education, so they would have experienced Catholic clergy as teachers. In both cities and towns, ordinary people viewed the priesthood or a monastery or convent as a chance for a fulfilling career.

Because of its centrality to everyday life, the church became the most important controversial issue of the eighteenth century and the Revolution. This controversy happened for several reasons. First of all, relations between the church and the royal government were not always easy, especially over church property. Every five years, the clergy paid their royal taxes, collectively; as the royal debt grew across the eighteenth century, French kings sought a greater contribution. Within the church, intense cultural and political conflicts broke out, especially between two different clerical movements, the Jesuits and the Jansenists. At the beginning of the eighteenth century, the members of the Order of Jesus, known as Jesuits, became increasingly influential in French society, especially in education. Jesuits also gained many of the most important positions within the clergy, such as the confessor to the king. The growing influence of the Jesuits disturbed the other major orders, such as the Dominicans (who had been the largest clerical order in France since the sixteenth century), and the Jansenists. Jansenists emphasized personal piety and a greater role for lay people in the church. This movement exerted particular influence among the noble magistrates of the royal law courts. These judges, as we have seen, exercised great influence on social life and on royal policy, and they brought their Jansenist education to bear on these questions. Parlementary magistrates tried to limit both the authority of the higher clergy over the laity and of the royal government over the rest of the country. As Jansenists, these judges considered too much power at the center—of the government or the church—to be a sure sign of corruption and immorality. They attempted to prevent corruption by opposing royal taxation and by defending the independence of France from Papal authority; these views made them very popular in the middle decades of the century.

The Jansenists and the Jesuits were two cultures in conflict in the most important controversies of the century, over such questions as whether to accept the Papal decree known as *unigenitus* (which asserted the authority of Rome over any political authority in France); over who should control the Parisian General Hospital (the Jesuits, the church proper, or the royal government); and over the attempt to assassinate King Louis XV in 1759 by Robert Damiens (who was rumored to have been prompted by the Jesuits). At the heart of this conflict was whether authority should come from the center (that is, the king, the higher clergy, and the traditional, military, or sword nobility, or be more dispersed (among the royal *parlements*, the parish clergy, and the better-educated, more recently ennobled, service, or robe, nobility).

The other great cultural conflict revolving around religion prior to the Revolution involved the legitimacy of the church itself. The Enlightenment, led by a group who described themselves as lovers of wisdom, or *philosophers*, challenged the authority of the clergy. Led by the writer Voltaire, this movement brought to light the abuses of clerical authority. For this reason, many reformers within the clergy, especially abbots educated in the Jansenist tradition, supported the Enlightenment and hoped that the use of reason to better understand nature would lead to reforms within the Catholic Church.

The Revolutionary leaders who came to power in 1789 and after placed high on their agenda religious reform to better promote morality. To achieve this goal, they took such actions as confiscating church lands and auctioning them off to generate revenue for the national treasury. They hoped this transfer of land would generate support for the Revolution among the peasantry by putting more land into their hands. In return, the clergy were to be paid an increased salary by government in return for swearing a loyalty oath to France (rather than to the Pope in Rome or to the king.) The Revolutionary leaders passed the Civil Constitution of the Clergy, a law that generated the greatest cultural conflict of the Revolution. In the later and more radically democratic period of the Republic, the Jacobins sought to replace the Catholic Church outright with civic festivals and a new civic religion.

Outside of religion, cultural life in France prior to 1789 revolved around the theater, and this form of entertainment became even more popular and important during the Revolution. Whereas disputes over literature, theater, and the arts generated some of the most widely discussed controversies prior to 1789, these controversies took on important political overtones during the Revolution, when more French citizens than ever attended theater and opera. Such debates took place in newspapers and in coffee shops and other public places where people gathered to discuss—and on occasion to fight. Because of the importance of these debates and their tendency to be linked directly to political questions, successive Revolutionary governments closely monitored conversations in coffee houses through a network of police informants.

Despite the emphasis on the political content of literature during the Revolution, and despite the prospect of disputes in the theater, the press, and the coffee shops, writers found a great many opportunities in this period to express their ideas and to have greater influence than ever on French culture.

## RELIGIOUS TOLERANCE AND INTOLERANCE

In the sixteenth century, religion had become synonymous in France with conflict—resulting in 30 years of hostility known as the Wars of Religion. At the end of this bloody conflict, in 1589, the victorious Duke Henri of Navarre became King Henri IV and decreed that Calvinists (known in France as *Huguenots*) could now worship openly in specified regions of the country. He intended through this religious policy for regional nobles and city governments to retain their traditional independence from the royal government without needing to fight for control. This policy enjoyed great success until the middle of the 1600s, when civil war briefly broke out again.

Fearing further unrest, Henri IV's great-grandson, King Louis XIV, revoked the limited tolerance in 1685. Louis limited the political independence of regional noble assemblies and instead pursued a policy of "one king, one law, one faith" across all of France. To his supporters, Louis had taken a step away from the traditional form of government in Europe—rule by regional elites—and towards a more modern, rational, and centralized state government. To critics, including the Enlightenment philosophers, this policy led to the repression of otherwise peaceable Huguenots. Moreover, they argued, it gave Catholic priests and bishops too much influence over questions of morality and politics in society. Nevertheless, Louis's successor, Louis XV, continued this policy of non-toleration.

When King Louis XVI took the throne in 1775, he appointed many Enlightened thinkers to his government. Among the reforms they proposed was religious toleration, which led to a royal edict issued in November 1787. This edict granted "non-Catholics" full eligibility for public offices and membership in royally sanctioned bodies. Enlightened reformers celebrated this change, by which Louis XVI intended to restore traditional liberties to the small (and relatively isolated) Huguenot minority, as a benefit to all of France. However, devout Catholics, especially higher-ranking clergy and court nobles, worried that toleration of religious minorities would lead to immorality and religious conflict, and they used their considerable influence to oppose the policy. In the documents that follow, we see some of the unexpected cultural conflicts that arose for ordinary French people, even before the Revolution, as a result of this decree.

The decree granted legal recognition to Calvinist marriages. But since obviously no Catholic priest would officiate, who would record these marriages? And since Calvinists did not consider marriage a sacrament and thus accepted divorce, would the decree authorize divorce? The royal decree did not specify answers, so leading prominent Huguenot citizens appealed for clarification to the Ministry of the Royal Household (which was responsible for, among other matters, record-keeping for marriages). The documents that follow are letters to the government from a prominent Huguenot lawyer, Mr. Baillanvilliers, in the city of Nîmes, home to one of the largest Huguenot populations in France.

## DOCUMENT 1: PROTESTANT MARRIAGES: EQUALITY FOR ALL OR SPECIAL RIGHTS?

Letter from Mr. Ballainvilliers, [Huguenot Lawyer], to the Baron de Breteuil [Minister of the Royal Household], 21 March 1788:

"The intent of the royal edict concerning non-Catholics does not leave any doubt about the approval given for marriages and baptisms [of Calvinists]...to be performed by or before clergy or by civil government officials in the domicile of one of the parties.

But it is not the same thing for conjugal unions declared before the effective date of the edict....In that case, the spouses must present themselves, with four witnesses, before a priest or a royal judge...and make a new declaration of their marriage. This provision for presentation before a judge is to ensure that non-Catholics are not prevented, where allowed by law, from withdrawing from already contracted marriages. [In some regions with large Protestant populations, local custom authorized divorces, which Catholic clergy refused to recognize.] This may present a problem in [rural regions] where the population is generally very poor and the royal courts are very far away...so as it stands, this will make it impossible for a great number of people of this sort [that is, Protestants from poor, rural regions] to take advantage of the [new royal edict]...."

[Source: Archives departementales de l'Hérault (ADH), C 647; translated from P. Angers, *L'Édit de 1787 et son application dans la Sénéchaussée de Nîmes* (Nîmes: Chastanier, 1925), 210–11.]

Letter from government official in Ministry of Royal Household to Mr. Ballainvilliers, [undated, March 1788]:

"In response to your letter on the worries of Protestants...about the execution of the edict of November 1787, and your letter to M. d'Augier, Lieutenant-General [of Police for the region] asking him to travel to certain [remote] places to receive the marriage declarations of those who live too far from a royal court, [I write to inform you that the Minister of the Royal Household has told me that] the priest of Bréau [a town in the region] is willing to receive the declarations of marriage of Protestants, and so if it is less costly for them [than to travel to a royal court], they can also address themselves to...Mr. d'Augier."

[Source: ADH, C 1917; translated from Angers, 224.]

***

Prior to the decree, religious minorities had been frustrated by the problem of burying their dead. Since city governments did not recognize Calvinist churches, Huguenots had been forced to use secret cemeteries outside of town. So, in response to the edict of 1787, the Huguenots immediately began to seek locations to build new cemeteries. Hoping to put aside years of exclusion, they naturally sought plots within the city limits. Yet city governments, throughout the eighteenth century, had been trying to move cemeteries out of town centers for health reasons. Moreover, not all Catholics wanted the Huguenots to have new cemeteries. This conflict of culture divided ordinary citizens of the town of St. Gervasy, near Nîmes, as we see in this next exchange of letters between Ballainvillers and the Chancellor, the head of the royal judicial system.

## DOCUMENT 2: DISPUTE OVER A PROTESTANT CEMETERY IN ST. GERVASY

Letter from a deputy to the Chancellor to Mr. Ballainvillers, 22 August 1788:

"I have received, Sir, the letter you had sent to me with the order from the city council of St. Gervasy that Mr. Castilhon should be forced to cede to the estimate of the experts on the land needed for a new cemetery... but after consultation with the royal council of state, the King himself has decided not to approve this order.

[The King] recognizes the truth of the claims of [the Calvinists] that it is within the power [of the royal government] to force individuals to sell land at a price established by experts, but this is usually for projects such as the widening of roads or the construction of public buildings... His Majesty has decided this power should not be applied for a project that concerns only one community rather than the good of the entire society. So that if the town council of St. Gervasy wants to buy the land from Mr. Castilhon, it will have to negotiate with him until they agree on a price or else find another location where the price will not be as expensive."

Letter from a deputy to the Chancellor to Ballainvillers, 2 December 1788:

"In response to the memorandum you kindly sent me asking to be authorized to have a price fixed by experts for the plot of land that would be a suitable place for a cemetery for non-Catholics and then to be able to buy it from the current owners... the difficulty is not convincing the owners to sell it but dealing with the objections of many of the neighbors who seek to block the project.... They object that the plot is not far enough away from their homes and that the wind from the north will carry all the smells [from the cemetery] to the city... and that the roads by that plot are not large enough for carriages [carrying coffins]... and that burials there could infect the water wells for the entire city....

There is, however, another location that does not raise these objections and which would not be much more expensive and not really too far, but the [Calvinist] community finds it too small. But I think it will be much easier to overcome that problem later, by adding adjacent plots of land, than it will be to deal with the objections of the entire city to a cemetery for non-Catholics in the center of town]."

[Source: Archvies Departementales de l'Herault, C 457; translated from Angers, 193.]

***

The decree had used the term *non-Catholics,* but the king had not necessarily intended it to apply to the other religious minority in France, the Jews. Most Jews had been expelled from France during the fourteenth century; those who lived in France in the 1700s were found almost exclusively in two regions—Alsace (formerly a German territory) and the city of Bordeaux. Jews had a special status in Old Regime Europe; in many countries, they were tolerated as long as they remained outside all social institutions. Jews were considered to be an ethnic group (that is, a nation) that had different language, traditions, and laws and beliefs, and neither wanted to nor could intermingle with the rest of the population. At least one Jew in Nîmes, however, wanted to assimilate, as we see in this next exchange of letters involving the city government, the regional governor (or *Intendant,* appointed by the king) of Languedoc, the Catholic bishop, and the royal sub-delegate for the city (who answered to the *Intendant.*)

## DOCUMENT 3: ADMISSION OF JEWS TO GUILDS IN NÎMES

Memorandum from mayor of Nîmes to the royal *Intendant* of Languedoc:

"The man in question [Izaac Monteil] has lived in the city of Nîmes for many years, he has paid his personal taxes [to the royal government] as well as his business taxes [to the city] and even contributed to the cost of the province's draft of soldiers, so he has upheld his part of the responsibilities of all citizens of the city.

Until now, he has been limited in his business by royal laws [that prevented him from entering the guild]...and he believes that he has acquired greater liberty from the decree of November 1787...since that edict has gone into effect, he has made his application to be recognized [by the leaders of the tailors' guild] as an authorized seller of all textiles in the city of Nîmes, and he has offered to pay his entrance dues and even to help pay off the debts of the guild. This offer was refused.... The leaders of the guild refused to admit him, arguing that he is Jewish and that the edict of November 1787 [declaring full civic rights for 'non-Catholics'] was not for those who profess his religion...."

Letter to the Chancellor from...the *Corps* of master taylors of Nîmes, 13 March 1788:

Dear Sir:

Izaac Monteil, taylor, sent us yesterday the document that is enclosed. This individual is Jewish and asks, based on the edict of last November, to be received as a master craftsman in our guild.... We have never had an example of a Jew received as a master craftsman in any guild of Nîmes, so we ask you, Sir, to let us know if we should admit him or refuse him.

Letter from a deputy to the Chancellor to Mr. Phéline, royal subdelegate at Nîmes, 14 March 1788:

...Based on the letter and petition you sent us, there does not seem to be any reason to deny him....

Letter to the Bishop of Nîmes, from Mr. Phéline, royal subdelegate at Nîmes, 23 March 1788:

"I have asked the leaders of the guild of master taylors...to explain to me why they refused to admit as a master Mr. Izaac Monteil, Jew. They told me that these people [Jews] have never before been admitted to any guild, and therefore, they believed themselves authorized to refuse him. But they said that if you [as a Catholic religious leader] decide that he should be admitted, they would follow your orders.

This affair is delicate under the edict of November 1787. The first article expressly permits non-Catholics living in the kingdom...to exercise all professions and not to be excluded on the basis of their religion.... This law is general and seems to include all those who do not profess the Roman Catholic religion and so would include Jews and all other religions.

Yet there is the repugnance of Christians to associate with Jews that could create difficulties within several guilds, so what do you think would be the better[policy] of the government on this matter?..."

Letter to the Bishop from the *Corps* of master taylors of Nîmes, 6 April 1788:

"This article [of the decree of November 1787] does not appear to us to be applied to Jews who, not being naturally French, cannot be considered subjects of the King. They are foreigners even if they live in the kingdom. Thus, they can only claim to be covered by article 5 of the edict, which allows...foreigners living in France [who are not Catholic] to contract marriages legally.

In effect, *Monseigneur* [a term of address reserved for high-ranking clergy], the Jews form a separate nation, with its own theocratic government [referring to Jewish customs and religious laws] that isolates it and makes Jews always foreigners in whatever country they live in.... They are also foreigners in any city. They cannot therefore hope to be admitted to any commercial corporations [guilds], which are reserved for true subjects of the king. We therefore reject and find repugnant this invocation of royal law by the Jews to their own advantage."

Second Letter from a deputy to the Chancellor to Mr. Phéline, royal subdelegate at Nîmes, 21 April 1788:

I have spoken to the Baron de Bretuil [Minister of the Royal Household] of the difficulties raised there by the application of Izaac Monteil, Jewish taylor, to be admitted as a master craftsman to the guild of master taylors of the city of Nîmes. The Minister told me that this question has already come up in Paris, where two Jews have sought to be admitted to the merchants guild...and it was decided that...under the edict of November 1787, Jews must continue to adhere to the specific laws under which they are permitted to live in France [which do not consider them subjects of the king, eligible for civic rights or admission to *corporations*].

I ask you therefore to inform the leaders of the taylors' guild of this decision as well as Mr. Izaac Monteil.

[Source: ADH, C 2818; translated from Angers, 224–25.]

***

This issue of Jewish civil status, then, remained unresolved at the outbreak of the Revolution. In September of 1789, the Declaration of the Rights of Man and Citizen assured all French people the right to worship openly without interference. At this point, not only individual Jews but the entire Jewish populations of Bordeaux and of Alsace petitioned to be accepted as active citizens.

The National Assembly took up the debate. Those opposed made the traditional argument that Jews were not ethnically French and thus were not eligible for citizenship, even if they met all other requirements. Speaking against admission of Jews to citizenship was the abbot Jean Maury, who supported the Revolution and the Declaration of Rights of Man. Yet on this question, he spoke in defense of the Catholic Church's traditional role in society and against the idea that Jews would ever regard France as their homeland or the French people as equal individuals under a common law:

## DOCUMENT 4: AGAINST CITIZENSHIP OF JEWS

"The Jews have been in Europe for seventeen centuries without involving themselves with others. They have never undertaken any relations with others based on something other than money... none of them know how to work the land or drive a plow... their religious holidays are so many that they work much less than Christians... They live off the sweat of Christians... [Now that we are making a Revolution] we must regard them as brothers and ensure they are not persecuted.... We must assure them protection as men but not as French citizens."

[Source: Translated from *Archives Parlementaires* X, 776.]

***

On behalf of admitting Jews to full citizenship, a liberal-minded nobleman known as the Count de Clermont-Tonnerre gave a speech calling on his fellow deputies to accept the Enlightened idea that society should consider all citizens equally over the more traditional belief that any society had to be based on one religion to function:

## DOCUMENT 5: FOR CITIZENSHIP OF JEWS

"There is no middle way. Either you admit a national religion, and all laws derive from it. In that case, you... exclude those who profess another religion and have no freedom [of religion]. Or you permit everyone to his own religion opinions and then you cannot exclude anyone from [voting and holding office] on this basis... The only test of a religion should be if it encourages morality... Those who oppose [citizenship for Jews] argue that they are not a sociable people [meaning they do not want to interact with the rest of society]... They say that Jews [want to] have their own judges and laws. I respond that... we should not allow it, [because everyone must be equal under the law.] For that reason, we must refuse [any specific rights] to the Jews as a nation, and accord [full legal equality] to the Jews as individuals. There should be no legal recognition of their judges... and no legal recognition of Judaic laws... they will be citizens individually.... Otherwise, we will have an association of non-citizens, a nation within the nation... The presumed status of every man resident in the country [who meets the requirements] must be that of a citizen."

[Source: Translated from *Archives Parlementaires* X, 754–55.]

***

Ultimately, the National Assembly agreed and voted to grant full citizenship rights to Jews. This became known as the emancipation of Jews; ever since, this act has been celebrated as an example of reason triumphing over prejudice and, moreover, of the idea of a society of equal individuals as the essence of modern citizenship.

## SEPARATION OF CHURCH AND STATE

The French Revolutionaries wanted to assure individual liberty as a way of strengthening, rather than suppressing, religion. They believed that a society with many different religions would offer many different ways to improve human morality. So while some worried that any organized religion—at least one that had a clergy—would always amount to a form of oppression, others expressed optimism that the government could tolerate all religions and openly support those that its citizens found the most moral. We find that argument in the following editorial from the official newspaper, *Mercure de France:*

### DOCUMENT 6: THE UTILITY OF RELIGION

"Is religion useful to creating a good government or is it not? If it is not useful, why do we need to bother about differences of opinion and about religious tolerance?... To say it is not useful is to say it has no influence at all on the social order. This is obviously not the case, so we must be concerned to encourage good morality by increasing religious toleration....

So whether the people love God or a cat, this liberty must not be restricted by legislation, because the government cannot be indifferent to the people's morality. If everyone has the freedom to bow down before a fetish or to worship the devil, they do not have the right to demand that their beliefs become a public religion....

[Should the government recognize all religions?] Not all doctrines encourage morality, support for the weak, or consolation for the unhappy. Religion should be a supplement to laws and to morality, and the government should authorize only those that pursue these goals. It cannot be indifferent towards all religious beliefs [that it tolerates.]...All religions that do not damage the public interest should not be deprived of the right to be known and to be celebrated, but who determines [whether they should be authorized]? Public opinion? That produced the St. Bartholomew's Day Massacre [of Protestants by Catholics in Paris in 1572]. Enlightenment? That did not stop eight thousand fanatics from nearly taking over London in 1780 [referring to the Wesleyan Methodist Connection revival, in which followers of Wesley's alternative to the official Anglican Church of England held very emotional and active religious services including gathering to pray under tents and in the open]. Only the legislator can make that determination. If he is Enlightened, there is nothing to fear. If he is not, the nation will become as intolerant as he.

Religious tolerance is a law and an institution and embraces all with equal protection all religious beliefs...but society must never allow any group of believers to create public altars [that is, an official religion] which would be an offense against reason and liberty and would put itself above the law as the judge of the actions of the people."

[Source: *Mercure de France* (5 September 1789) 77; reprinted in Legg, 118–19.]

***

The patriot newspaper, *Revolutions of Paris,* was less encouraging:

"We cannot hide our disappointment that the National Assembly, rather than stuffing out the virus of [religious] intolerance, has given it pride of place in the Declaration of Rights...by declaring that the demonstration of religious opinion [rather than the opinion itself] cannot be limited and that for reasons of public order, the law can restrict that liberty...These are false, dangerous principles of intolerance on which the Dominicans [a Catholic order of monks founded during the Counter-Reformation] and Torquemada [the legendary Spanish Inquisitor] can base their own bloody doctrines...."

[Source: *Révolutions de Paris* (5 September 1789) 2; reprinted in Legg, 119.]

***

Most critics of the Catholic Church attributed the problems of the Old Regime to the clergy. The Revolutionaries wanted to address this problem by retaining those members of the clergy who were most committed to improving morality and teaching ideals of individual liberty, equality under the law, and toleration—and to remove those who abused their office and did little work on behalf of the people. At the same time, the National Assembly knew that the church controlled a large amount of land (roughly 10 percent of the cultivated land in the kingdom) and wanted to put that land to the service of the people. These goals led to the law of June 1790 known as the Civil Constitution of the Clergy. By this law, land belonging to the church became national property; it would be auctioned off, with the proceeds going to the national treasury to retire the national debt. Those clergy who pledged to support the Revolution by swearing an oath would become civil servants, paid a salary by the nation for their work. The following document is an excerpt of the law establishing this change.

## DOCUMENT 7: REFORMING THE CLERGY TO SERVE THE NATION

"All clergy exercising a ministry [that is, assigned to a parish or to a cathedral rather than in a monastery], in recognition that theirs is among the most important functions in society, will be obliged to instill confidence in the people by residing continually in a place where they can serve the people [that is, reside in their parish or diocese, which was not always the case for clergy under the Old Regime]. The Nation will defray the cost of their residence.

Each deserving bishop, priest, and vicar... will be given an appropriate lodging and... all their expenses will be covered by a stipend [depending on rank and location].... Vicars who, due to age or infirmity, cannot take up their functions will notify the [local government] which will engage a new vicar and pay [the retired vicar] a pension."

[Source: Translated from Michelle Vovelle, ed., *De la France monarchique á la France républicaine: Documents de travaux* (Paris: Université de Paris I, 1997) 80.]

***

The Civil Constitution of the Clergy proved very controversial, and a great deal of cultural conflict erupted from its application. When roughly half the clergy refused to take the oath, the government removed these refractory priests from their pulpits and replaced them with juring priests. In some regions, the replacement priests met with open resistance from their new parishioners, who remained loyal to the former priests. In the following document, once again from Nîmes, we see how the Catholic priests—many of whom had already resisted civil rights for Calvinists and Jews—fought openly against the Civil Constitution of the Clergy, leading to the first violent resistance to the Revolution:

## DOCUMENT 8: RELIGIOUS STRIFE OVER THE CLERGY IN NÎMES

"Aristocracy and fanaticism have not yet excited such bloody scenes as those which just took place in Nîmes. We remember that [recently] certain [members of the clergy] made statements [against the Revolution] that caused a wave of indignation across the country, and this response should have brought the supposed Catholics of this city to accept principles of patriotism and tolerance that all French people must profess in this moment of liberty and reason. These fanatics, seeing that a clear majority of the five hundred people elected to the new city council [created in the fall of 1789] were known patriots who would keep [the conservative clergy] out of office, [the clergy] did everything they could to dissolve the new city council and overthrow the city.

These priests and the nuns who supported them . . . deceived some of the people and convinced them to murder, in the name of a religion that abhors bloodshed. The uprising began the twelfth [of June, 1791] and in the days that followed, the city fell victim to all the horrors of a civil war. Martial law was declared but did not help end the disorder. The patriots received reinforcements from nearby towns, until the fanatics, wearing red hoods [symbols of the upper ranks of the clergy] and white cockards [symbols of support for the monarchy] were obliged to leave the field of battle, only after having taken the lives of numerous patriots . . . of distinguished virtue.

The evening of the fourteenth, some two thousand Cévenols [men from a region near Nîmes, and one of the principal Calvinist regions of France] arrived to help defend the constitution. The faction [of opponents of the city government and of the revolution] retreated into convents and into a tower over the old city walls . . . from which they fired on all the passersby and killed several citizens . . . until the National Guard units from Arles and Montpelier [two larger cities in the region] arrived with canons and besieged the tower and the convents . . . By the sixteenth, calm had been re-established by about thirty thousand armed men who had arrived with various National Guard units to aid the city.

Everyone took a civic oath promising to see to the defense of the homeland everyone that enemies of the Revolution sought to make trouble . . . Many cried at the number of victims killed by the ambition and the fanaticism of those priests."

[Source: Translated from *L'Observateur Marseillais* (19 June 1791) 11.]

***

After the establishment of the Republic, many French patriots no longer hoped to reform the Church but instead to suppress it. As we saw in chapter 5, zealous sansculottes massacred hundreds of refractory priests in September 1792, just after the overthrow of the monarchy. At the height of the period of Revolutionary government, in early 1794, the Republic shut Catholic churches across France and tried to replace them with a national, patriotic religion without clergy. Some favored a Cult of the Supreme Being based on worship of a generic god; others called for a Cult of Reason based on human thought as the source of morality. Both cults staged public festivals celebrating revolutionary values rather than weekly services. Collectively, this program became known as dechristianization.

To some, dechristanization represented the final step of Enlightenment, the abandonment of all unnecessary traditions and superstitions. But others, such as the author of the next document (who went on to become a bishop after the Revolution, when the Catholic Church would be restored in France), regretted the closing of the churches in 1794.

## DOCUMENT 9: THE CLOSING OF THE CHURCHES

"All the Churches of the diocese were seized upon and converted to profane uses. Some were used as storehouses for . . . hay, some were converted into *casernes* and stables; some into manufactories and some altered into dwelling houses by those who bought them; some were leveled with the ground in order that the materials might be sold or to make room for new streets; some were . . . changed into temples for the festivals of the national calendar . . . or for the clubs and political assemblies of the time. . . . It was forbidden by law and under penalties of fine and imprisonment to observe Sunday or to distinguish it in any way from common days whilst the *decadi* or every tenth day [in the new Revolutionary calendar], had been...made the legal day of rest. As each *decadi* came around, they endeavored to make it more attractive by new inventions of shows or...sentimental exhibitions, mixing with them special speeches and songs, civic banquets, and public games."

[Source: Bruté, 97.]

***

## FESTIVALS AND CIVIC RELIGIOUS LIFE DURING THE REVOLUTION

Revolutionary festivals were elaborate public celebrations, involving extensive planning. The following description of the first festival, which commemorated the one-year anniversary of the taking of the Bastille, gives us a sense of the scale of the festival and of the way it incorporated elements of Catholic mass, such as altars and priests, with new values, such as unity and patriotism. Ordinary people experienced these festivals as a tremendous liberation—a chance to participate in a large spectacle rather than to listen passively to obscure prayers in Latin. At the same time, these festivals included many elements—large crowds in public places, parades, music, symbolic presentation of the leader—of what would become mass politics of the twentieth century, in democracies as well as other political systems.

### DOCUMENT 10: FESTIVAL OF FEDERATION

"The day of the taking of the Bastille will never be equaled in the history of the French nation. [We will always remember] the devotion, courage, and ardor of all the citizens—their agreement, their perfect equality, their respect for the rights of all and for justice...the vanquishing of tyrants who were put to death [the governor of the Bastille and the mayor of Paris] while the true heroes were crowned...the inspiration of the people who threw off their chains and reclaimed their rights; all of this is what sets apart that sublime day...and would be commemorated and revered by the Festival of Federation.

The contingent from Brittany arrived [in Paris for the Festival] on Saturday the tenth [of July 1790]...The Parisian National Guard sent a detachment before them to parade into Paris with drums beating. At the Tuileries Palace, the Bretons paraded before the King and the commandant gave a speech of respect for this 'citizen-king.'...Cries of 'Long live the King' were heard from every window. The commandant of the recently arrived contingent of National Guardsmen from the city of Tours followed and presented the king with a ring that Henri IV had given to the [people of Tours] in recognition of their fidelity [during the Wars of Religion two hundred years earlier]. Sunday, there was a parade of the Paris National Guard before the National Assembly and then the King. The next day, four Assembly deputies from each department [province] of France were invited to attend a ceremony at the Saint-Roche Church...On the thirteenth, the king reviewed the passage of all the contingents of Guard units, led by Mr. de Lafayette [leader of the Parisian National Guard].

Meanwhile, an army of workers were preparing hastily the *Champ du Mars* [Marching Field, in front of the royal Military Academy], despite abundant rain, and distributing tickets all across the city for the ceremonies [on July 14]....

[Then the report describes the ceremonies of July 14.] At daybreak, the people began to march towards the *Champ du Mars* [Marching Field] while the Federated [Guard Units] formed up on the wide boulevards....Citizens watched the guard units form up and perform small drills to warm up...On one side [of the field] the deputies [of the National Assembly] assembled with 83 banners [each with the name of their home department]...The oldest form each department had the honor of holding the banner.

The parade began at seven o'clock in the morning in the following order: the Parisian cavalry unit, then the infantry unit with a corps of drummers at the front, then the city councilors of Paris, and a company of 240 citizen-soldiers [that is, those in the royal army rather than in the National Guard]...the presidents of each of the districts of Paris and then the Committee of the Federation [National Assembly delegates who had organized the Festival]. Next, a battalion of children and of older men followed...then came [National Guard units from] forty-two departments in alphabetical order....At the rear, a detachment of infantry soldiers and guardsmen on horseback.

[When this procession entered the Marching Field] a great spectacle struck the eyes of the [marchers]: three hundred thousand spectators, men and women, all wearing ribbons printed "To the nation." They marched through three triumphal arches arranged on an incline...and [through] an alley of trees to an immense platform with a raised altar in the center. [The platform was] raised twenty feet from the ground, accessible on each side by a large staircase . . . four smaller platforms, each with four staircases, had smaller altars with incense burning on them. In the middle of the field was the altar dedicated to the Homeland, around which a number of patriotic clergy, wearing red, white and blue sashes.

In the middle of the spectators' gallery was an immense covered gallery decorated in blue and gold drapes . . . over a pavilion for the King and behind him, the royal family . . . The King entered the pavilion from the Military School [behind the Marching Field] and took his throne without scepter, crown, or royal coat to show that he had renounced those trappings [of his former rule, now replaced by a constitutional monarchy].

It took until three thirty [eight and one-half hours after it had begun] for the procession to complete its arrival on the Marching Field . . . Cannon shots, as at the beginning of the procession's arrival, now announced [its completion]. Eighty-three flames were lit behind the royal pavilion. . . .

After all this, Mr. de Lafayette climbed to the altar and gave a speech ending with an oath sworn by all ten thousand of the Federated guardsmen. . . . He had great difficulty riding his horse off the field, because it seemed like all ten thousand guardsmen wanted to embrace him; [as he rode past] they reached out to touch his face, his legs, his arms, his coat, his boots, the horse harness, and even the horse itself.

Then, the National Assembly rose and swore an oath. The crowd cried 'Long live the King!' and several voices added 'Long live the National Assembly!' . . . Finally, the King rose . . . and more cries of 'Long live the King!' were heard. The Queen raised their son towards the people, and the covered parts of the gallery—where one had needed tickets to enter—shouted 'Long live the Queen!' and 'Long live the Prince!' Several more cannon shots announced the end of the festival around six o'clock.

Altogether, it was impressive how many people were there, as participants and spectators, how many flags waved in the breeze, how orderly everything was, and how beautiful the scene was. Of all the memories and ideas of this day, [we will most remember] the oath sworn by four hundred thousand men [spectators and participants] to defend the constitution that was being written [by the Assembly] . . . But nothing about the details. . . . "

[Source: *Révolutions de Paris* (16 July 1790) 53.]

***

Another Revolutionary approach to cultural life as a means to promote new values and regenerate society was to create the first public museums. The Revolution organized into collections many historic documents, artifacts, and works of art that had belonged to nobles or the church. Whereas most works of art under the Old Regime had been viewed in a church or an aristocratic home—and owned by the Church or an aristocrat—the French Revolution made important works into public property, available for all citizens to see.

Moreover, the revolutionaries wanted people to understand their history—not only to know about the lives of former kings or the occurrence of great battles but to understand the struggles for social change of ordinary people like themselves. To that end, they organized the documents of the Revolution itself, from its very first days, into collections available to the public in archives and museums. The formation of the first museums, and of the idea of art and history for public use, is described in this document:

## DOCUMENT 11: THE BIRTH OF THE PUBLIC MUSEUM

"Amidst the struggles of the French for their political existence, nothing has marked their superiority over... their enemies more than the calm confidence with which they have founded various institutions for the civilization and refinement of the people. Independent of the general organization of public education throughout the Republic, great care has been taken in forming vast repositories of monuments, of art, and of documents of government... [to be displayed to the people for their knowledge and enjoyment].

When the Assembly decreed the land of the clergy was to become property of the Nation, the committee [formed to oversee this transfer of land] was ordered also to ensure the preservation of any monuments and works of art on those ecclesiastical domains... The committee designated the convent of the Augustins [in Paris] to receive these objects, and it was soon in the possession of a large number of monuments and works of art. This responsibility was then taken up by the Committee of Public Instruction [another committee of the Assembly]... for the preservation of these monuments and works of art....

In the autumn of 1795, this collection was, by a decree of the Assembly, organized into a museum of French monuments with two parts—one on history in general and the other on the history of France . . . and of its Revolution."

[Source: Williams, 224–27.]

***

The most important cultural reform through which the Revolutionaries sought to improve the lives of citizens was the creation of public schools. Prior to the Revolution, the Catholic Church had run most schools, primarily to train future clergy. The eighteenth century had seen the development of a series of church-run private high schools, known in French as *collèges,* that catered to the sons of upper-middle class families. Revolutionaries wanted to expand education further, so all individuals could develop new skills and advance socially, could develop better morals, and could become more patriotic.

To this end, the Revolutionaries hoped to establish free, secular public schools throughout the country. They also sought to shut down private schools, which provided education only for those who could afford it. To avoid this fate, one of the most prestigious private schools of the Old Regime, known as the *Collège of King Louis-the-Great,* changed its name to the *Collège of Equality* and opened its doors to poor boys on scholarships. Nevertheless, the revolutionary desire for cultural equality brought this school under suspicion, as described in the following documents.

## DOCUMENT 12: AN ARISTOCRATIC SCHOOL IS DENOUNCED

Observations of Citizen Rolin on Equality College [September 1793]:

"Most of the professors in this establishment are as much aristocrats as they could possibly be. It was said yesterday at dinner in the dining hall that the prisoners were in danger of their lives and that the prisons were mined and might be blown up. In the Rue Saint-Jacques, across the street from the door used by the professors of Equality College, is a perfume dealer with a wooden leg. This man is a pronounced aristocrat; there is no term he will not use to ridicule the Republic. He goes to impossible lengths to propagate his detestable sentiments; to have reliable information on these two matters you can turn to Citizen Germain, a tenth-grade teacher.

Some washerwomen in this *section* [of Paris, known as the Section of the Panthéon] stopped five sacks of coal coming from [the town of] Choisi [to be delivered to the College]. The owner [of the coal cart] said he had *livres* in coin [the Old Regime currency that was replaced by *assignats*], which the College administration believes it cannot use without authorization. There are also about five hundred silver table settings, including drinking cups, which were used by the scholarship students. Lastly, in the sacristy of the College, there is a large quantity of silver objects that no longer serve any purpose."

Deliberation of the General Assembly of the Section of the Panthéon:

"Considering that the objects in question are of no use to Equality College, and that in the present circumstances it is important not to leave in private hands such national properties as may be valuable to the Republic, to repel the last efforts of the enemies of liberty, [the general assembly of the *section* of Panthéon in the part of Paris where the University and many other schools were located, now known as the Latin Quarter] orders that the sum in coin now at the College shall be transported to the National Treasury and converted into paper money. This money will be returned to . . . the College for its daily expenses.

[The *section*] further orders that the silver table service and mugs, together with the silver objects in the chapel, should also be transported [to the National Treasury] and that a receipt shall be given for them to the [College] as evidence of its patriotic contribution. . . . Citizen Dubois . . . shall proceed to Equality College, to oversee the execution of the present order."

Account of recent operations by Citizen Ameilhon of the Temporary Commission on the Arts, 15 Floréal An II [May 4, 1794]:

"The library of Equality College, rue Saint-Jacques, has been transported to the Cultural Depot. I estimate that this library, on which . . . work can be done, may contain at least thirty-five thousand volumes, printed and in manuscript. The latter are few in number, and I have noted none of any great interest. It is otherwise with the printed books. They offer an assortment of the best works in all fields. It is evident that learned men brought together this collection of books.

Four Coronelli globes that adorned the library, two of ordinary size and well preserved, and two smaller ones, have been taken to the

Depot of the Petits Augustins, along with a relief model of the building that was once planned as a central office of the University, to be erected at the former Place Sainte-Geneviève. All paintings have been taken to the same place. No medals were found, but in one dark corner I discovered two old microscopes with various pieces used in optical operations, among which I noticed some lenses whose special qualities showed their merit; also a magnet that seemed strong enough to lift ten pounds or more, a glass cage for objects in natural history, and finally some animal horns or claws, and some seals or stamps. I have had all these articles most carefully transported to the Cultural Depot, and I am ready to turn them over to whichever members of the Commission are in charge of such matters."

[Source: Translated from Vovelle, ed., 145–50.]

***

## THEATER-GOING IN THE REVOLUTION

The most common cultural activity in the eighteenth century for all social levels and cultural groups was going to the theater. From parodies, pantomimes, and puppet shows in fair theaters to elaborate musicals in the highly popular comic opera to classical tragedies in the royal French Comedy to the most prestigious and expensive royal opera, there was a theater and a genre for every taste. Under the Old Regime, many of these theaters were also sites of cultural conflict, where debates and, occasionally, riots broke out. After 1789, the royal regulations limiting the number of theaters and types of plays were lifted, providing even more opportunities for new plays—and for more active audience responses. Different political clubs even organized group outings to the theater to support or oppose plays based on what they perceived to be the political meaning.

The following documents describe how theater retained its appeal as a place to see and be seen, even during the Terror. A regular theatergoer describes the intense cultural conflicts that broke out at a performance of Charles Laya's play *Friend of the Law*. This play was performed during the period of revolutionary government, when the foreign and civil wars were their most intense, and divisions were increasing between supporters of the Terror as necessary to save the Republic and opponents who considered it unlawful.

## DOCUMENT 13: FASHIONS AND THEATER IN A TIME OF CRISIS

"Anarchy has reached its climax. The *sections* and the clubs re-echo with constant calls to insurrection. The Commune [the city government of Paris] is openly conspiring against the majority in the Convention [the National Assembly of the Republic]...The Revolutionary Tribunal sends fresh [convicts] to the scaffold every day. Civil war is laying waste to our western departments, and the Austrians are menacing our northern frontier.

Paris, meanwhile, goes on amusing itself....This spring, the streets are crowded with people, especially women, conspicuous by their gorgeous and tasteful make-up....The wardrobe of a fashionable woman contains [dresses of fine materials in] the national colors [red, white and blue]...The men, not wanting to be left behind in this display of elegance and patriotism, have been [dressing themselves] in Jacobin garb with remarkable care white pants and tie blue and red [shirts]...and blue coats of Indian silk; some wear trousers with wide stripes of alternating red and blue...even the dandies carry in their jacket or coat pockets as fashionable decorations one or two pistols.

All the theaters are packed every night...Some go to comedies, others to musicals, while many applaud patriotic tragedies...The Theater of the Nation [formerly the French Comedy, which had been the royal theater prior to 1791] still remains the best playhouse in Paris. It has lost some of its most famous actors [who left to form their own Theater of the Republic] but it retains...a company of the most excellent actors, of true-hearted people, who perform with great success. They hope not to bring upon the theater the displeasure of the [municipal government, which saw itself as representing the sansculottes].

Before the most recent performance on Friday, at four o'clock in the afternoon...the audience had the opportunity to witness a spectacle of a different kind on the other side of town. At one o'clock, a woman was guillotined in the Revolution Plaza [formerly, the Place Louis XV, today known as the Place de la Concorde, or Peace Plaza]. She was a poor servant, fifty-six years old, condemned to death for having spoken anti-revolutionary expressions, while drunk."

[Source: Biré, 66–69.]

## DOCUMENT 14: THE POLITICS OF THEATER

"On the second [January 1793], the Theater of the Nation performed a new comedy, in five acts and in verse, entitled *Friend of the Laws,* written by Mr. Laya. It is not a very interesting play; the plot makes no sense, and the verses are harsh and too long. Nevertheless, the audience responded to this play enthusiastically [by an] immense audience.

Before three in the afternoon, impatient crowds blocked all streets leading to the theater.... The excitement and curiosity were due to the author's reputation for attacks on the current rulers of Paris and of France and on those who are false patriots [who claim to be more patriotic than anyone else. Biré then describes how the characters in the play satirize leading Jacobin politicians.] He has dared to say openly what many people have long thought, and all the excitement [for his play] results from the daring of expressing those sincere feelings [of opposition to the Jacobins.] With an ardor and an energy we have not seen for a long time, the crowd was able to express distaste for pro-revolutionary dialogue...and to applaud the principles of moderation, justice, and responsibility. It is impossible not [to see that] it is a striking protest against the trial of Louis XVI [which had begun in the National Assembly the month before] and against those who want to send him to the scaffold.

During the first four performances, not a single spectator expressed the least disapproval [of the play]; enthusiasm reigned in every part of the playhouse. There is no doubt that this vast audience included supporters of Robespierre [one of the better-known Jacobin leaders] and of Marat [the patriotic journalist who edited *Friend of the People* and who had been elected to the National Assembly the previous fall]. But in spite of their opposition [to Laya's play] they kept silent....The republican newspapers [that is, those that opposed the monarchy] were furious and demanded that the play be suppressed by the government and that the author and actors be arrested and the patriotic clubs have been as adamant,...exhorting true patriots to proceed to the theater and put an end to the scandal [by demonstrating against the play]. But these calls produced no results. There were no disturbances and the [city government] therefore had no reason to interfere. Nevertheless, on the eleventh [of January], the city council approved a motion by Citizen Hébert [leader of a group known as the 'Rapid Dogs' or 'ultra'-patriots], to suspend performances of the play.

That evening, in Odéon Place, where the theater stands, there was a crowd of thirty thousand people who prevented the mayor's carriage from arriving [so he could announce the suspension of the scheduled performance]. Finally, after a great deal of commotion, he was able to enter the theater but when he began to address the crowd, he could not be heard. Hardly had he set foot in his box seat when the crowd began chanting, 'Friend of the Law! Friend of the Law!' [He] appealed to the crowd to obey the law and respect the decision of the elected city council to suspend the performance. However, the public refused...a deputation, headed by citizen Laya, was sent to the National Assembly to demand that the liberty of the theaters be respected [and the city council be over-ruled]....The mayor is blocked from leaving the theater.

Shortly thereafter, Santerre [leader of the Paris National Guard] and a band of more than a hundred fifty Jacobins rushed into the theater with swords and pistols...to defend mayor and to announce that the play will not be performed; when members of the audience shout in protest, the men in uniforms of the National Guard silence them by threatening to use their weapons.

When the deputation [to the National Assembly] returned, Laya had an order [from the Assembly]. The mayor is allowed to leave his box to read it aloud: 'The [National Assembly] proclaims that there is no law authorizing the municipal government to censor plays.' The crowd breaks out with shouts of joy; the curtain rises, and the performance begins. Throughout the performance, perfect order is maintained in the theater. The Jacobins, with their pistols and swords, disappeared. [At the end,] the crowd hailed the courage of the author and the actors...with an indescribable ovation....People in the theater fell into each other's arms with shouts and tears of joy. When we left the theater at one o'clock in the morning, the square outside was full of...true citizens who shouted, 'Long live liberty!'

The next day, *Semiramis* [a classic tragedy by Voltaire, written long before the Revolution] was scheduled to be performed. Before the performance, the audience again chanted for *Friend of the Law*. Dazincourt [the leading actor of the troupe, who was very popular with all sides] announced it would be performed again in a few days [as was standard at the theater]....But the crowd would not allow any delay and threatened to riot; to calm the storm, Dazincourt promised that the troupe would perform *Friend of the Law* the next day....

The next day, once again, the city council issued a decree ordering [the National Guard] to take proper precautions to prevent the play from being performed. So the posters that morning advertised [other plays]. To be sure that there would no mistake this time, Santerre positioned the National Guard in front of the playhouse and along all the streets leading to it, and patrols moved through the neighborhood of the theater [to prevent a crowd from gathering to demand the suppressed play]. In spite of al this, the audience in the theater persisted in chanting 'Friend of the Law!' ... When the Commissioner of Police arrived, several spectators from the pit [the open area in front of the theater, which were the least expensive tickets] made their way towards him and made many threats implying that that he would not be allowed to leave the theater. At that point, the National Guard entered, accompanied by a deputation from the city government, to restore order [by enforcing the decree of the city government] ... and defend the Commissioner of Police.... The crowd cried out 'murderers' and shouted for the play to be read from the stage. Someone began to read the play, and each line was met with furious applause. Santerre [the leader of the National Guard] said that 'the theater must be full of aristocrats'."

[Source: Biré, 249–55.]

***

In the Old Regime, the opera was the most expensive, elaborate, and prestigious form of theater. For this reason, it attracted a more upscale audience than other theaters, including many aristocrats. After 1789, government subsidies made opera admissions affordable for ordinary citizens, and opera audiences began to change. While many celebrated this trend as a sign that France was becoming more equal and democratic, some opposed it. They missed the sense of exclusivity and prestige formerly associated with the opera. In this document, Edmond Biré describes his evening at the opera with Jean-Baptiste Antoine Suard, who had been a leader of the Enlightenment Philosophes but also a cultural elitist. Suard favored reason but came to oppose the Revolution for having destroyed the cultural elite of the Old Regime.

## DOCUMENT 15: OPERA AS A SYMBOL OF THE OLD REGIME

"Yesterday evening [22 March 1793], we were on our way to hear Mozart's opera performed at the National Music Academy [formerly

This engraved portrait of the playwright Marie-Joseph Chenier shows him as a romantic poet, looking upward for inspiration, and was used as a frontispiece to multiple editions of Chenier's collected works, beginning in 1802. The engraving is based on Horace Vernet's portrait of Chenier at age 30. Courtesy of the Library of Congress PQ 1966 A1 1824, v.1.

known as the Royal Music Academy] when [Jean-Baptiste Antoine] Suard, who had been a censor of plays and operas under the Old Regime and is now an editor of [a political newspaper], reminded me that 'in 1778, as today, there had also been great parties that conflicted in the opera house . . . ' over which composer was better, the Italian Puccini . . . or the Austrian Gluck. . . . . . . [Suard continued]: What fine quarrels we had on warm summer evenings! I remember how humiliated we [the supporters of Gluck, of whom Suard had been one of the leaders] were when the receipts of [Gluck's operas] were less than those of Puccini. . . . But now there are no longer Gluckists and Puccinists; there are only Rolandists and Robespierristes [Roland was a leader of the Girondin party, which had been the majority between 1791 and 1792 but had lost in the most recent elections to the Jacobins, of whom Robespierre was among the best-known leaders.] . . . The field of battle is now more serious; there are cries of vengeance and death.'

We then reached our seats in the theater. Suard was the only one to associate this opera hall with happy memories [of the Old Regime], since most of the citizens in attendance had not been able to afford opera tickets prior in those days. . . . At the intermission, Suard remarked, 'Today is Friday. Before [the Revolution], you know, it was considered the proper thing only for high-class people to go to the opera on Friday; the king's entire entourage would come from Versailles . . . but now, Friday is like any other day [when anyone might attend the opera]. Such is equality.' Suard's face grew darker, and he looked sad as he glanced around the hall. He pointed out to me the box seats that had belonged under the Old Regime to nobles and to the king and queen.

When the curtain rose for the second act, the audience was surprised that the first scene was entirely spoken [and not sung, as ordinarily would be the case at the opera]. . . . It was the first time for many to hear a comic opera [a work that mixed spoken and sung lines. These works had been very popular since the Old Regime, but many in the audience evidently had never been to the opera before.] . . . When it was all over, the audience dispersed. . . .

We returned to the boulevards. The evening papers were being sold, and I bought the *National Gazette*. When I arrived at home, I read that Marat had given a speech [in the Assembly] which made me unhappy, and I wanted to be back at the opera listening to Mozart instead . . . "

[Source: Biré, 383–89.]

***

## PRINTING AND READING: BOOKS AND NEWSPAPERS DURING THE REVOLUTION

Newspapers today are expected to remain neutral, other than in their editorials. But in the eighteenth century, readers expected newspapers to reflect a specific point of view. A reader, by following events in several newspapers, could get not only the news but also different interpretations of events. Under the Revolution, censorship of the press ended, and the number of newspapers increased drastically. Several hundred papers appeared in Paris each day. Even more widely read were broadside posters, which became a constant source of news for ordinary people.

### DOCUMENT 16: POSTERS IN REVOLUTIONARY PARIS

"There was a time when the posters seen on the walls of buildings in Paris announced nothing more exciting than the auction of some . . . property of a deceased nobleman or the upcoming departure of a ship for overseas . . . But those days of ignorance [about politics] are long past. Now the poster has become a source of power, greater perhaps than anything else. The public speaker or the newspaper may hold [the interest of the public] for a few hours only, but the poster attracts attention for several days. A newspaper costs two *sous*, but it costs nothing to read a poster. [Political leaders] are well aware of this, and when they want to make a point, they have it printed on posters and have them stuck up on the walls. Marat has done this several times, and the brightly colored posters always draw a gaping crowd. . . . They are printed in all the colors of the rainbow, and the opinions they promote are as varying as their hues. Every day, there is a different call for the people of Paris to revolt and attack, and others to be moderate and peaceful."

[Source: Biré, 159.]

***

For those seeking a more thorough discussion than could be found on a poster, newspapers were available in many coffee shops. A reader, for the price of a hot chocolate or coffee, could peruse several different newspapers and get a variety of views on leading events of the day. Moreover, the reader would ordinarily find others happy to discuss and debate different interpretations of the day's news. Many contemporaries viewed Parisian coffee shops as the ideal place for cultural conflicts to be addressed in fair-minded and rational debate.

The writer Réstif de la Bretonne describes in the next two documents the active discussions in coffee shops—and how the government (anxious to know what people were thinking and to suppress any dissent that might develop) closely monitored the coffee shops. As a self-described philosopher, Réstif thought of himself as acting out the Enlightenment ideal of open debate through which he hoped to win over those who held extreme views. His own testimony, though, suggests that many in Parisian coffee shops during the Revolution did not have the temperament for rational debate or the open-mindedness to other opinions necessary to be convinced by rational argument:

## DOCUMENT 17: NEWSPAPERS AND POLICE SPIES IN PARISIAN COFFEE SHOPS

"As I entered...the café on the Place de l'École, I noted that the clientele comprised four different kinds of people: the checker players, the chess players, the passersby, and the loafers. The checker players ranked highest; while the chess players, rejects from the [more fashionable] Café of the Regency, were given short shrift. The passersby were of three kinds: the strangers who entered out of need; those who came in to change their boots...and who ordered nothing; and swindlers looking for an opportunity to scam. Finally the loafers, who neither played nor read the newspapers, did nothing but gather about the stove and gossip among themselves, awaiting their bedtime. This large group also fell into three categories: the...coffee-drinkers, who ordered breakfast in the morning but nothing in the evening except perhaps a little glass of Hendaye [a less expensive form of brandy]; the gossips, who came only in the evening and never ordered anything; and the beggars. These last were poor devils, more than limited in resources, who would attach themselves to some talker with money, would listen to him, and praise what he had to say until the conversationalist would order something and offer his parasite a cup of coffee; the poor devil would usually say that black coffee was bad for his stomach and would ask for some milk in it and for a roll. What with five or six cups, and as many rolls, and on some days, a custard or on another, a bottle of cider or beer...the poor devil would manage to feed himself....

The Café de Paris [a large, well-known café] dates from 1705. It was run by a foreigner, who at first served coffee [newly introduced into

Europe] without sugar, which brought a grimace to the faces of the first people to taste it. But the cleanliness of the cups and the tables and the caliber of the company were such that respectable people came. Most of them did not order coffee and preferred wine. But the sense of well-being and the clarity of mind that coffee induced soon became widely known, and then everyone ordered it. There was a certain fear, however, that putting sugar into it would cause over-excitement of the senses.... It was only realized much later that a generous helping of sugar...added a nutritional element [since most people in eighteenth-century Paris, as we have seen, rarely had enough to eat, the additional calories from sugar were considered an important improvement in their diet].... Nonetheless, the prejudice that sugar overstimulates persists even now among [middle-class] people [who ate better and did not need extra sugar for energy during the day].

The cafés have long been the meeting place for respectable people. This is a much more appropriate place than a cabaret, where one was obliged to shut oneself into a room [in early restaurants and bars, small groups were seated in private rooms and only individuals sat in the open dining room.] It is also better than the barbershop, where one was spattered with powder and treated to the awful spectacle of soapy beards.... Barbershops, by the way, have fallen a long way in the past twenty years.... I believe that as of today I am the only [middle-class] man who still goes to a barbershop rather than have a barber come to my house.... I find it useful to know barbers in every quarter of Paris. Also, since 1760 I have worn my sideburns pulled back [in a style so out of fashion that no private barber knows how to do this.]

To return to the subject of the cafés, here is the conclusion I have reached: Most ordinary Parisians as well as people from the provinces bring to them the harsh and thoughtless manners of the streets. It is really only the foreigners or...[middle class] people of good senses who behave politely there. The worst is when some young fool simply comes over and stands in the light when you are reading a paper...so badly printed that it is [unreadable]...There are others who rudely hold on to the newspaper while you are waiting for it...or who chat without releasing it. Others ask you for a paper that you were about to read, and then do not return it to you. Still others read their papers aloud, which should be prohibited except for a very short and very noteworthy item. Others shout, swear, and generally disturb and deafen peaceful coffee-drinkers who have come in for a short rest. This lack of civility is gradually driving all decent people away from the cafés. Already men of letters no longer dare to appear there...The cafés are frequented by a crowd of arrogant young men who never suspect that before the age of thirty...they lack maturity and sound judgment....These arrogant youngsters would provoke and enrage any real man of letters...And yet I, madame, I shall continue to go to the cafés, because I know that my kind of work [being a writer of articles about everyday life] requires it, just as I go to the barbers, and as I sometimes look into the cabaret.... "

[Source: Restif, *Nuits de Paris,* 134–38.]

"The truth is that spies are necessary to the government. It is up to wise people to realize this and to behave accordingly in public places....Here is a story about spies in the coffee shops.

I had gone into one in the gardens of old Royal Palace [which had been renamed Palace of the Nation] where I heard politics being discussed openly...I even noticed that certain persons whose faces gave no sign of education expressed themselves more freely than others and made extreme statements....I approached two of these men. I tried to talk about philosophy to them, but...they did not bother to listen. Then I made a casual reference to politics. At that point, they began to listen very attentively. I knew who they were then, and I watched them. They stirred up a young man from the provinces, who seemed quite hot-headed in his opinions. I approached this young man and proposed to talk about philosophy with him. Immediately he took fire and gave me a whole speech on the subject, which seemed to be poorly thought out. More importantly, I saw that we were being observed [by the two men], so I continued to speak in a loud voice.

Then a little political brawl flared up at the other end of the room, and when everyone ran over to see it, I took the opportunity to tell the reckless youth to slip away and to meet me later...He left unnoticed; I went over to listen to the dispute. It was about the revolution. Two different sides were being argued, so one side...simply had to be true. With a little deliberation, one is almost certain to make the right choice when there are only two possibilities. Those who were listening began to bet for or against the success of the revolution. A great many people made bets, as if it were a kind of game.

Afterwards the two [uneducated] men were looking around for the young man. One of them asked me if I knew what had become of him. I conducted myself exactly as this man had done when I had spoken about philosophy to him [that is, he showed no interest.] He seemed surprised...'Why should you complain?' I said to him. 'Earlier, when I spoke of *my* profession [philosophy] to *you*, you yawned, turned your head away and changed your seat. So now I return the favor when *you* talk to me of *yours* [spying]. I'm only being fair....' He grew angry at my words. 'My dear sir,' I said to him in a very low voice, 'watch your temper! If you make a scene here, it will do you more harm than me.' He thought better of quarreling and went to confer with the other man. I found myself under heavy scrutiny. I took little notice. I went to join the political idiots, and whenever I saw them on the point of saying something they would regret, I cut them off sharply...[so the police spies would not hear them say dangerous things].

The evening drew to a close. We left the café. At the door, the men I had provoked surrounded me, and one of them said, 'We don't know who you are., but you speak very well!' 'Yes, gentlemen!' I replied. 'We have each this evening plied our trade: you, that of seeking out indiscretions and...criticisms in order to report them; I, that of reprimanding those persons who would do much better to support the judicious aims of the government than to kindle mistrust and discontent in the heart of the citizens.'"

[Source: Réstif, *Nuits de Paris,* 134–38.]

***

A final cultural conflict of the French Revolution arose between oral culture, or the spread of knowledge through word of mouth, and print culture, or the spread of knowledge through print and reading. To understand how print began to overwhelm oral culture during the Revolution, we can compare the number of new writers and new books published after 1789 with those published during the Old Regime. The following statistics suggest the growing opportunity for writers, men and women, to publish their ideas. They also suggest the growing importance of reading as a necessary skill for citizens to be active in their society. The greater openness and opportunity to read afforded by the Revolution is one of its lasting cultural legacies.

## DOCUMENT 18: STATISTICS ON BOOK PRINTING DURING THE FRENCH REVOLUTION

| Year | Male authors | Female authors |
|---|---|---|
| 1755–66 | 1,187 | 73 |
| 1767–75 | 2,367 | 58 |
| 1777–88 | 2,819 | 75 |
| 1789–1800 | c. 5,000 | 329 |

[Source: Robert Darnton, "The Facts of Literary Life in Eighteenth-Century France," in Keith Michael Baker, ed., *The Political Culture of the Old Regime* (Oxford: Pergamon Press, 1989) 295; Carla Hesse, *The Other Enlightenment: How French Women Became Modern* (Princeton: Princeton University Press, 2001) 37.]

***

All these new authors and books suggest a more vibrant debate. These statistics perhaps give us some reason to see the Enlightenment ideal of a gradual expansion of debate and spread of knowledge through print as taking shape amid a period of intense political and cultural conflict. So, we see, literacy and knowledge may well have increased during the Revolution, even amid the violence.

# Glossary

**assignat:** This term referred originally to the promissory notes issued in 1790–91 by the National Assembly. It was backed by the value of church lands that had been nationalized and were soon to be auctioned. As food shortages continued and prices rose, the Assembly issued more and more assignats as paper currency. Under the Republic, these bills became the official currency of the Revolution.

**bourgeois:** Prior to 1789, this term referred to those among the commoners who were better educated, better off, and more acculturated than workers or peasants. The term meant literally "a citizen," and it implied those who lived in cities without lords to govern over or protect them. After 1789, *bourgeois* was applied to those who did not defend or benefit from traditional Old Regime privileges but did own, defend, and benefit from private property, especially commercial, industrial, or financial property (rather than land).

**clergy:** The first in the three orders of traditional European society, this group had the responsibility for the spiritual salvation of society. In France, *clergy* refers specifically to the priests, monks, bishops, archbishops, and bishops of the Roman Catholic Church. The clergy was distinct from the rest of society in several respects: they followed their own laws (known as canon law), they had their own assembly to determine their collective tax payment to the crown, and they were exempt from royal laws and law courts. The French Revolution ended the distinct status of French clergy with the Civil Constitution of the Clergy in June 1790.

**commoners:** The third of the three orders in traditional European society, this group constituted approximately 85 percent of the population in Old Regime France. The commoners included all those who worked, ranging from peasants to urban artisans to professionals. The great variety of economic status, educational level, and cultural development meant that the better-off commoners, known as *bourgeois,* generally felt closer to the nobles than to the working people. The representatives of this group briefly unified in 1789 to eliminate the traditional European society.

**corporations:** This term referred to social institutions under the Old Regime that combined people who worked in the same trade or profession. The term literally means "a body," and legally, the members of a corporation functioned as a single body—following their own traditions and rules to govern how they did their work and went about their business. In effect, all of Old Regime society consisted not of individuals but of *corporations,* ranging from urban, artisanal guilds to professional societies such as the legal bar to the three orders of society, which were also corporations. The Revolution abolished all these corporations in its first few years, so that individuals could use reason to form voluntary associations based on mutual interest.

**courtiers:** The men and women who, by virtue of noble status, political office, or great wealth, or a combination of all three, had been invited to reside at the royal residence in Versailles. Courtiers throughout early modern Europe shared a common culture, which led them to think of themselves as the political, social, and cultural leaders of society. However, many people in eighteenth-century France became increasingly critical of courtiers as aristocratic parasites, whose culture consisted primarily of immoral self-indulgence paid for by the work and taxes of others.

**Directory:** This term refers to the modified republican form of government in France from late 1795 to late 1799. To establish greater stability, this government included a five-man executive committee that was responsible for keeping the peace and preventing too much political participation. It did this by restricting the right to vote, by using force to suppress demonstrations, by promoting private property and commerce, and by promoting foreign wars. This government enjoyed moderate success but by preventing citizens from taking an active interest in politics; it lost much of its popular support and was easily overthrown in a military coup by Napoleon Bonaparte.

**empire:** Three years after Napoleon Bonaparte arrested the elected legislature and made himself First Consul of France (1799), he crowned himself emperor (1802). By tradition, an empire differed from a monarchy because it included many different lands and ethnic groups, and it governed through force rather than consent. Napoleon's rule of 1802–14, known as the French Empire, did indeed use force to conquer other lands and people. It also created a much more powerful government within France that more efficiently collected taxes, drafted soldiers, and administered a universal legal code. It did not allow for any political participation and sharply limited individual freedoms.

**Estates General:** By tradition, this body, when summoned by the king, combined the three orders—clergy, nobles, and commoners—into a parliamentary body, made up of three separate chambers. As part of their absolutist program, the French Bourbon kings ceased to call the Estates General, which did not meet from 1614 until Louis XVI called it in 1789 to resolve the crisis of debt his country faced.

**Girondins:** This term referred to a political grouping whose leaders came from the commercial city of Bordeaux on the Gironde River. In the early years of the Revolution, especially during the constitutional monarchy (1789–92) and the first months of the Republic (September 1792–May 1793), the Girondins controlled a majority in the National Assembly. They defended policies designed to promote commerce and foreign trade, including more power for the king and preemptive war against France's rivals. The Girondins favored individual liberty (especially the individual right to private property) but distrusted too much democracy, especially for those who did not own property, and opposed such policies as the price maximum designed to alleviate poverty.

**hobereaux:** This term, meaning literally "old birds," referred to nobles who had lost much of their land and wealth but retained their political privileges, such as exemptions from taxation. The hobereaux resented the gentlemen who, though not noble, had surpassed them in wealth, education, status, and power.

**Huguenots:** This term refers to Calvinists in France. In the sixteenth and seventeenth century, Calvinism had spread rapidly in France and attracted about 10 percent of the population and as many as 40 percent of the nobles. This movement particularly attracted those who worked in law and finance, a small but important sector of society. However, the Bourbon monarchs—though descendants of a Huguenot family—gradually suppressed the movement until finally outlawing it in 1685, leading more than one million to flee France. A minority remained, covertly practicing their religion and hoping that enlightened ideas of tolerance would eventually allow them to regain their legal status. This did happen in 1787, on the eve of the Revolution.

**Jacobins:** This term referred to members of the Society of Friends of the Constitution, a network of political clubs that favored greater democracy, greater individual liberty, and a greater degree of civic spirit, or patriotism, and of national unity, as the keys to the Revolution. This group remained a minority in the National Assembly until June 1793, when its rivals, the Girondins, were expelled from the Assembly. Thus, the Jacobins governed during the tensest period of the Revolution, from June 1793 to July 1794, a period when France faced invasion, civil war, and runaway inflation. In response, the Jacobin policies included a price maximum to keep food affordable, a mass levy and requisition of property to supply soldiers and material to the army, centralization of power in the hands of the Committee of Public Safety (the "revolutionary government"), and the use of jury trials ("revolutionary tribunals") to suppress enemies of the Republic.

**National Assembly:** Many deputies from the Third Estate considered the Estates General an anachronism, since it divided society into three parts. They preferred instead the idea of a single body to represent all the people—the nation. Only one month after the Estates General met in May 1789, these deputies announced they were reconstituting themselves into a national assembly—they would meet as a single body, they would serve the people who had voted for them rather than the king, and they would possess sovereign authority to pass laws and write a constitution. This idea eventually prevailed, and from June 1789 until 1795, the National Assembly named the elected legislature that governed France.

**nobles:** The second in the three orders of traditional European society, the nobles had the traditional responsibility for defense and government of the society. Nobles held, by birth, a privileged status that gave them certain powers—such as the power to serve as military officers and judges, the power to inflict violence on commoners, and the power to be exempt from royal taxation on their land—and set them apart from the rest of society. The French Revolution abolished the nobility in June 1790.

**parlements:** These were the highest law courts in Old Regime France, made up of noble magistrates. These magistrates not only heard appeals and all cases involving nobles but also considered themselves advisors to the king, to whom they claimed to represent the nation. The 12 regional *parlements,* plus the *Parlement* of Paris, claimed the authority to reject royal decrees that violated the traditional liberties of their region or the nation.

**patriots:** This vague term referred to those who considered themselves defenders of the French homeland (or *patrie*) and its people (the nation). The term *patriot* in early modern Europe meant two things: one who defended the liberty of his or her homeland (from foreign enemies and domestic despots) and one who was willing to sacrifice personal wealth or personal freedom to defend the liberty of the *patrie*. In the French Revolution, this term came to mean those who were willing to sacrifice in order to defend and advance the cause of the Revolution, against both foreign enemies and against those in France who endangered the Revolution by conspiring against it. Patriots were particularly concerned about some who claimed to support the Revolution but who were not willing to sacrifice—by serving in the military, paying taxes, and remaining politically aware and active. Patriots thus criticized not only the king and his court but also all who argued to defend personal property and liberty rather than sacrifice it for the good of the entire country.

**republic:** In September 1792, a crowd stormed the royal palace, and the legislature ended the constitutional monarchy. It was replaced with a republic, or a government ruled directly and completely by the legislature, without a king. In early modern European culture, a republic required all citizens to become patriots and take an active role in defending the country's liberty, by self-sacrifice (or virtue). This idea influenced the Jacobins, who governed from mid-1793 to mid-1794 and sought to promote patriotism and virtue among the citizens. After the fall of Robespierre, the government remained a republic, but its leaders emphasized defense of private property and economic development over political participation or patriotism.

**sansculottes:** Literally meaning "without breeches," this term referred to the artisans of Paris who became politically active during the Revolution by participating in local section meetings. Sansculottes, though relegated to passive citizenship status between 1789 and 1792, considered themselves the leading patriots of the Revolution, whose bravery and willingness to take direct action had begun the Revolution by storming the Bastille on July 14, 1789, and then had continued it afterward. For this reason, sansculottes regularly petitioned and demonstrated for greater democracy and worried that the revolutionary government's policies were not doing enough to defend France from its foreign and domestic enemies or to alleviate hunger and shortages in the cities.

**seigneurs:** Literally meaning "lords," this term referred to landowners who held traditional authority not only over their land but also over anyone who worked on it. Though lords in eighteenth-century France did not have serfs, they did hold powers over the peasants who lived on and worked their estates. Seigneurs collected dues from peasants for each use of the land: to harvest, to buy or sell, to inherit, to weigh and mill grain, and to bake bread. Peasants had to make a payment, or due, to the lord. The Revolution ended the distinct status of seigneurs on August 4, 1789.

**sous:** A unit of currency under the Old Regime corresponding roughly to the English shilling. A *livre* (pound) could be divided into 20 *sous*. A skilled worker earned approximately 4 pounds, or 80 *sous,* per day. Though the Revolution introduced a new currency, known as the *assignat,* the term *sous* continued to serve as a slang term for money.

**tithe:** Payment of 10 percent of the value of anything produced on the land, collected by the church on all land. This payment differed from seigneurial dues and royal taxes, though peasants who owed the tithe as well as dues and taxes generally did not draw such distinctions.

# Study Questions

These questions will help students think about the larger issues raised by the Revolution. There are no correct or incorrect answers, though students should be able to find useful information throughout this book to develop thoughtful responses.

1. The National Assembly delegates who began writing a constitution in the fall of 1789 were very concerned with rights. But this was a new idea for most people at that time. Where in European thought prior to 1789 might they have drawn their ideas about rights? What different traditions of thinking about rights were available to them?
2. How "absolute" was the absolute monarchy in France prior to 1789? What was meant by absolute monarchy and to whom did this idea appeal? How practical does this idea seem to have been? Why did the monarchy want to be absolute? What kinds of resistance existed?
3. What were the reasons for the overthrow of the monarchy—the so-called second French Revolution—on August 10, 1792?

   Consider the following events to understand why the Revolution reached this second, more radical stage: the emigration of nobles, the flight of the king, the Civil Constitution of the Clergy, and the distinction between active and passive citizens under the Constitution of 1791.

4. How would you characterize the Jacobin conception of the Republic?

   Consider the Constitution of 1793 (which was never put into effect) and some of the measures the Jacobins enacted during the period of revolutionary government, such as the price maximum, the abolition of the slave trade, free compulsory education, the creation of the revolutionary calendar, the Festival of the Supreme Being, and the declaration of the Terror and the accompanying legislation, including the Law of Suspects and the Law of Prairial.

5. Were women's experiences during the French Revolution different from men's? To what factors might these differences, if any, be attributed? What consequences might be attributed to these differences, if any?

   During the period from the Old Regime to the Napoleonic Empire, consider such factors as economic and social differences among women; policies specifically aimed at women; women's political activism; and the way women were portrayed.

6. During the period of the Republic, from 1792 to 1799, the most important issues in French political and social life were the striving for (or resistance to) some form of democracy and the on-going civil and foreign wars. Do you think that the question of democracy led to and influenced the waging of war or, conversely, did the war influence the form of democracy? Ultimately, what conclusions can you draw about the relationship of democracy and war in eighteenth-century France?

   Consider different meanings of democracy and different forms of government during the Republic; consider also the different kinds of wars being fought and the different strategies pursued by the French Republic in waging these wars.

7. To what extent might the presence, or shortage, of basic subsistence (bread, work) have influenced the course of the Revolution from 1789 to 1799? Do you think that the shortage was a central factor in the course of the Revolution or were other factors more important?

8. Consider the economic situation in France in the eighteenth century (such as different factors involved in the production and distribution of food across the country), the cultural importance attached to work and to bread, the policies proposed to address shortage of work and of bread (such as national workshops and the price maximum), and the different ideas of property and wealth that we have encountered in our study of the Revolution. Alternatively, you may want to consider other factors besides bread and work—such as religious differences, political theories of law and the general will, and the cultural differences among middle-class gentlemen, artisanal workers, and peasants.

# Resource Guide

## BOOKS

### General works on the Revolution:

William Doyle, *The Oxford History of the French Revolution* (3rd edition, 2002); Christopher Hibbert, *The Days of the French Revolution* (2nd edition, 1999).

### On the Enlightenment, the Old Regime, and the Outbreak of the Revolution:

Roger Chartier, *Cultural Origins of the French Revolution* (1989); William Doyle, *Origins of the French Revolution* (3rd edition, 1999); Daniel Roche, *France in the Enlightenment* (1998); Peter Jones, *Reform and Revolution in France* (1995).

### On social change during the Revolution:

David Andress, *French Society in Revolution* (1999); Peter Jones, *The Peasantry in the French Revolution* (1988); John Markoff, *The Abolition of Feudalism* (1996); Dominique Godineau, *The Women of Paris and their Revolution* (1998); William Sewell, *Work and Revolution in France from the Old Regime to 1848* (1980).

### On politics during the Revolution:

Patrice Higgonet, *Goodness Beyond Virtue* (1999); Isser Woloch, *The New Regime* (1994); Lynn Hunt, *Politics, Culture, and Class in the French Revolution* (1984); Olwyn Hufton, *Women and the Limits of Citizenship in the French Revolution* (1992); David Jordan, *The King's Trial* (1979).

### On protest, violence and the Terror during the Revolution:

Arno Mayer, *The Furies* (2000); George Rudé, *The Crowd in the French Revolution* (1967); Richard Cobb, *The People's Armies* (1987); Albert Soboul, *The Sans-Culottes* (1972); R.R. Palmer, *Twelve Who Ruled* (1941).

### On the military and warfare during the Revolution:

Ken Alder, *Engineering the Revolution* (1999); T.C.W. Blanning, *French Revolutionary Wars* (1996); Alan Forest, *Soldiers of the French Revolution* (1990); Owen Connelly, *Blundering to Glory: Napoleon's Military Campaigns* (1999).

### On French Revolutionary culture:

Antoine de Baecque, *Glory and Terror* (2001); Lynn Hunt, *The Family Romance of the French Revolution* (1993); Jeremy Popkin, *Revolutionary News* (1990); Mona Ozouf, *Festivals of the French Revolution* (1988).

## FILMS/ VIDEO/ AUDIO

"Bastille" (1989). This four-hour radio program, produced by the University of Chicago's Benton Broadcast Project, features interviews with prominent historians, and dramatic readings of historical documents—including a memorable interpretation of Robespierre by William Shatner. It is both highly informative and thoroughly entertaining.

*The French Revolution* (1989). Directed by Robert Enrico and Richard Heffron, starring Jane Seymour and Klaus-Maria Brandenauer. This is really two different films, each three hours long. Together, the two halves constitute the most accurate and detailed film version of the Revolution.

*Dangerous Liaisons* (1988). Directed by Stephen Frears, starring Glenn Close, John Malkovich, and Michelle Pfeiffer. This film is based on an eighteenth-century novel by Choderlos de Lacos. It is the story of two decadent aristocrats who set out to corrupt a virtuous and pure young girl. This melodramatic story line derives directly from eighteenth-century popular culture and remains influential today. This film gives a good sense of how many eighteenth-century patriots—and many historians since then—have viewed the Old Regime aristocracy.

*Death in the Seine* (1988). A short, documentary film by noted English avant-garde director Peter Greenaway, this film draws on historical documents to describe and show in detail what bodies that had drowned in the Seine river in the age of the Revolution would have looked like. This film is not directly about the Revolution, but it provokes thoughts about the fragility of life in that age.

*Danton* (1982). Directed by noted Polish filmmaker Andrzej Wajda and starring the leading French actor of the 1980s, Gerard Depardieu. This French feature film dramatizes the conflict between Robespierre and Danton at the height of the Terror. The film very subtly implies comparisons to twentieth-century politics.

*La Marseillaise* (1938). Directed by Jean Renoir, this black-and-white, French film is a visually stunning, highly patriotic version of the story that emphasizes the unity of the people. The French government subsidized this film to celebrate the 150th anniversary of the Revolution.

*Napoleon* (1927). Written and directed by French film legend Abel Gance, this silent film is one of the all-time film classics and a dramatic portrayal of Napoleon's rise through the ranks during the Revolution. The fully restored version (released in 1981) runs six and one-half hours.

## MULTI-MEDIA ELECTRONIC RESOURCES

Andress, David. "Links on the French Revolution." http://userwww.port.ac.uk/andressd/frlinks.htm. An annotated directory of links to Web sites on many different aspects of the Revolution.

Censer, Jack and Lynn Hunt. *Liberty, Equality, Fraternity: Exploring the French Revolution* (Penn State University Press/American Social History Project: 2000). This CD-ROM contains 10 chapters of analytical work by two leading historians on the French Revolution. Plus over 1,500 pages of primary documents (translated and edited), over 600 images from the period of the Revolution, 12 Revolutionary songs (with words in English and French), and a series of multimedia slide shows and short instructional videos, all packaged in an accompanying workbook. Also, there is an accompanying Web site at http://www.chnm.gmu/revolution.

Halsall, Paul. "The Modern History Internet Source Book: The French Revolution." http://www.fordham.edu/halsall/mod/modsbook13.html. A very useful collection of public domain, primary documents on the French Revolution. For another, similar collection (with some overlap of documents), see the Dartmouth College Department of History collection at http://history.hanover.edu/modern/frenchrv.htm.

Jones, Colin. "French Revolution Reading List." http://history.hanover.edu/modern/frenchrv.htm. A very thorough bibliography organized by topic, for advanced study of the Revolution.

# Index

## About the Author

GREGORY S. BROWN is Assistant Professor in the Department of History, University of Nevada, Las Vegas.